FILM
MAKERS
ON
FILM
MAKING

INDIANA UNIVERSITY PRESS

BLOOMINGTON & LONDON

FILM MAKERS
ON
FILM MAKING
*

Statements on

their art by

thirty directors

Edited by

HARRY M. GEDULD

THIRD PRINTING 1971

First Midland Book edition 1969
Copyright © 1967 by Indiana University Press
Library of Congress catalog card number: 67–25134
Manufactured in the United States of America

253-20104-7 pa   253-12600-2 cl

For Marcus,
* and in Spite of His Objections*

ACKNOWLEDGMENTS

MY SINCERE THANKS are due to Mr. Royal Brown of Queens College, New York City, for his expert translation of the article by Ingmar Bergman; to Mrs. Edith Greenburg Albee for her assistance and encouragement; to Mr. Michael Aronson, who suggested the idea of this book without realizing all that he was letting himself in for, and who also provided much useful advice and many pleasurable hours of conversation; to Mr. Herman G. Weinberg for his advice and suggestions; to Mr. John H. Gagnon for helping to trace one of the copyright holders; to Mr. Dan H. Laurence for his generous assistance; to Carolyn for much encouragement and the constant reminder to justify my surname; and to all the directors represented in this book as a small and quite inadequate appreciation of their work.

Grateful acknowledgment is also made to the following for permission to print the material listed:

To M. Georges Sadoul and *Sight and Sound* for "Lumière—The Last Interview," originally published in *Sight and Sound,* XVII, no. 66 (Summer 1948), pp. 68-70.

To Mr. Raymond Rohauer, Film Curator and Program Director of the Gallery of Modern Art, New York City, for "How to Throw a Pie," from *King of Comedy* by Mack Sennett as told to Cameron Shipp (New York: Doubleday, 1954), pp. 135-46.

Mr. Rohauer kindly grants this permission as copyright holder of all interests pertaining to films and publications by Mack Sennett.

To Mrs. Frances H. Flaherty, Mr. Erik Barnouw, and International Film Seminars, Inc., for "How I Filmed Nanook of the North," by Robert J. Flaherty, originally published in *The World's Work,* XLIV (September 1922), pp. 553-60.

To Mr. Max Reinhardt and The Bodley Head, Ltd., for the excerpts from *My Autobiography* by Charles Chaplin (London: The Bodley Head, Ltd., 1964).

To M. Jacques Ledoux (Royal Film Archive of Belgium) and Mr. Peter Morris (Canadian Film Institute) for "Von Stroheim Introduces the Merry Widow," published in *Hommage à Erich von Stroheim,* a brochure of the Canadian Film Institute, issued in February 1966.

To Penguin Books Ltd., Penguin Books Inc., Mrs. Sandra W. Smith, and Mrs. Linda Posey for "Happily Ever After," by Fritz Lang, originally published in *Penguin Film Review* no. 5 (January 1948), pp. 22-29; for "Those Were the Days," by Cecil Hepworth, originally published in *Penguin Film Review,* no. 6 (April 1948), pp. 33-39; and for "About Stereoscopic Cinema," by S. M. Eisenstein, originally published in *Penguin Film Review* no. 8 (January 1949), pp. 35-44. And to the authors and translators, living and dead.

To *Film in Review* and Miss Jeanne Stein for "Color and Color Films," by Carl Th. Dreyer, published in English in *Films in Review,* April 1955.

To Mr. Pete Martin for his interview, "I Call on Alfred Hitchcock," originally published in the *Saturday Evening Post,* July 27, 1957, pp. 36-37, 71-73.

To Mr. P. E. Dosse, Hansom Books Ltd., and *Films and Filming* for "The Bitter Life—of Money," by Federico Fellini, from *Films and Filming,* January 1961, pp. 13, 38; for "The Two Worlds of the Cinema," by Tony Richardson, from *Films and Filming,* June 1961, pp. 7, 41; for "Destroying the Commonplace," by Andrzej Wajda, from *Films and Filming,* November 1961, pp. 9, 40; for "Trying to Understand My Own Film," by

ACKNOWLEDGMENTS ix

Alain Resnais, from *Films and Filming,* February 1962, pp. 9-10, 41; for "Last Words on Last Year," by Alain Resnais and Alain Robbe-Grillet, from *Films and Filming,* March 1962, pp. 39-41.

To Dobson Books Ltd., and Mr. Alan England for the excerpts from *Cocteau on the Film* by Jean Cocteau and André Fraigneau, translated by Vera Traill (London: Dobson, 1954), pp. 12-21, 104-17.

To Mr. Jonas Mekas and *Film Culture* for "A Statement," by Luis Buñuel, from *Film Culture* no. 21, Summer 1960, pp. 41-42; for "Reflections on the Film Actor," by Michelangelo Antonioni, from *Film Culture* nos. 22-23, Summer 1961, pp. 66-67; for "A Talk with Michelangelo Antonioni on His Work," from *Film Culture* no. 24, Spring 1962, pp. 45-61; and for "The Writings of Dziga Vertov," from *Film Culture* no. 25, Summer 1962, pp. 50-65. The "Kinoks-Revolution" manifesto, part of the Dziga Vertov material, was first published in 1919. It reappeared in an extended version in *LEF* magazine, no. 3, 1922, ed. Vladimir Mayakovsky, from which the translation published here was taken. The "Notebooks" material first appeared in *Iskusstvo Kino,* no. 4, 1957. The "Kino-Eye" lectures were first published in English in *Filmfront,* New York, 1935.

To *Cahiers du Cinéma* for "Qu'est-ce que faire des Films?" by Ingmar Bergman, originally published in *Cahiers du Cinéma,* XI no. 61 (July 1956), pp. 10-19. The article appears here in an English translation, titled, "What is 'Film-making'?"

To Mr. Josef von Sternberg, The Macmillan Company, Martin Secker and Warburg Ltd., and Mr. Jonas Mekas for "Acting in Film and Theatre," by Josef von Sternberg, from *Film Culture,* I nos. 5-6, Winter 1955, pp. 1-4, 27-29. This article has been incorporated, with some changes, in Mr. von Sternberg's book, *Fun in a Chinese Laundry* (New York: Macmillan, 1965).

To Mr. Francis Koval and *Sight and Sound* for "Interview with Welles," from *Sight and Sound,* December 1950, pp. 314-16.

To *Sight and Sound* and Miss Penelope Houston for "A Long Time on the Little Road," by Satyajit Ray, from *Sight and Sound,* Spring 1957, pp. 203-205.

To *Show* magazine, Symphonette Square, Larchmont, New York, for "Kurosawa: Japan's Laureate of Film," from *Show Business Illustrated,* April 1962.

To Mr. Robert Hughes for the excerpts from "The Film-maker and the Audience," originally published in *Film: Book I,* edited by Robert Hughes (New York: Grove Press, 1959).

To Mr. Kenneth Anger and Mr. Stephen De Canio (editor of *Spider*) for "Spider Interviews Kenneth Anger," from *Spider* I, no. 3, April 15, 1965, pp. 5-7, 9-11, 14-16.

The editor and publisher have made every effort to determine and credit the holders of copyrights of the selections in the book. Any errors or omissions may be rectified in future editions.

H.M.G.

LINDSAY ANDERSON (1923-   ), British director; contributed
to the Free Cinema movement of British documentary. His
best-known film is *This Sporting Life* (1963).

KENNETH ANGER: one of America's leading avant-garde film-
makers. His work includes: *Fireworks* (1947), *Inauguration
of the Pleasure Dome* (1954), *Scorpio Rising* (1962-63), and
Kustom Kar Kommandos (work in progress).

MICHELANGELO ANTONIONI (1912-   ), Italian director. His
films include: *Il Grido* (1957), *L'Avventura* (1959), *La
Notte* (1960), *L'Eclisse* (1962), and *Il Deserto Rosso*
(1964).

J. A. BARDEM (1922-   ), Spanish director. His films include:
Death of a Cyclist (1955) and *La Venganza* (1957).

INGMAR BERGMAN (1918-   ), Swedish director. His many
films include: *Sawdust and Tinsel* (1953), *Smiles of a Summer
Night* (1955), *The Seventh Seal* (1956), *Wild Strawberries*
(1957), *The Virgin Spring* (1959), and *The Silence* (1963).

LUIS BUÑUEL (1900-   ), Spanish-born director; has worked
infrequently in Spain, extensively in Mexico, and more recently in France. Among his numerous films are: *Un Chien
Andalou* (made in collaboration with Salvador Dali, 1928),

L'Age d'Or (1930), *Los Olvidados* (1950), *El* (1952), *The Criminal Life of Archibaldo de la Cruz* (1955), *Nazarin* (1958), *Viridiana* (1961), and *Diary of a Chambermaid* (1963).

CHARLES CHAPLIN (1889-   ), British-born actor and director; the world's most famous comedian. Most of his films have been made in the United States, and since 1915 he has directed every movie in which he has appeared. Among his many films are: *The Kid* (1920), *The Gold Rush* (1925), *City Lights* (1931), *Modern Times* (1936), *The Great Dictator* (1940), *Monsieur Verdoux* (1947), *Limelight* (1952), *A King in New York* (1957), and *Countess from Hong Kong* (1966).

JEAN COCTEAU (1899-1963), French director. His films include: *Blood of a Poet* (1930), *Beauty and the Beast* (1945), and *Orpheus* (1949).

CARL TH. DREYER (1889-   ), Danish director; best known for his *Passion of Joan of Arc* (1928), *Vampyr* (1931), *Day of Wrath* (1943), and *Ordet* (1954). His most recent film is *Gertrud* (1964).

SERGEI M. EISENSTEIN (1898-1948), the greatest of Soviet film directors and a leading theoretician of the art and technique of motion pictures. His films include: *Strike* (1924), *The Battleship Potemkin* (1925), *October* (1927), *The General Line* (1929), the unfinished *Que Viva Mexico!* (1931), *Alexander Nevsky* (1938), and two parts of *Ivan the Terrible* (1945-46).

FEDERICO FELLINI (1920-   ), Italian director. His best-known films are: *La Strada* (1954), *The Nights of Cabiria* (1957), *La Dolce Vita* (1959), *8½* (1963), and *Juliet of the Spirits* (1964).

ROBERT J. FLAHERTY (1884-1951), American pioneer of the documentary film. His most celebrated motion pictures are: *Nanook of the North* (1921-22), *Moana* (1926), *Tabu* (1929), *Man of Aran* (1934), and *Louisiana Story* (1948).

D. W. GRIFFITH (1875-1948), America's first great motion picture director, the "Father of Cinematographic Art," whose major films include: *Birth of a Nation* (1915), *Intolerance*

(1916), *Broken Blossoms* (1919), and *Way Down East* (1920).

CECIL HEPWORTH: (1874-1953), pioneer British director and one of the founders of the British film industry. His best-known films were: *Rescued by Rover* (1905) and two versions (1916 and 1923) of *Comin' through the Rye*. See further his autobiography, *Came the Dawn* (London, 1951).

ALFRED HITCHCOCK (1899-   ), British-born director, often called the "Master of Suspense." His many famous films include: *Blackmail* (1929), *The Lady Vanishes* (1938), *Saboteur* (1942), *Lifeboat* (1944), *Spellbound* (1945), *Strangers on a Train* (1951), *Dial M for Murder* (1953), *Rear Window* (1953), *Vertigo* (1958), *Psycho* (1960), *The Birds* (1963), and *The Torn Curtain* (1965).

AKIRA KUROSAWA (1910-   ), leading Japanese director. His film *Rashomon* (1950) was the first Japanese motion picture to receive widespread attention and acclaim in the Western world. His numerous other films include: *Living* (1952), *The Seven Samurai* (1954), *The Lower Depths* (1957), *Throne of Blood* (1957), *The Bad Sleep Well* (1959), *Yojimbo* (1961), *Sanjuro* (1962), and *The High and the Low* (1962).

FRITZ LANG (1890-   ), distinguished Austrian director whose career as film-maker began in 1919. His silent films include: *Dr. Mabuse, the Gambler* (1922), *The Nibelungen* (in two parts, 1924), *Metropolis* (1926), and *Woman in the Moon*. His earliest sound films, *M* (1931) and *The Testament of Dr. Mabuse* (1932), were, like all his silent films, made in Germany. After fleeing from the Nazis he settled in Hollywood, where, during the period 1936-1956, he made numerous films, including: *Fury* (1936), *You Only Live Once* (1937), *Hangmen Also Die* (1942), *Woman in the Window* (1944), *Scarlet Street* (1945), and *The Big Heat* (1953). Since his return to Germany, in 1956, he has made several films, including *The 1000 Eyes of Dr. Mabuse* (1960).

DAVID LEAN (1908-   ), British director. His films include:

Brief Encounter (1945), *Great Expectations* (1946), *Oliver Twist* (1947), *The Bridge on the River Kwai* (1957), *Lawrence of Arabia* (1962), and *Doctor Zhivago* (1964).

LOUIS LUMIÈRE (1864-1948), French film pioneer; brother of Auguste Lumière (1862-1954), with whom he gave the first public motion picture demonstration in 1895. They named their apparatus the "Cinematograph."

EDWIN S. PORTER (1869-1941), pioneer American director, discovered some of the basic elements of film language and the fundamentals of editing as a means of storytelling through motion pictures. Between 1902 and 1910 he made about 600 films, the most famous being *The Life of an American Fireman* (1902) and *The Great Train Robbery* (1903).

SATYAJIT RAY (1922-   ), leading Indian director, best known for his "Apu" trilogy, comprising *Pather Panchali* (1954), *Aparajito* (1956), and *The World of Apu* (1959). His other films include: *The Music Room* (1958) and *Devi* (1960).

JEAN RENOIR (1894-   ), French director, son of the artist, Jean Renoir. He has worked in France, Italy, the United States, and India. His films include: *Une Partie de Campagne* (1936), *La Grande Illusion* (1937), *La Règle du Jeu* (1939), *The Southerner* (1946), *Diary of a Chambermaid* (1946), *The River* (1950), *French Can-can* (1954), and *Le Déjeuner sur l'Herbe* (1959).

ALAIN RESNAIS (1922-   ), French director. His films include: *Night and Fog* (1955), *Hiroshima Mon Amour* (1959), *Last Year in Marienbad* (1961), and *Muriel* (1963).

TONY RICHARDSON (1928-   ), British director; began filmmaking as part of the Free Cinema movement. His films include: *Look Back in Anger* (1958), *The Entertainer* (1960), *A Taste of Honey* (1962), *Loneliness of the Long-Distance Runner* (1962), *Tom Jones* (1963), and *The Loved One* (1964).

MACK SENNETT (1880-1960), American producer; master of slapstick comedy during the silent film era. The stars of Sennett's numerous movies included: the Keystone Kops, Ben Turpin, Chester Conklin, Mabel Normand, "Fatty" Arbuckle, Larry Semon, Louise Fazenda, Harry Langdon, Charlie Chaplin, Buster Keaton, and W. C. Fields.

JOSEF VON STERNBERG (1894-   ), Austrian-born director; worked mainly in the United States. His films include: *The Salvation Hunters* (1925), *The Last Command* (1928), *The Docks of New York* (1928), *The Blue Angel* (made in Germany, 1930), *An American Tragedy* (1931), *The Scarlet Empress* (1934), *The Devil is a Woman* (1935), and *The Saga of Anatahan* (1953).

ERICH VON STROHEIM (1885-1957), Austrian-born director and actor. During the 1920's he combined a career as director of powerful works of film realism with that of actor (usually in villainous roles). As an actor he became known as "The Man You Love to Hate." Stroheim's major films as a director were: *Foolish Wives* (1922), *Greed* (1924), *The Wedding March* (1927), and *Queen Kelly* (1928). Stroheim's career as an actor continued well into the sound period, and he gave notable performances in many Hollywood films as well as in such European pictures as *La Grande Illusion* (1937) and *Les Disparus de Saint-Agil* (1939).

DZIGA VERTOV (1896-1954). The name was a pseudonym of Denis Arkadyevich Kaufman, Soviet film-maker and film-theorist. Dziga Vertov was leader of the Kinoks (Kino-Eye) Group during the 1920's. He directed many of the Group's early experimental documentaries and newsreels, including: *Kino Pravda* (1922), *Kino Eye* (1924), *The Sixth Part of the World* (1926), and *Man with a Movie Camera*. His most celebrated sound film was *Three Songs about Lenin* (1934).

ORSON WELLES (1915-   ), American director; one-time "enfant terrible" of American theatre and motion pictures. His main films are: *Citizen Kane* (1940), *The Magnificent Ambersons* (1942), *The Lady from Shanghai* (1947), *Macbeth* (1948), *Othello* (1952), *Confidential Report* (1955), *Touch of Evil* (1957), *The Trial* (1962), and *Chimes at Midnight* (1965). Welles has also played major roles in numerous films.

ANDRZEJ WAJDA (1926-   ), Polish director. His best-known films are: *A Generation* (1954), *Kanal* (1956), *Ashes and Diamonds* (1958), and *The Innocent Sorcerers* (1960).

CONTENTS

FILM
MAKERS
ON
FILM
MAKING

INTRODUCTION

HARRY M. GEDULD

THIS BOOK is a collection of statements by film directors. With few exceptions most of the directors represented here are not widely known as writers on their métier. Charlie Chaplin and Erich von Stroheim are familiar to us as actors, but what they have to say about their craft is little known. The films of the other film-makers represented here are shown and admired universally, but before the general public their names suggest, for the most part, nebulous and inarticulate figures working obscurely beside cameramen and various technicians. Nevertheless, experienced filmgoers know that in the hands of a master the film is anything but an impersonal medium. Such films as Cocteau's *Orpheus* and Fellini's *8½* are as intensely personal as *The Cantos* of Ezra Pound or the *Duino Elegies* of Rilke.

In what follows I wish to comment briefly on some of the ways in which the film director may express himself through his chosen medium. I shall then discuss some of the unique characteristics of this medium, considering in turn first what Gilbert Seldes has called the "physical essentials" of the motion picture, then the major directions in which the methods of the film-maker differ from those of the dramatist and play producer, and finally some of the problems of adaptation, especially with respect to the adaptation of novel into film, a recurrent problem that the majority of professional film-makers have to face.

I

Because great directors individualize their work, to those who are sensitive enough to be able to discern all the characteristics of a particular director's style or technique, every shot or sequence will be recognizable as part of the personal expression of the film-maker. However, such powers of discernment are not given to the majority, not even of intelligent filmgoers. In a whole film or in particularly striking sequences or in characteristic choices of subject or theme, the intelligent film audience may be aware of certain stylistic qualities—the "Hitchcock touch," unusual camera angles, or reminiscences of silent film values in a movie by Orson Welles—but often the impact of the film story and the performances of the actors will obscure the individual "voice" of the director. For many film-makers such self-effacement is actually desirable. And for the majority who work on the Hollywood conveyor-belt it is unavoidable—for strictly commercial reasons the package has to be tied with all the usual clichés. There remain the comparatively few for whom the film is indeed a direct means of self-expression and for whom, triumphing over economic pressures, self-effacement is neither desirable nor unavoidable.

It may be objected here that insofar as the making of films is a group activity, individual self-expression is virtually impossible to the film-maker. By contrast with the intricate and highly technical collaborative effort that goes into the making of a motion picture, the novelist and painter work alone, potentially, if not actually, in control of their creative material. How then can the director, surrounded by technicians and actors, achieve any comparable control over *his* material? How can he mold the skills, arts, and sciences of so many other persons into a tool for his self-

expression? Mainly by force of personality, by the ability to impose his vision, and his alone, on the others working with him.
"Surrounded," writes Grierson," by a thousand technicians and a
thousand interests which conflict with his job of pure creation, a
director has to have something of a Lenin in him to come
through." More specifically, the director is able to achieve self-
expression through his choice of subject, story, or theme (or his
characteristic handling of these even when the choice is not his)
through his focus on details that characteristically interest him,
and sometimes, as in the instances of Chaplin and Orson Welles,
through his personal presence in the film.

Chaplin's *City Lights* (1931), Orson Welles's *Citizen Kane*
(1941), and Buñuel's *Diary of a Chambermaid* (1965) may serve
as examples. Aficionados will recognize each of these films as
highly characteristic of its director. How?

Well, even if one could overlook the presence of Chaplin
(admittedly a pretty tall order!), *City Lights* would distinguish
itself as his work because of its story, its slapstick devices, its
unabashed sentimentality and pathos, and its elaboration of well-
worn silent film themes and plot material from Victorian melodrama. Technically the film is fairly primitive. (Eisenstein's
Battleship Potemkin, made six years earlier, is a more sophisti-
cated film in every way.) But this very lack of sophistication, this
comparative indifference to elaborate stylistic devices (the very
antithesis of Welles's methods) is also characteristic of Chaplin
as a film director. It expresses, as do his choice and treatment of
story, an elemental simplicity and innocence, heart reaching out
to heart, unobstructed by intellectual pretensions.

Orson Welles, like Chaplin, plays the major role in his film;
but *Citizen Kane* is not "individualized" so much by his performance as by the extraordinary technical devices he uses in telling
his story: the exceptional lighting effects, the faked newsreels,
shots taken from unusual angles, bizarre mirror effects, low shots
revealing elaborate ceilings (features rarely seen in studio sets),
and the long traveling dolly shot at the end of the film, when the
camera ranges across the débris of Kane's life before coming to
rest on "Rosebud." Welles's technique provides a rich array of

devices for ironically contrasting Kane as he sees himself with the frustrated child who lives on inside him. Over and above this, they provide him with a means of suggesting with remarkable insight some of the profound driving forces behind megalomania.

By contrast with *City Lights* and *Citizen Kane,* Buñuel's *Diary of a Chambermaid* is based not on an original idea, but on a work by Octave Mirbeau, first filmed by Jean Renoir in 1945. Buñuel himself does not appear in the film. Nevertheless, anyone who has not already seen it, but knows other pictures by Buñuel, could with very little difficulty distinguish his version from Renoir's. How? Certainly not by choice of theme or story, nor by any unusual technical devices, but by characteristic details singled out for special attention: the old man's shoe fetishism, shots of snails crawling over the body of a dead girl. Buñuel "interprets" Mirbeau's story not only by directing the actors, but also by directing our attention to details that characteristically interest him.

Like all great motion pictures, each of these films testifies to its director's creative vision and singleness of purpose. Less obviously, but no less fundamental to the making of a great film, each of them testifies to its director's firm control over his actors and technicians. Thus, inspiration and the ability to control and give meaningful form to creative material—terms one usually associates with the novelist and painter—are equally applicable to the film director. In their recent book, *The Cinema as Art,* Ralph Stephenson and Jean R. Debrix comment on the director's role in the group activity that is basic to film-making. "Artistic creation in a group has certain difficulties, but also certain advantages, and it by no means rules out the possibility of great art . . . for the best results the artistic intuition has to be shared; other people have to be won over and infused with something of the original inspiration . . . an idea may catch fire from the contact of other minds, and an enthusiasm be generated in a group which an individual working alone would lack."

But for most of us who see rather than make motion pictures, Roger Manvell's comment on the director's role has more immediacy. In his book *Film* Manvell observes that "the film can be used to its full potentialities only by men who have the imagination to do so. The average director is satisfied with average results. So is the average public. But the average public is pleasantly surprised when the more-than-average artist arrives and shows the possibilities of the medium in a new light. Shakespeare and Shaw did this for the average public of the theatre. Griffith, Pudovkin, Eisenstein, Chaplin, Disney, von Stroheim, Lubitsch, Pabst, Hitchcock, Capra, Ford, Welles and some others have done this for the average cinema public."

II

Gilbert Seldes in his book *The Public Arts* lists as follows the physical essentials of the motion picture:

(1) A series of photographs so taken and so projected as to give the illusion of motion;

(2) the ability to control the attention of the spectator by showing as much or as little of any given scene as suits the purpose;

(3) a variety of ways to go from one scene to another (the fade, the dissolve, the direct cut are the familiar ones);

(4) control of the time-sense by breaking any action into many parts, showing the audience some of it, skipping other portions;

(5) creation of various feelings of movement by riding the camera or panning;

(6) creation of a sense of beat or rhythm by the system of cutting.

Seldes maintains that these have been the physical essentials of the motion picture from the outset. They were, more accurately, the physical *potentials* of primitive film. In fact, the last five belong to the techniques of motion picture editing, those methods of organizing film material which did not begin to dawn upon the consciousness of film-makers for more than a decade after the motion picture was invented. The earliest films were simply "actualities"—moving pictures of real objects or scenes taken from one unchanging vantage point, invariably at medium shot distance, and without any editing. The "actualities" of the

Lumière brothers, for example, consisted of single-shot films and nothing more. The Lumières' *Train Entering a Station,* the movie sensation of 1895, consisted of one uncut, unspliced film strip about fifty feet long, showing a locomotive entering a station—as photographed by a stationary camera placed at a vantage point behind the terminal buffers. Early film drama was simply the photographing of plays, with insert titles to take the place of spoken dialogue—as sound was not in general use in the cinema until after 1927. Such films, prior to Griffith, were shot from a vantage point equivalent to that of a spectator in the best seat in the orchestra. Each shot was uncut and its footage was limited only by the capacity of the camera. If the camera capacity had been unlimited, the *whole* film would have been taken in one uncut shot. However, the limitation on shot footage determined the need for a primitive kind of editing: the splicing of one uncut shot to the next in the temporal sequence of the acted play. But the camera was not moved during the shooting of each scene and the shots were almost invariably medium shots. As Pudovkin has said, the early film-maker merely photographed the art of the actor; his continuity was confined to the linkage of separate shots and he did nothing to rearrange the order of his material, to indicate that it could be viewed from many vantage points, or to cut and splice his film footage into rhythmic arrangements. In brief, he had not discovered the special nature and potentialities of the film medium.

However, Edwin S. Porter discovered and D. W. Griffith developed and enlarged these potentialities. And in the twenties the Russians, notably Kuleshov, Dziga Vertov, Eisenstein, Pudovkin, and Dovzhenko, analyzed the work of Griffith and constructed theories of film from which the techniques employed in their own motion pictures were derived.[1] The techniques of the Russians, of Porter, and of Griffith were those of constructive editing or montage, to which Seldes was referring in the last five essentials

[1] See further Karel Reisz, *The Technique of Film Editing* (London: Focal Press, 1966). Section One of this book, concerned with the history of editing, provides a lengthy analysis of the techniques of Porter, Griffith, Pudovkin, and Eisenstein.

mentioned on his list. Without going into the ramifications of the leading theories of montage, I shall outline briefly some of the most important editing devices usually employed in film-making. For a fuller discussion, to which I am indebted as the basis of the following summary, the reader is referred to Rudolf Arnheim's *The Film as Art.*[2]

1. *Sequential montage:* the arrangement of film material in a succession of sequences—usually in simple temporal order. The familiar story film relies heavily on sequential montage. Two notable variations are (a) the insertion of a sequence, such as a flashback episode, into an arrangement of material in simple temporal order, and (b) the cutting up of two or more sequences and the interweaving of the pieces, thereby producing a cross-cutting effect, as at the end of many of Griffith's full-length movies.

2. *Rhythmic montage:* a kind of editing involving the arrangement of shots or film strips of equivalent length. A succession of long strips gives a slow rhythm; a succession of short strips gives a hectic effect, as in Keystone comedies. Another kind of rhythmic montage is produced by alternating long and short strips to achieve a balanced effect.

3. *Editing in terms of the kind of shot* rather than the length of shot or the arrangement of sequences. By this method a long shot might be followed by a close-up focusing on a detail of the scene indicated or "established" in the long shot. Conversely, cutting from close-up to long shot could be used to reveal the whole of which the detail in close-up is a significant part. A variation on this method of editing is to give a succession of detail shots that built up a whole event or scene from a succession of small pieces.

4. *Synchronic editing:* the arrangement of shots or sequences in terms of parallel events or occurrences in different places. Among variations on this method are (a) the building up of details or shots occurring in the *same* place at the same time, and (b) shots showing the "before" and "after" of the same place or person.

---

[2] Berkeley: University of California Press, 1957.

5. *Symbolic or commentative editing.* Arnheim vividly exemplifies this by referring to the film *Strike,* in which Eisenstein cuts from a shot of soldiers shooting down strikers to a shot of an ox being slaughtered in a stockyard.

6. *Editing in terms of content or subject-matter relationships.* This kind of editing involves the arrangement of shots that are related (a) through similarity of shape or movement, (b) through contrast of shape or movement, or (c) through a combination of similarity and contrast.

It should be added that many or all of these methods may be used in the same film.

III

Now, having briefly surveyed the film-maker's methods of organizing the material that he shoots, it is possible to point out the major directions in which the methods of the film-maker differ from those of the dramatist and play producer. Unique to the film-maker is the advantage of using the potentialities of his medium to achieve freedom of vantage point, manipulation of space and time, and the selection of and focus on expressive detail.

In the theatre it is usually difficult or impossible to isolate expressive or significant details from the mass of material presented in a stage setting. The film-maker can, however, move into extreme close-up from a long shot or medium shot position and exclude all the details of lesser significance which would remain visible throughout the scene in a stage presentation. The close-up disclosure of hidden or generally unobserved but significant detail is something that the film can do *par excellence.* The film-maker's selection of detail serves not only to eliminate insignificant material from the focus of attention but also to retain only dramatic or climactic points. In brief, the selection of and focus on expressive detail serves as the film-maker's method for focusing the spectator's attention exclusively on what he is expected to see, and in this respect the film may be said to do the selection for the audience that they would have to do for themselves if they were in a theatre.

The audience in the theatre—and also the camera in the period of primitive cinema—function as motionless spectators. From Porter and Griffith onward, however, the camera was transformed from a motionless spectator to an active observer. The cameramen would henceforth change the viewpoints or vantage points of their cameras in order to get the best or most intimate view. The whole range of shots was developed out of the discovery of the possibilities of shifting viewpoints offered by the camera. Hence we have close-up, medium shot, long shot, and all the intermediate shots between these main divisions—as well as pan, track, zoom, high, and low shots, etc.

Through editing emerges the method of temporal concentration, which Pudovkin called the basis of film representation. The producer of a play is working with actual material and in general the material he uses is subject to the laws of space and time as we familiarly experience them. However, the film-maker is working not with actual material but with photographs of it on strips of celluloid that can be rearranged at will. The celluloid strips of, say, a man falling out of an airplane can be arranged or cut so that the time interval of the fall is reduced or eliminated. In the theatre, time intervals cannot be easily eliminated, except between the acts or scenes. Cutting and editing of the film, however, creates a new kind of time, filmic time, subject only to the will of the director, or film-maker. Slow-motion and fast-motion photography can also be used to distort time at the will of the film-maker.

In addition, the film-maker can bring together places that are remote from one another by joining strips of film showing these places. In this way he can create a filmic space that is different from real space. Thus a movie could show its hero going into the White House and a moment later emerging from the Kremlin. The film-maker manipulates space and time by (a) eliminating time intervals, and (b) selecting and juxtaposing key scenes which are not juxtaposed in reality. In short, unlike the dramatist and play producer, the film-maker does not adapt reality; he fixes certain elements of reality on celluloid film, cuts the film as he desires into numerous strips, and rearranges these strips and the elements of reality fixed on them, into a new *filmic reality*.

IV

Professionally, the scenario-writer, particularly in Hollywood, has a threefold function. He prepares original screenplays, writes additional dialogue, or turns out scenarios based on literary work in various genres. About 60 percent of the annual Hollywood output consists of the filming of original screen material. Perhaps 10 out of the remaining 40 percent consists of the filming of literary work of some distinction.

During the past decade, money from movie companies has begun funneling into the publishing business in a big way—and particularly into the paperback book business. Increasingly, novels that are extensively promoted by modern advertising techniques or that are expected to hit the best-seller lists are published according to schedules that coincide with the release of movie adaptations. The promotion of the paperbacks of *The Prize, The Group, Ship of Fools, Lord Jim, Exodus, Tom Jones, Lolita,* and the James Bond novels will serve as well-known examples, selected at random. It is evident that the film is increasingly directing public reading habits, especially in the area of prose fiction, and that for many the film adaptation takes the place of the novel, which they have not read and will not read. With the aid of television we are approaching the time when, for the majority of people, an experience of literature will be primarily an experience of filmed adaptations of literature; we may already have reached this period! From this viewpoint alone, what the film-maker does with works of literature is not a negligible matter. And thus it should be unnecessary to emphasize the need for the inclusion of the study of film "grammar" and techniques in the basic high school and college syllabus.

There is, of course, an intrinsic interest in exploring the problems of adaptation. But whatever our motives for such an inquiry, some understanding of the problems of adaptation will obviate the kind of so-called criticism that condemns a film adaptation out of hand because it is not 100 percent faithful to the letter and spirit of the novel. This is the kind of criticism that complains because so much was left out of the movie, because the ending of the story was changed, because Gregory Peck wasn't the incarnation of Captain Ahab, etc. We tend to tolerate this in film criticism. In criticism of literature or art we should find it objectionable, superficial, irrelevant, or ridiculous—as ridiculous, for example, as this excerpt from a review of D. H. Lawrence's *Lady Chatterley's Lover:*

> Although written many years ago, *Lady Chatterley's Lover* has just been reissued by the Grove Press, and this pictorial account of the day-by-day life of an English gamekeeper is full of considerable interest to outdoor-minded readers. . . . Unfortunately, one is obliged to wade through many pages of extraneous material in order to discover and savor those sidelights on the management of a midland shooting estate, and in this reviewer's opinion the book cannot take the place of J. R. Miller's *Practical Gamekeeping.*
>
> (*Field and Stream* magazine.)

All too frequently the film critic persists in telling us what we know already: that the film of a novel is not the same as the novel. He seldom tries to tell us why such differences exist, even when there are very sound reasons for them. He seldom explains how some of the differences, at least, might have something to do with the nature of the film medium, or with constricting censorship codes, or with the fact that the film-maker may be attempting a creative interpretation and not a slavish imitation. In fact, it is only to the film-maker himself that a film adaptation of a novel is likely to seem 100 percent faithful to the letter and spirit of the book. This is because each reader's conception of a novel is based on his unique, subjective experience in reading it. *Oliver Twist* is not the same book to you as it is to me, or as it was to David Lean, who made a film based on it. And our dissatisfaction with this film —as with any other adaptation—is likely to be grounded on the fact that the film-maker has not achieved the impossible and realized *our* unique conception of the book, when, in actuality, he may have succeeded quite admirably in giving expression to *his own* vision of the novel. The moral for critics is that they are treading safely only when they deal with adaptations as films *per se,* and forget about the novels on which they are based.

Many problems of adaptation do not become apparent until

one examines the scenario in conjunction with the novel on which it is based—or, better still, unless one tries to write a scenario-adaptation for oneself. Unfortunately, the number of available published scenarios is pitifully small, and many of those in print are "doctored" play versions and not shooting scripts—although it is the shooting script that the student of adaptation really requires.

One of the most important of all scenarios is not at present available to us. This is Erich von Stroheim's adaptation of Frank Norris's *McTeague,* which Stroheim filmed in 1924 under the title of *Greed*. The importance of Stroheim's film as an adaptation is that it is the only attempt ever made to film a novel with utter fidelity to the book. The completed film ran for ten hours; but only a handful of people saw it in its entirety because MGM, the producers of the film, took it out of Stroheim's hands and cut the forty-two reels down to a marketable ten. Rumor has, however, persisted to the effect that an uncut print of *Greed* survives in the vaults of MGM. However, it was assumed by MGM in 1924 that the film-going public would not endure a ten-hour movie or even a serialization of it no matter how brilliant the film's conception nor how faithful the adaptation is to the novel. The acceptable length of a feature film is thus a primary factor in determining the nature of an adaptation. Even a four-hour film like *Gone with the Wind* is limited by this factor, and it is worth mentioning here that not more than 10 percent of the plot material of Dumas' *Monte-Cristo* has been used in making any of the film versions of that novel.

Censorship codes account for another restrictive influence on the film-maker; censorship often forces a film-maker to suggest where a novel may be explicit or to omit altogether what the novel may elaborate upon at great length. Public taste as assessed by consumer research branches of the film industry often exerts considerable influence on the kind of story-line and cast accept-able to the film producer or backer. This kind of influence is discussed at length by Leo Handel in his book, *Hollywood Looks at Its Audiences*. Public taste may persuade the film-maker to let Professor Higgins marry Eliza Doolittle or to cast Charlton Heston as Michelangelo. However, there are other, more subtle problems of adaptation.

In one shot, a film can present what may take pages of description in a story. Scott's long account of Waverley Castle could be dealt with in about a dozen shots, occupying less than two minutes of screen time. "In an instant," writes Marshall McLuhan, the film "presents a scene of landscape with figures that would require several pages of prose to describe. In the next instant it repeats, and can go on repeating, this detailed information. The writer, on the other hand, has no means of holding a mass of detail before his reader in a large bloc or *gestalt*. . . ." But though the screen may present in one shot what may take many pages of descriptive writing, it cannot simultaneously convey the allusive depths of verbal description. T. S. Eliot's "The Love Song of J. Alfred Prufrock" is an almost ready-made scenario: all of its images could be embodied in a film, but the rich and complex associations of the imagery, the allusive interrelationships of the poem's verbal patterns would be entirely lost. The same loss is discernible in most film adaptations of prose fiction. As John Howard Lawson puts it: "An accurate film adaptation of a novel cannot avoid being prosaic in the literal sense: having the quality of prose without its magic."

In general, the film has excelled from the outset at presenting external detail. In the silent period, the film-maker had to rely primarily on visual images even when presenting nonvisual experience. I say "primarily" because even the silent film could often rely on musical counterpoint to supplement the visual image. Yet even where it attempted to be most faithful to the novel, the silent film adaptation seldom got beyond the stage of being a moving cartoon-strip version of the original, like a comic book treatment of *Hamlet*. Significantly, few of the great films of the silent period are adaptations of novels, and the outstanding adaptations—such as Pudovkin's film based on Gorki's *Mother,* Griffith's treatment of Dixon's *The Clansman* in *The Birth of a Nation,* or Fritz Lang's films of the Nibelung legend—are important as exploitations of the resources of the film medium and not for their fidelity or otherwise to their literary sources.

The coming of sound brought hope, to Eisenstein at least, that the divergence of novel and film would diminish. He wrote in his essay, "A Dialectic Approach to Film Form," of the "formal possibility of a kind of filmic reasoning . . . a purely intellectual film, freed from traditional limitations, achieving direct forms for ideas, systems, and concepts, without any need for transitions and paraphrases." This is evidently the direction in which the French New Wave film-makers are or have been moving with such films as *Last Year in Marienbad* and *Muriel*. Lawson notes that "A new school of French novelists who reject a plot structure in favor of moods and sensuous impressions is closely connected with similar tendencies in cinema. There has been fruitful collaboration between fiction writers and film-makers, notably in the work of Alain Resnais with Marguerite Duras and Alain Robbe-Grillet." Resnais' *Last Year in Marienbad* approaches closer to Eisenstein's ideal of the film freed from traditional limitations than any work of the Russian film director. But it is clear that Eisenstein himself would have proceeded in a similar direction. He prepared a scenario for Joyce's *Finnegans Wake*, a project that he was never permitted to realize as a motion picture. With the completion of such a film the esthetic possibilities of adaptation and a true interrelationship of film and novel might have been achieved. This much seems implicit in the "Anna Livia" section of the screenplay, the only fragment that has been published.

In his well-known essay on Dickens and D. W. Griffith, Eisenstein revealed many of the ways in which the film is indebted to the techniques of prose fiction; but in one major direction the film has influenced the techniques of the modern novelist. As Marshall McLuhan observes: "In modern literature there is probably no more celebrated technique than that of the stream of consciousness or interior monologue. . . . The stream of consciousness is really managed by the transfer of film technique to the printed page."

PIONEERS

AND

PROPHETS

*

Part
One

Louis Lumière

*
THE
LAST
INTERVIEW

Georges Sadoul

I HAD NOT the honor of knowing the great inventor who has just died when I received from him in August, 1946, a manuscript consisting of some dozen pages entitled, "Observations suggested to Louis Lumière by reading Georges Sadoul's book entitled: 'L'Invention du Cinéma.'" In this monograph he had taken the trouble to rectify certain errors in the first volume of my "Histoire générale du Cinéma," completing my data on a number of points.

M. Louis Lumière received me a few weeks later at Bandol. In the course of this long interview—and of those which followed— he furnished me with a large body of information concerning his Cinematograph, and this enabled me to prepare a very much augmented and corrected edition of "L'Invention du Cinéma." . . .

In January last [1948] M. Louis Lumière, whose health had been steadily declining since 1946, was kind enough to allow me to interview him for the French television service.

This interview was recorded and filmed by M. Bocquel. A lengthy afternoon's work was required. M. Louis Lumière, who at that time scarcely left his bed, had to make a considerable physical effort in reading, at the cost of great exertion, the text which he held before his almost sightless eyes. However, under the pro-

Originally published in *Sight and Sound*, XVII, no. 66 (Summer 1948), pp. 68-70.

jectors and in front of the microphone he maintained his usual smiling affability. This was the last time he was confronted by the apparatus on which he had bestowed the name "Cinéma."

Last March [1948] this interview was televised; it opened the series of remarkable broadcasts which Georges Charensol devoted to the history of the cinema, with the collaboration of Pierre Brive. It is thanks to their initiative that the cinema is able to retain among its archives a final picture—and an extremely touching one—of Louis Lumière.

* *

SADOUL: M. Louis Lumière, what were the circumstances in which you began to be interested in animated photographs?

LOUIS LUMIÈRE: It was during the summer of 1894 that my brother Auguste and I commenced our first work. At that period, the research of Marey, Edison and Démeny had caused those inventors to arrive at certain results, but no projection of film on a screen had yet been accomplished.

The main problem to be solved was that of finding a system of driving the strip of film pictures. My brother Auguste had thought of using for the purpose an indented cylinder, similar to that proposed by Léon Boully in another apparatus. But such a system was clumsy. It couldn't work and it never did.

SADOUL: Did M. Auguste Lumière then put forward other systems?

LOUIS LUMIÈRE: No, my brother ceased being interested in the technical side of the cinematograph as soon as I had found the right driving device. If the cinematograph patent was taken out in our joint name, this was because we always signed jointly the work reported on and the patents we filed, whether or not both of us took part in the work. *I was actually the sole author of the cinematograph*, just as he on his side was the creator of other inventions that were always patented in both our names.

SADOUL: What was the driving system you proposed?

LOUIS LUMIÈRE: I was rather indisposed and had to remain in bed. One night when I was unable to sleep, the solution came clearly to my mind. It consisted of adapting to the camera the mechanism known by the name of "presser foot" in the driv device of sewing machines, which device I first carried out with the aid of a circular eccentric; this I soon replaced by the same part but triangular in shape, which is known in different applications by the name of Hornblower's eccentric.

SADOUL: You then constructed an experimental apparatus on the principles you had just discovered?

LOUIS LUMIÈRE: M. Moisson, chief mechanic at our works, assembled the first apparatus in accordance with the sketches which I handed him as the invention took shape. As it was then impossible to obtain transparent celluloid films in France, I conducted my initial tests with strips of photographic paper manufactured in our works. I cut them and perforated them myself. The first results were excellent, as you may have seen.

SADOUL: As a matter of fact I have held in my hands with considerable emotion that long strip of paper which you presented to the "Musée de la Cinémathèque Française." The pictures are of perfect clarity.

LOUIS LUMIÈRE: Those strips were purely experimental. The negatives on paper could not be cast on the screen owing to their excessive opacity. I nevertheless succeeded in animating them in the laboratory by looking at them with the transparency effect produced by a strong arc lamp. The results were excellent.

SADOUL: Did you have to wait long before using celluloid films similar to those employed by the modern cinema?

LOUIS LUMIÈRE: I would have used celluloid strips at once had I been able to obtain in France a flexible, transparent celluloid which gave me satisfaction. However, no French or British firm was then making any. I had to send one of our departmental managers to the United States, who purchased celluloid in non-sensitized sheets from the New York Celluloid Company, and brought them back to us at Lyon. We cut them and perforated them with the aid of an apparatus whose feed device was based on that of the sewing machine, which apparatus was perfected by M. Moisson.

SADOUL: What was the date when you were able to make your first film on celluloid?

LOUIS LUMIÈRE: It was at the end of the summer of 1894 that I was able to make my first film, "Workers leaving the Lumière Factory." As you may have noticed, the men are wearing straw hats and the women summer dresses. Moreover, I needed strong sunlight to be able to make such scenes, for my lens was not very powerful, and I should not have been able to take such a view in winter or at the end of autumn. The film was shown in public for the first time at Paris, rue de Bennes, before the "Société d'Encouragement pour l'Industrie Nationale." This was on 22nd March, 1895. This showing ended a lecture which I had been asked to give by the illustrious physicist, Mascart of the Institute, then President of the Society. I also showed on the screen the formation of a photographic image in course of development; this involved certain difficulties which I will not go into here.

SADOUL: Was your apparatus already called the Cinematograph?

LOUIS LUMIÈRE: I do not think we had already baptized it. Our first patent, taken out on 13th February, 1895, did not adopt any particular name. In that patent we merely referred to "an apparatus for obtaining and showing chronophotographic prints." It was not until several weeks afterwards that we selected the name of Cinematograph.

However, my father, Antoine Lumière, thought the word Cinematograph was impossible. He was persuaded to adopt for our apparatus the name of DOMITOR by his friend Lechère, the representative of the Moet and Chandon champagnes.

SADOUL: What was the meaning of that word?

LOUIS LUMIÈRE: I don't exactly know; it was a portmanteau word devised by Lechère. It was probably derived from the verb "to dominate"—dominator—domitor. This name was never accepted by my brother or by myself, and we have never used it

SADOUL: Did the perfection of your cinematograph involve you in technical problems that were difficult to solve?

LOUIS LUMIÈRE: One of the points which received my attention was that of the resistance of the films. Celluloid films were then, to us, a new product of whose qualities or properties we were ignorant. I therefore, embarked on methodical experiment by piercing the strips with needles of different diameters, to which

I suspended increasing weights. I thus arrived at important conclusions, for instance that the hole might, without inconvenience, be larger than the pin passing through it and have equally as good resistance as if the hole and pin were the same size.

SADOUL: Did your factory undertake the industrial manufacture of your cinematograph?

LOUIS LUMIÈRE: No, and what is more we did not make any apparatus, for we were not equipped to carry out such manufacture. After the lecture which I gave at Paris at the beginning of 1895, the engineer Jules Carpentier, who became one of my best friends and remained such until his death, asked if he might manufacture our apparatus in his workshops, which had just placed an excellent camera on the market. I accepted this suggestion but it was not until the beginning of 1896 that Carpentier was able to supply us with the first ten machines. Up to then I had to be content with the apparatus we had built at Lyon.

SADOUL: Since in 1895, you only had a single apparatus which served both for taking pictures and for showing them, during that year you were the sole operator taking pictures for your cinematograph?

LOUIS LUMIÈRE: That is correct. All the films which were shown in 1895, either at the Photographic Congress of Lyon in June, for the Revue Générale des Sciences at Paris in July or in Paris, in the basement of the Grand-Café, from 28th December, 1895, onwards, were films in which I had been the operator. There was a single exception, "Les Brûleuses d'Herbes" was taken by my brother Auguste, who was on holiday at our estate in La Ciotat. I should add that not only did I make these films, but the first strips shown at the Grand-Café were developed by me in enameled iron slop-buckets containing the developer, then the washing water and the fixative. The relevant positives were similarly printed, and I used as source of light a white wall with the sun shining on it.

SADOUL: Can you, M. Lumière, tell us about the "Partie d'Écart"?

LOUIS LUMIÈRE: The partners are: my father Antoine Lumière, who lights a cigar. Opposite him his friend the conjurer Trewey who is dealing the cards. Trewey was, moreover, the organizer in London of showings of our cinematograph, and he is to be seen in several of the films, "Assiettes tournantes" for instance. The third player, who is pouring out some beer, is my father-in-law, the brewer Winckler of Lyon. The servant, finally, was a man attached to the house. He was born at Confaron—a pure-blooded southern Frenchman, full of gaiety and wit, who kept us amused with his repartees and jokes.

"L'Arrivée du Train en Gare," which I took at the station of La Ciotat in 1895, shows on the platform a little girl who is skipping along, one hand held by her mother and the other by her nurse. The child is my eldest daughter, afterwards Mrs. Trarieux, and she is now four times a grandmother. My mother, Mrs. Antoine Lumière, can be identified by her Scotch cape.

SADOUL: What can you tell us about the famous "Arroseur Arrosé"?

LOUIS LUMIÈRE: Although my recollections are not very accurate, I think I may say that the idea of the scenario was suggested to me by a farce by my younger brother Edouard, whom we unhappily lost while an airman during the 1914-1918 war. He was then too young to play the part of the urchin who treads on the garden hose. I replaced him by a young apprentice from the carpenter's workshop of the factory, Duval, who died after performing his duties as chief packer of the works for almost forty-two years. As regards the waterer, the part was played by our gardener M. Clerc, who is still alive after being employed at the works for forty years. He retired and is now living near Valence.

SADOUL: How many films did you make in 1895?

LOUIS LUMIÈRE: I must have made nearly fifty. My memory is not very reliable with regard to the number of these subjects. These films were all 17 metres long and it took about a minute to show them. This length of 17 metres may seem odd, but it was merely governed by the capacity of the spool-boxes holding the negative film when the pictures were taken.

SADOUL: Can you mention a few titles of films which you made in 1895?

LOUIS LUMIÈRE: We produced a few comic films in which relations, friends, employees, etc., took part, such as "Chez le Photographe," a little farce in which the actors were my brother Auguste and the photographer Maurice, who was soon to become the concessionnaire of our cinematograph at the Grand-Café. Then there was "Charcuterie Americaine," in which we showed a sausage machine; a pig was put in at one end and the sausages came out at the other, and vice versa. My brother and I had great fun making this fictitious machine on our estate at La Ciotat, and we inscribed on the instrument "Crack, pork butcher, Marseilles."

I should also mention the "Landing of Members of the Congress" at Neuville-sur-Saône, which was in a way the first news film, for I took it on the occasion of the Photographic Congress in June, 1895, and showed it next day before the members of the congress.

SADOUL: Have you made any films since 1895?

LOUIS LUMIÈRE: Very few. I left this to the operators whom I had trained: Promio, Mesguich, Doublier, Perrigot and others. In a few years they had entered on our catalogues over twelve hundred films made in all parts of the world.

SADOUL: How long is it since you have ceased to be interested in the cinematograph?

LOUIS LUMIÈRE: My last work dates back to 1935, at which time I perfected a stereoscopic cinema which was shown, in particular, at Paris, Lyon, Marseilles and Nice. However, my work has been in the direction of scientific research. I have never engaged in what is termed "production." I do not think I would fit into a modern studio. Moreover, I have been incapacitated for some time and can scarcely leave Bandol.

Cecil Hepworth

*

T H O S E
W E R E
T H E
D A Y S

WHEN ONE WANTS to talk about the early days of film-making it is extremely difficult to know where to begin. You know so much already about present-day methods; about producers, directors, actors and actresses, cameramen, art directors, technicians, electricians, musicians, cutting-room experts and continuity girls, that it is practically impossible for you to visualize a time when not one of these people existed. And yet we made films—of a sort. Crude they were in the extreme, but we like to think that their halting steps led gradually to better things and pointed in the end to that near perfection which is your heritage today.

I think I must begin with the Royal Polytechnic Institution in London's Upper Regent Street. If that were in existence now, it would be about 120 years old, but I am thinking of some sixty-five years ago, when it was to me, and to thousands of other small boys, the place of our utter delight. For gathered under that one roof were examples of all the latest scientific achievements of the day. There was a model electric railway with trains that ran all by themselves, and alongside that railway were a couple of Wheels of Life, Zoetropes, which gave movement to drawings of living figures. There was a famous automaton which walked a tight rope

Originally published in *Penguin Film Review*, no. 6 (April 1948), pp. 33-39.

along the whole length of the great hall—I never found out how that was done. There was a monster induction coil giving a spark which they said would kill a horse, and a huge frictional electricity machine from which, turning it slowly, you could draw miniature lightning into your small and rather scared knuckles. And then for sixpence you could take your seat with a dozen other small boys in the big Diving Bell and be completely submerged, with your feet dangling just above the surface of the water which the contained air was pressing down. I have heard it said (with complete disregard of the truth) that the band played particularly loudly while the diving bell was going down, so as to smother the screams of the drowning people inside!

In the optical theatre, which was a notable part of the old Polytechnic, all that was known of magic-lantern projection was demonstrated to the full, and in its operating-room, which, I remember, ran the whole width of the theatre, some twelve or more lanterns were installed, many of them using hand-painted slides, not photographs, of various sizes up to ten inches in diameter. Beale's Choreutoscope was shown here frequently (an early form of very crude Living Pictures), and there were many other optical devices of great popular appeal. In this theatre there were daily lectures, mildly instructional but always entertaining, by such men as B. J. Malden, my own father T. C. Hepworth and Professor Pepper. Here the famous "Pepper's Ghost" was born, also the very clever ghost illusion invented by J. J. Walker, the organ builder. Indeed, the very air about that spot is filled with ghosts for those whose memories will carry back so far. I am told that on the day the old Polytechnic was closed forever, I was found, a very forlorn little boy, lying on the stone steps before the closed front door, weeping my heart out.

Who can doubt that if the old Polytechnic had lived it would have been the very place to have welcomed and honored the new art-science which was destined, though no one knew it then, to be the greatest medium for education and entertainment the world has ever known? It seems almost like a sensate act of fate that when a clever Frenchman was searching London for a suitable hall in which to exhibit his new invention of Living Photographs, he should have drifted to one built on that very spot and set up his apparatus there.

The name of that Frenchman was Louis Lumière: the date, 20 Feb., 1896.

That was the date of the first public showing of films in this country. Without counting some earlier, very brave, but not successful attempts; without counting many inventors' pipe-dreams which never came to birth, that was, so to speak, the official birthday of the cinematograph here.

I am not going to attempt to delve into the actual history of cinematography, partly because the history of an invention is, for most people, very dry and uninteresting; partly because I don't myself know much about it—it is so largely a matter of vague rumor and conflicting memories—and partly because the real interest starts with the showing upon a screen in a public assembly. But it is not to be supposed that Lumière is to have the whole credit, or anything like it. The courage of the early experimenters, even the pipe-dreamers who only conceived but went no further, all contributed something—and who knows that it wasn't important?—to that notable birthday.

Me? I had no share in it. There was nothing of courage in what I did. It was always just a lark for me. Even now, after fifty years of it, what little I do is still something of a lark! I was suckled on amyl acetate and reared on celluloid.

Did I say the beginners were very crude? Here is an example of it. The stage was a back garden at Walton-on-Thames. The scenery was three flats painted by me. It represented the side wall of a little house with a practicable window. I (the only actor), as a burglar with a black beard, climbed in at the window (scene 1) and climbed out again with the swag (scene 3). Then the three flats were turned round, for the interior of the same house was painted thereon, and the burglar was seen inside (scene 2). It was, I think, the first time that a "story" had been produced in separate scenes. The drawback was that in the middle scene the burglar was clean-shaven, for in the excitement of changing the scenery I had entirely forgotten to put on my beard. We held a little inquest on it afterwards and decided that it wasn't sufficiently important to warrant a retake, and though we sold many copies we never had a complaint!

There were only two or three of us in the little company at Walton, and we did everything ourselves. First we thought of a story; then we painted the scenery if it wasn't all open air, as it usually was. Then we acted and photographed it, the one who was not acting turning the handle. Then we developed and printed it, and took it out to our fairground customers—there were no "Electric Palaces" in those days, not even converted shops. After that we reassembled and put our heads together to think of another story.

Story pictures were only part of our output. For instance, I photographed Queen Victoria's visit to Dublin, and that was No. 96 in our catalog!

A very great deal of what would now be called newsreel material was made by the little company from Walton and helped to swell our catalog, and in among it we made trick pictures, comics, dramas (rather small ones at first), and almost every kind of film you could think of. And while we were gradually building up from the crudity of the first fifty-footers (showing-time, fifty seconds) to bigger, better, and more worthwhile pictures, other people were feeling their way from the circus tent, through the village hall, the converted shop, and the glaring "Electric Palace" towards the comfort and magnificence of the modern picture theatre. I had a tiny share in that movement too, for before I even dreamed of making pictures myself I bought a terrible mechanism for a guinea, fitted it on to a limelight lantern and, with half a dozen throw-out forty-foot films of R. W. Paul's and about a hundred lantern slides of my own, I toured the country and gave an hour and a half's entertainment in church rooms, mechanics' institutes, and the like. It took some little ingenuity to make those six miserable little films fill out the time. I showed them, repeated them, showed them backwards, showed them again and argued with the people in them or stopped them in peculiarly awkward attitudes. Anyway, I got away with it and had many repeat engagements, building up the repertoire with the money I earned.

I thank the special providence who looks after amateurs and fools for the fact that I never had an accident, for my little machine was set up on a borrowed table in the middle of the audience, and there were no safety precautions of any kind.

Once, when I had progressed to the dignity of many more films, joined together and wound upon a spool, I was showing from the very front of the gallery in a chapel of some kind, turning the handle for the films and talking through my hat—well, lecturing, between whiles. About the middle of the show the take-up spool fell off its spindle and dived into the audience below, unwinding as it went. I had to haul the film in hand over hand talking all the time. Meanwhile, a terribly anxious man, the friend who had engaged me, kept calling in a loud whisper: "Tell Cecil not to strike a match. Tell Cecil not to strike a match." A boy from downstairs brought me my empty spool with a sad tale of an irate gentleman immediately beneath me who had two lovely tram-lines cut on his bald head by the edges of my spool.

My brief mention a moment ago of R. W. Paul and his basket of throw-out films will have suggested to you that there were other film-makers before I started. . . . Indeed, I was by no means the first, although I was among the early ones. It is a strange coincidence, and one which must be carefully noted by historians, that Paul actually showed in London some films of his own make on the same day that Lumière gave his first exhibition at the Polytechnic. But Paul's show was a private one and, besides, as he freely admitted to me, his pictures were not as good or as steady as those of the Frenchman.

The question of steadiness is important. It is, of course, chiefly a matter of the accuracy of the perforations down the edges of the film by which it is drawn through the mechanism. Lumière used one pair of holes per frame. Moreover, he used the same pair for taking, printing, and projecting, and it mattered very little, therefore, whether the holes were very really accurately spaced. Paul and the other Englishmen used the four-hole perforation inherited from Edison, and most of the early English films were dreadfully unsteady. It showed up alarmingly on "scenics"—rivers and hills, and so on. It was said at the time that thus the

Scriptures were fulfilled and the mountains skipped about like young rams.

One of my cherished possessions is an early film of Paul's of the Race for the Derby in 1896—Persimmon's Derby. It is interesting rather than good. The last time I used it in public an old showman who had been in the audience came up to me afterwards and pointed out, what I hadn't noticed, that all the policemen in the picture were wearing beards. I asked him how it was that he seemed to know more about the picture than I did myself, though I had shown it so often. And then the old rascal unblushingly admitted that he had shown it not only for the Derby of 1896, which it really was, but for eight succeeding Derbys afterwards.

Many strange things happened in those early days, and sometimes one had to think pretty quickly to meet an unexpected situation. I was giving my lecture once in a large hall built underneath a chapel. My apparatus was set up as usual in the heart of the audience, and while I was waiting beside it for the hour to strike when I was to begin, the dear old parson came and sat down beside me. He said he was quite sure that my entertainment was everything that it ought to be, but he knew I would understand that, as shepherd of this little flock, it was his duty to make doubly certain and would I let him see my list of pictures. So I handed him the list and watched him mentally ticking off each item until he came to the pick of the whole bunch, a hand-colored film of Loie Fuller in her famous serpentine dance. He said at once that he could not allow that—a vulgar music-hall actress. I said rather indignantly that there was nothing vulgar about it; that it was indeed a really beautiful and artistic production, but he was adamant and insisted that it must be omitted. Then I had to begin. Apart from my reluctance to leave out my best picture, I was faced with the practical difficulty of how to do it. For this was the last picture but one on the spool. There was no earthly means of getting rid of it except by running it through in darkness, and I didn't think the little flock would stand for that. Then, just as I came to the danger-point, I had a sudden brainwave. I announced the film as "Salome Dancing before Herod." Everyone was delighted. Especially the parson. He said in his nice little speech afterwards that he thought it was a particularly happy idea to introduce a little touch of Bible history into an otherwise wholly secular entertainment.

And he added that he had no idea that the cheenimartograph had been invented so long!

Edwin S. Porter

*
E V O L U T I O N
O F
T H E
M O T I O N
P I C T U R E

LOOKING BACK upon the past eighteen years in the motion picture business—back to the day when no one knew what a motion picture was—and realizing the wonderful strides the industry has taken since then, I am more than impressed. I am thrilled. Artistically and mechanically the motion picture has forged its way forward until today it is recognized as the greatest amusement factor in the world and the greatest educational force in the history of civilization.

Today the motion picture does even more than entertain and instruct; it has already gone beyond the present needs and desires of men, and will exert a tremendous influence upon posterity. It will record the histrionic achievements of the dramatic geniuses of the contemporary stage; it will chronicle and reproduce history as no other medium ever could or possibly will. As an illustration, the present Mexican conflict, through the motion picture, can be exhibited to future generations with such realism and exactitude as the spoken or written word could never convey.

In its artistic development alone, the motion picture has progressed within ten years to a stage reached by the oral drama only

Originally published in *The Moving Picture World,* July 11, 1914, p. 206.

after thousands of years of development and evolution. In passing, however, we must record the assertion that the development of the stage greatly assisted the advancement of the film, because even at an early date in the history of the industry it was commonly recognized that the introduction of general dramatic principles in the production of motion pictures was desirable and necessary. The problem, however, remained as to the best means of utilizing the science of the drama so as to conform with the mechanical limitations of the film, and later, with the vast possibilities that these same mechanical factors presented.

What does the development of the motion picture first suggest?

Natural evolution, an evolution assisted and enhanced by the demands of the millions who sought, and long sought in vain, clean entertainment at a minimum cost. Step by step, obstacles were overcome, difficulties surmounted, growth and development realized, not because there was money to be made through such development, but rather because the public demanded and made necessary the advancement that has been attained in the motion picture art. To the public, more even than to those who labored and struggled to give artistic presentations of the popular drama on the screen, is due the credit for the measure of improvement that has already rewarded the efforts of film producers.

My contention is this: if the public were content to receive and support the mediocre films that marked the inauguration of the business, this standard would still be acceptable. The public owes thanks only to itself for its ability today to see the beautiful, refined and artistic presentations of the screen. As for the producers, they should be content to know that public encouragement proved the inspiration that it did, and should be thankful that they were given the strength and the light to accomplish the great things which that public encouragement suggested.

I see as in a vision on the screen itself the days of 1899, the embryonic age of the motion picture. Today we hear that the picture is still in its infancy; if this general statement is true, at that time it was only a germ. There was no guide toward the right methods nor the pitfalls to avoid. The making of a picture depended most upon guesswork. Incidentally, the pictures at that time proved it.

At just about this time, when forty- or fifty-foot lengths was the vogue, I often wondered why it was not possible to produce a dramatic story in motion pictures. At this period I was chief producer of the Edison Company and it seemed peculiarly proper to me for the Edison Company to inaugurate this innovation. Accordingly, I conceived and prepared a story called "The Life of An American Fireman," a complete 800-foot story based on a fairly good dramatic element and introducing the fireman's life in the engine house and in his home. The subject became instantly popular, and continued to run for a longer time consecutively than any film production previously. Encouraged by the success of this experiment, we devoted all our resources to the production of *stories,* instead of disconnected and unrelated scenes.

My mind jumps from this time to the early part of 1912, when the Famous Players Film Company was organized to present famous plays and celebrated stars in motion pictures. Between 1899 and this latter date the work of development and systematic formulation had been proceeding steadily, until at last it was possible not only to present short dramatic stories in motion pictures, but the great dramatic successes of the stage. These two dates must always represent decisive epochs in the history of the film. I am more proud than perhaps I should be to have been responsible for the first connected story in film and later to be associated with the first concern to undertake the presentation of celebrated dramas for the photoplay public.

What the future holds in store none can say. But its possibilities are as unlimited and incalculable as the difficulties and dilemmas that beset the producer in the early days of the art. That the men who have been largely responsible for this present excellence of motion pictures will reach out for better things seems certain.

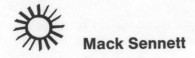**Mack Sennett**

WHEN I STARTED these recollections, I opened up with some remarks that might be taken as unbecoming and even downright immodest. I claimed that it had been a long, tired time since any citizens had been rolled in the aisles of a motion-picture house or had been doubled up with laughter while watching television comedians. I was implying, of course, that my own comedies truly murdered the people.

Don't get me wrong. It wasn't me, the Old Man, who was so funny; it was the comical people I had around me. I called myself "King of Comedy," a solemn and foolish title if there ever was one, but I was a harassed monarch. I worried most of the time. It was only in the evenings that I laughed.

I sat in a heavy, creaking rocking chair in the rear of my screening room at Keystone and examined our dizzy productions with a hard eye. When there was anything to laugh at I rocked back and forth with the contented rhythm of a broad-beamed Percheron in a bareback riding act. I seldom needed to say much to my writers, gag men, and actors. They watched the rhythm of the rocker. When I was in full gallop, they assumed that every-

From Mack Sennett, *King of Comedy* (New York: Doubleday, 1954), pp. 135-46.

thing was as ridiculous as it should be. If I didn't rock and roar as the rushes went on the screen, everybody took it for granted that the work of art under eye was no good. Then we'd shoot scenes over again.

My main contribution to motion-picture comedy seems to have resided in my boiling point. I was equipped with a natural, built-in thermostat. It turned out that when I got up a full head of steam over a film and began to roll and spout, millions of movie-goers were likely to react the same way. I was a reliable one-man audience.

Since I did produce the Keystone Comedies, it turns out that I have been credited with considerably more inventiveness than I actually possessed. For instance, historians of the drama put me down for the creation of what was once a distinguished facet of cineplastic art—pie-throwing. I'd be glad to claim this honor, if I could claim it honestly, since a pie in the face represents a fine, wish-fulfilling, universal idea, especially in the face of authority, as in cop or mother-in-law. Also, these sequences in which we started building from the tossing of one pie, quickly increasing the tempo and the quantity until we had dozens of pastries in flight across the screen simultaneously, were wholesome releases of nervous tension for the people and made them laugh. But honor for the pie is not mine. It belongs to Mabel Normand.

Mabel was always shown on the screen as a comely girl, usually poor and unfashionable, whose fate was to find herself surrounded by ruffians, villains, and amiable boobs such as Ben Turpin, Ford Sterling, or 285-pound "Fatty" Arbuckle. As our story would begin to release doses of our stock commodity, pandemonium, Miss Normand would invariably be caught in the middle.

But one afternoon in Edendale we were having trouble shooting the simplest possible kind of a scene. Ben Turpin had to stick his head through a door. Since Mr. Turpin's eyes were aimed in all directions, we thought the scene would be funny. It wasn't.

"Don't look into the camera," I instructed Ben. "This is the kind of quick scene we throw away, casual-like."

Turpin stared at me, or approximately at me, with the affronted dignity of a Wagnerian soprano ordered to conceal her tonsils.

"Shoot the eyes! Shoot the eyes!" he squalled. "What do millions of people go to movies for?"

If Turpin had ever seen the Mona Lisa he could have explained an ancient mystery. He would have claimed she was about to break out laughing at him.

Ben squinted, peered, and mouthed, but still the scene was not comical. Suddenly it was one of the funniest shots ever flashed on any motion-picture screen.

Mabel, who had nothing to do with this sequence, had been watching. She was sitting quietly, minding her own business for once, when she found a pie in her hand. It was a custard pie.

Miss Normand was not startled. At Keystone you were likely to find anything in your hand from a lion to a raw egg. You were as likely to meet an ape on the sidewalk as Gloria Swanson. If you were unwary you were likely to get a shock treatment in the seat of the trousers, mustard in your make-up, or a balloonful of water on your head. We lived our art.

As it turned out, the projectile in Mabel's hand was neither a joke nor an accident. Two carpenters were having custard for dessert. Mabel sniffed, and was inspired.

She weighed and hefted the pastry in her right palm, considered it benevolently, balanced herself on the balls of her feet, went into a windup like a big-league pitcher, and threw. Motion-picture history, millions of dollars, and a million laughs hung on her aim as the custard wabbled in a true curve and splashed with a dull explosion in Ben Turpin's face.

No one expected this memorable heave, least of all Turpin. The grinding camera, going sixteen frames to the second, was full on him. When the custard smote him, Ben's face was as innocent of anticipation as a plate. His aplomb vanished in a splurch* of goo that drooled and dripped down his shirt front. As the camera held on him his magnificent eyes emerged, batting in stunned outrage in all directions.

Worse luck for scholars, I don't remember the name of the

_____

* *Splurch:* A technical and onomatopoetic word coined by Mack Sennett; applies only to the effect of sudden custard in the puss.

picture in which the first custard was thrown. The date would have been sometime in 1913. But if we failed in later years to understand the long words laid on us by heavy-duty professors who explain our art to us, we knew a good thing when we saw it, seized upon pie-throwing, refined it, perfected its techniques, and presented it to the theater as a new art. It became, in time, a learned routine like the pratt-fall, the double-take, the slow burn, and the frantic leap, all stock equipment of competent comedians. When the Turpin pie scene was shown that night in a screening room we saw at once why it was funny.

It was funny, not only because a pie in the face is an outrage to pumped-up dignity, but because Turpin received the custard without a flick of premonition. Nonanticipation on the part of the recipient of a pastry is the chief ingredient of the recipe. And it takes an actor with a stern artistic conscience to stand still and innocent, never wagging an eyelash, while a strong man takes aim at him with such ammunition.

If you don't run with show people you may find this incredible, but it is a fact that many actors are frustrated because they never had a chance to display their integrity and facial control by taking a pie. Franklin Pangborn, for instance, a gentle comedian and a fine artist, pined for many years to receive a custard. When he finally worked for me, we had to write in a scene for him in which he got splurched. Frank did well, too, but he said being pushed backwards into swimming pools while wearing top hat and cutaway was more in his line.

We became scientists in custard. A man named Greenburg, who ran a small restaurant-bakery near the studio, became a throwing-pie entrepreneur. Our consumption was so enormous that this man got rich. After several experiments he invented a special Throwing Pie, just right in heft and consistency, filled with paste, and inedible. He lost most of his eating customers when he began to sell them throwing custards by mistake.

Del Lord, my ace comedy director, soon became the world-champion pie tosser. And "Fatty" Arbuckle, who in spite of his suet was an agile man—the kind of fat man known as light on his feet—became a superb pie pitcher. Arbuckle was ambidextrous and had double vision like a T-formation quarterback. He could throw two pies at once in different directions, but he was not precise in this feat. The Christy Mathewson of the custard was Del Lord.

"This is a delicate and serious art," says Mr. Lord, "and not one in which amateurs or inexperienced flingers should try to win renown. Pie-throwing, like tennis or golf, which depend upon form, requires a sense of balance and a definite follow-through.

"Actually, you don't throw like a shortstop rifling to first base. You *push* the pie toward the face, leaning into your follow-through. Six or eight feet is the limit for an artistic performance.

"You must never let the actor know when you're going to give him the custard in the choppers. Even the most skillful actor, José Ferrer or John Gielgud, for instance, finds it difficult to conceal anticipation.

"The wisest technique is to con your victim into a sense of security and then slip it to him.

"In my day, when I was the acknowledged world-champeen pie heaver, I developed a prejudice for berries with whipped cream. After the actual whomp in the face, the berries trickle beautifully down the actor's shirt and the whipped cream besplashes his suit. This is muddy, frothy, and photogenic."

Soon after we discovered that a pie is as theatrical a device as Bette Davis's handkerchief or Cyrano's nose, we made a picture called *The Great Pie Mystery*. Pies were thrown every time the heavy would try to do dirt to the girl or the comic. Pies came from everywhere and the audience couldn't see who was throwing them. Our pay-off gag was that the fellow who began telling the story in the first scene was throwing the pies.

We also invented a way to throw pies around telephone poles. We did this by having an expert fly caster out of camera range atop a stepladder. After a little practice he could let fly with rod and reel and make a pie do a figure eight before it hit a guy in the face.

As I was saying a while back, we demanded at least some kind of motivation in our pictures. Always the improbable, never the impossible. The introduction of pie-throwing was no stumbling block at all to our scenario writers. They simply inserted a restaurant or a bakery into the scene whenever it seemed like a good idea to fling a pie.

In speaking of the impossible, one of our most notable laugh-making scenes was one in which we had Charlie Murray tied to a steam boiler in a basement. The boiler actually expanded before the audience's eyes. Now that would be impossible, but that is how the boiler would *seem* to a man who was tied to it.

This rudimentary notion seems to be beyond the capacity of movie makers today. With my boys it was merely the beginning of a laugh sequence. They went on from the expanding boiler and had the *whole house* expand.

There are four kinds of laughs in the theatre: the titter, the yowl, the belly-laugh, and the boffo, according to Mr. James Agee, poet and motion-picture critic.

I don't want to create the impression that the titter, the yowl, the belly-laugh, and the boffo were purely mechanical affairs, even when the switcheroo was as charming a device as a tastefully flung pie. Neither my rocking-chair responses nor the genius of my thinker-uppers in the gag room was responsible for all the fun. The Keystone studio was a university of nonsense where, if an actor or actress had any personality at all, that personality developed in full blossom without inhibition. Two of the most special performers who ever came my way were Harry Langdon and Ben Turpin, both prime comics, and as different in outlook, philosophy, and abilities as men could be. Like most of our people—it was some years before we employed the already famous—they came to us from the knockabout stage with no money and no fame.

Harry Langdon came from a small-town vaudeville act in which his specialty was helpless frustration with a balky automobile. Frank Capra, who had progressed from gag man to director, wanted Langdon as soon as he set eyes on him. Harry had a kind of dough-faced baby innocence about him, combined with malice, that delighted Capra. Harry Langdon actually was as innocent as an infant. He had his routines, well learned in vaudeville, and he could do them on demand, but he seldom had the mistiest notion of what his screen stories were about. Like Charlie Chaplin, you had to let him take his time and go through his motions. His twitters and hesitations built up a ridiculous but sympathetic little character. It was difficult for us at first to know how to use Langdon, accustomed as we were to firing the gags and the falls at the audience as fast as possible, but as new talent arrived, we found ways to screen it and to cope with it. I thought for a while Langdon was as good as Chaplin. In some of his pathetic scenes he was certainly as good.

Langdon was an oddly gifted fellow. He drew cartoons for *Judge* and *Puck,* was an expert designer, and curiously handy at carpentry.

On screen he resembled Chaplin in one kind of appeal. He was always the small figure of frustrated good will beset and bewildered by a cruel world of hard rules and economics. But Chaplin, who could be as pitiful as a kicked spaniel or as forlorn and brave as he was in that wonderful scene in which he ate his shoes in *The Gold Rush,* was a man. He was adult. His impulses were often venal. He chased girls with pretentious gallantry and they never took him seriously. He gave you to know, though, that, if ever a girl *had* taken him seriously, he might have made a fool of himself in her boudoir but he would have known exactly what to try to do. Langdon was infantile.

Ladies pursued him. He not only didn't know what was expected of him, he didn't even know they were after him. Everything from sex to money was college algebra to Langdon.

Like Charlie, Harry was a slow starter. Even after we learned how to use him—I mean, saw what his essential character was for screen purposes—we had to give him a hundred feet of film or so to play around in, do little bits of business, and introduce himself. The two were the same in their universal appeal. They were the little guys coping with a mean universe, and, since motion-picture audiences are seldom made up 100 percent of tycoons, heroes, or millionaires, a majority of people managed to identify themselves with these comedians. Charlie Chaplin, I suppose, carried out this appeal to the heights in the great pictures he made after he left me. But wonderful as Charlie was, or is, he didn't invent being a little man.

Being a little man was being laughed at and sympathized with long before Charlie, or Langdon, or Turpin arrived in the public eye. Like the fall of dignity, it is one of the essences of comedy. We didn't invent it any more than we invented those two other reliable stock characters, little David with his slingshot and little Cinderella with her pumpkin.

Langdon was as bland as milk, a forgiving small cuss, an obedient puppy, always in the way, exasperating, but offering his baby mannerisms with hopeful apology. Frank Capra's enormous talents first showed themselves when he saw all this as something that would photograph. Chaplin was a waif, but an adult waif who thumbed his nose at anything.

Under Frank's easy guidance Harry soon became a Keystone star in two-reel comedies. His salary went up to several thousand dollars a week. Langdon became important and unfortunately realized it. Suddenly he forgot that all his value lay in being that baby-witted boy on the screen. He decided he was also a businessman. His cunning as a businessman was about that of a backward kindergarten student and he complicated this by marital adventures, in which he was about as inept as he was on screen. He was soon behind in alimony payments.

He decided that if Harry Langdon pictures could make so much money for Mack Sennett, they could make all that money for Harry Langdon. He heard about the wonderful grosses of big pictures like *The Miracle Man* and *The Birth of a Nation* and concluded that this kind of enterprise was for him.

Other companies were always ready to grab my stars after they had been tested and proved profitable. Soon enough Langdon had an offer from First National. It was a wonder, too. First National offered him $6,000 a week and 25 per cent of the net provided he would make six pictures in two years with a limit of $150,000 production cost per picture.

Langdon was delighted by these fat figures, hired Harry Edwards as director at $1,000 a week, Capra at $750 a week, and Bill Jenner as his personal manager at $500 a week.

Then he forgot all this outgoing money was actually his own, merely his advance from First National. He blew the entire $150,000 production budget before he got his first story written.

Poor Langdon failed wretchedly as a producer, and lived brokenhearted and in near-poverty around Hollywood for many years. He did his last work at Columbia, where he attempted to dance in a musical comedy. But working and rehearsing all day exhausted the little fellow. He went into a coma and died of a stroke after lingering for about eight days.

He was bankrupt and neglected, forlorn and forgotten. His shy charm and his gentle humor have yet to be matched on the screen. I wish he had stayed with me. He was a quaint artist who had no business in business. He was hurt and bewildered at the end and he never understood what had happened to him.

Ben Turpin, the cross-eyed man, was an artist too, but another breed of cat.

All comedians, as I keep saying, are sensitive, egotistical persons. They require audiences, applause, security, and reassurance. Some are tender and some are tough. Some are both, but the combination of clown-poet-intellectual is a rare bird and occurs only once in a lucky generation, as in Chaplin.

Turpin came to us from the circus and the vaudeville stage. One of his demands on the studio as soon as his face became known all over the world was that we take out an insurance policy with Lloyd's of London which would pay him one million dollars if his eyes ever came uncrossed. It took only the simplest examination by an honest oculist to assure Lloyd's their money was safe. Ben's eyes were permanently fixed and so were his notions.

This skinny, strutting little man with a Polish piano player's mane of hair and a neck like a string was obsessed by money and by the conviction that he couldn't be funny after 5 P.M. He had a five-o'clock quitting time in his contract. When the bell rang he left no matter what it cost the studio.

Mr. Turpin had several wives. I was not acquainted with all of them, but he brought one to the studio and introduced her around. She was the one who was stone-deaf.

"Mr. Sennett," he said, "I want you to meet my wife. I got the old bag in trouble and had to marry her."

The deaf Mrs. Turpin smiled graciously and acknowledged the introduction.

Ben went on to find Mabel Normand.

"Mabel, I want you to meet the wife," he said. "She used to be a tattooed woman in a honky-tonk. Don't have anything to do with her. She's a blackmailer and a dope smuggler."

Mrs. Turpin beamed fondly on Ben and was delighted to meet his friends.

We paid Turpin $1,500 a week at the height of his powers. He invested all his money, bought apartment houses, and became a rich man. He always saved a few dollars a week by personally doing the janitor work at all his apartment houses.

He seldom drove an automobile—a frantic thought at that: who knows how many directions he would have tried to drive at once? He preferred to save money by traveling by streetcar. As he would enter the trolley, he would draw his wrenlike physique up to full strut and squeak at the top of his voice:

"I'm Ben Turpin! Three thousand dollars a week!"

Before taking a seat he would treat the passengers to a 108.

A 108 is an acrobat's term for a comic fall which only the most skillful athletes can perform without lethal results. One foot goes forward, the other foot goes backward, the comedian does a counter somersault and lands flat on his back.

I've seen Turpin perform the 108 not only on streetcars but on concrete sidewalks—if there was an audience handy to whom he could announce himself as three-thousand-dollars-a-week Ben Turpin.

Turpin was an emotional little man, especially under the influence of money or the bottle. Once when we had leased a special train to take a company to Lake Tahoe, scheduled to leave at seven in the evening, Del Lord found Mr. Turpin hitting crescendo in the throes of a crying jag. On such occasions Turpin demanded the attentions of his attorney, his business manager, and his priest.

When Del arrived at the roaring Turpin establishment, Ben had decided that *he* was all right, but that for reasons obscure to everyone else, his wife (the deaf one) was dying.

Since Mrs. Turpin was blooming with health, Del dismissed the lawyer and business manager, took the priest home, and called up Tommy Lofthaus, chief of the Los Angeles Motor Patrol. Mr. Lofthaus was a good friend because we often gave his cops jobs on off-duty days.

Turpin arrived at the station under full siren, delighted with his police escort. He dashed into his drawing room, belted down a scotch and soda, and went through the entire train announcing himself as Ben Turpin, $3,000 a week. He performed a 108 in each car.

We got him to Lake Tahoe in fancy fettle, but Turpin immediately became victim of a new terror. We had a scene in which the giant Kalla Pasha, wearing a black fur suit, worked interchangeably with a live bear which closely resembled him. The script called for Turpin to hop into bed with the fur-bearing Pasha. Ben winced and keened over this idea, said it was frightening enough to send a valuable actor to the looney bin just to think of getting into bed with Kalla Pasha, let alone a dangerous, man-eating critter. Anyway, Turpin complained, he had no faith whatsoever in the integrity or the human kindness of anybody connected with Keystone and Mack Sennett. He was dead sure he was being framed and would wind up in the embrace of the bear.

During this tantrum our bear got his teeth into his trainer's arm and almost chawed it off. This upset all of us to some extent. The accident was particularly dismaying to Turpin.

As things came out, we had to do away with that bear as a safety measure, but it seemed a shame to waste him. We put the warm corpse in Kalla Pasha's bed and inserted Mr. Turpin. Ben's histrionics made a notable scene for a few seconds. He never forgave us.

It is honorable to give credit where credit is due. It was Mabel Normand who connived the bedding of Ben Turpin and the bear

Turpin seldom invited guests into his home. On the few special occasions when he did you knew immediately how you stood with him the moment you entered his parlor. Unless you were an extremely welcome guest you never got to see his furniture. He kept every piece draped with white cloths which he removed only as a delicate compliment of friendship.

Ben could fall, tumble, and prank with the best of my rough-necks, but his special and universal appeal was, of course, like Langdon's and Chaplin's, the appeal of all undersized gents who stand up against Fate *anyway*. Ridiculous to everyone, yes, but never to himself. In Von Stroheim breeches and monocle Turpin reduced Von Stroheim and all domineering Prussians to absurdity. With cross-eyes batting with passion he could lie on a tiger-skin rug and make the heaving sultriness of Theda Bara (or all pretentious love-making) a silly joke.

The thing was, he seemed to take himself with utter seriousness. You never felt sorry for him no matter how you laughed. You had to see that Mr. Turpin was very, very brave.

This was true also of Buster Keaton. Keaton carried out comic courage to its ridiculously logical absurdity. He never batted an eye or changed an expression, no matter what catastrophies threatened him. "Fatty" Arbuckle brought him to me. The two worked funnily together for several pictures. But these films were so hilarious that Keaton was immediately swamped with offers of more money than I could pay him.

He went to Metro-Goldwyn-Mayer, where he became, in my opinion, the greatest comedian the greatest studio ever had. His pictures eventually cost $200,000 to make and always brought in at least a couple of million dollars—a long cry from our cut-rate productions. Keaton married Natalie Talmadge, sister of Norma, Metro's biggest star at that time.

I fondly claim Buster Keaton. We could have done improbable things together. But the Great Stone Face was cut out for larger works than we had to offer. He was one of the first to set the pattern that kept me in trouble the rest of my life: start with Sennett and get rich somewhere else!

Ben Turpin died rich and having fun. After his retirement it was his hobby to direct traffic at the intersection of Santa Monica Boulevard and Western Avenue. With eyes crossed and arms flailing he engineered some of the most outrageous automotive jams in the history of congested Los Angeles.

He yelled to every motorist, "Ben Turpin, three thousand dollars a week!"

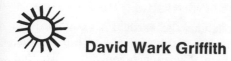

David Wark Griffith

*

THE

MOVIES

100

YEARS

FROM

NOW

THEY SAY I am a realist—a man who functions best when re-producing in the films life as he sees it or knows it. Whereupon the editor promptly assumes that fantasy will be perfectly easy for me, and propounds a question that scarcely can be answered by anything other than a dream. Fortunately, I have my fancies.

"What," asks the editor in substance, "will be the status of the motion pictures one hundred years hence?"

I have wondered that very thing many times myself, and since I am one of those persons who sometimes respond to their own imagery with answers, I can at least give an opinion. I may qualify this by adding that it is the opinion of one who has devoted a large part of his life to the subject.

In the year 2024 the most important single thing which the cinema will have helped in a large way to accomplish will be that of eliminating from the face of the civilized world all armed conflict. Pictures will be the most powerful factor in bringing about this condition. With the use of the universal language of moving pictures the true meaning of the brotherhood of man will

Originally published in *Collier's*, May 3, 1924, pp. 7 and 28.

have been established throughout the earth. For example, the Englishman will have learned that the soul of the Japanese is, essentially, the same as his own. The Frenchman will realize that the American's ideals are his ideals. All men are created equal.

It is not to be presumed that I believe one hundred years from now the pictures will have had time to educate the masses away from discord and unharmony. What I do mean to say is, by that time war, if there is such a thing, will be waged on a strictly scientific basis, with the element of physical destruction done away with entirely. My theory is that conflict, if and when it arises, will find itself governed by scientific rules and regulations to which both sides of the controversy will subscribe. Armies outfitted with boxing gloves, man to man, may, I think, go into "battle" to determine the victor. I am not smiling with you now. I am quite sincere. It will be a matter of science and fair play to the last letter. I am just as sincere when I predict that after the "battle" the warriors will repair to a prearranged cold-drink canteen and have grape juice. Just as the old English debtors' prison was wiped out by education, so will armed conflict be wiped out by education.

There is little question that a century ahead of us will find a great deal more of the so-called intimate drama presented on the screen, although there will always be a field set apart for the film with a vast background such as *The Birth of a Nation* and *America*.

You will walk into your favorite film theatre and see your actors appearing in twice the size you see them now, because the screens will be twice as large, and the film itself twice as large also. With these enlargements, "close-ups" will be almost eliminated, since it will be relatively easy to picture facial expression along with the full figure of the performer. It will always be necessary to picture the face in pictures. It is the face which reflects the soul of a man.

Our "close-ups," or "inserts," as I call them, are sometimes cumbersome and disconcerting. I invented them, but I have tried not to overuse them, as many have done. It is a mechanical trick, and is of little credit to anyone.

We shall say there are now five elaborate first-run picture

theatres on one New York street, Broadway. In 2024 there will be at least forty. Cities of 1,000 will average at least six. Cities of 20,000 and thereabout will have over a hundred. By virtue of its great advantage in scope, the motion picture will be fitted to tell certain stories as no other medium can. But I must add that the glory of the spoken or written word in the intimate and poetic drama can never be excelled by any form of expression.

In the year 2024 our directors of the better order will be men graduated from schools, academies, and colleges carrying in their curriculum courses in motion-picture direction. Our actors and actresses will be artists graduated from schools and colleges either devoted exclusively to the teaching and study of motion-picture acting or carrying highly specialized courses in acting before the camera. This is inevitable.

I am well aware of the fact that the present cumbersome and haphazard method by which screen talent is selected (and by screen talent I mean to say directors, designers, actors, and cameramen) will not endure long. Time will find this matter adjusted upon a basis of merit and equipment.

Probably on an average of a dozen times each week persons ask me if I think color photography in the motion pictures will be perfected and made practical. Most assuredly, I do think so. Certainly all color processes and tint methods at present in use are wrong. They are not arrived at with any degree of inventiveness, and they cannot last. At present the colored pictures we see are made by the use of gelatines on the film or by the use of varicolored lenses which fly before the film. Thus we find a great lack of harmony and accuracy. I am willing to confess that I have tried them. But I should be the last to speak of my color effects seriously. We have been merely exploring and speculating.

Only through one method will color be naturally and properly given to objects and persons in the motion pictures. This is a method which will develop a film so sensitive that it will record the natural tints and colors as the picture is being photographed.

Of course, to the man or woman untrained in these lines, this seems remote and hardly possible. Still, consider the conquering of the air—the discovery of a means whereby the human voice may be projected through air three thousand miles! When we realize what has been done in the wireless it seems utter folly to suppose that color photography—natural, permanent color photography—may not be found for the films. One hundred years from now the color of a woman's eyes and hair, the tint of the sea, the hues of the rainbow itself will be a natural part of every motion-picture play.

On the other hand, I am quite positive that when a century has passed, all thought of our so-called speaking pictures will have been abandoned. It will never be possible to synchronize the voice with the pictures. This is true because the very nature of the films foregoes not only the necessity for but the propriety of the spoken voice. Music—fine music—will always be the voice of the silent drama. One hundred years from now will find the greatest composers of that day devoting their skill and their genius to the creation of motion-picture music.

There will be three principal figures in the production of a picture play—the author first, the director and music composer occupying an identical position in importance.

We do not want now and we never shall want the human voice with our films. Music, as I see it within that hundred years, will be applied to the visualization of the human being's imagination. And, as in your imagination those unseen voices are always perfect and sweet, or else magnificent and thrilling, you will find them registering upon the mind of the picture patron, in terms of lovely music, precisely what the author has intended to be registered there. There is no voice in the world like the voice of music. To me those images on the screen must always be silent. Anything else would work at cross purposes with the real object of this new medium of expression. There will never be speaking pictures. Why should there be when no voice can speak so beautifully as music? There are no dissonant r's and twisted consonants and guttural slurs and nasal twangs in beautiful music. Therefore the average person would much prefer to see his pictures and let the voice which speaks to him be the voice of music—one of the most perfect of all the arts.

I seem a little emphatic on this particular point, and I mean to be.

In the year 2024 we shall have orchestras of many kinds playing for the pictures. Each motion-picture theatre will have several orchestras of diversified character. The big, robust, outdoor pictures will have more than one orchestra in attendance at all times. String quartets will play for the mood of a string quartet; sighing guitars and thumpety banjos will play for their mood in the picture play; symphonic orchestras of greater proportions than we now dream of will be employed for moods to fit the sublime and the grand.

We have scarcely an inkling of what the development of music is going to be in the film play.

It really seems to me a little bit humorous now to realize how narrow a place in our everyday life the film is playing, despite the great rise in attendance in the last few years. One hundred years hence, I believe, the airplane passenger lines will operate motion-picture shows on regular schedule between New York and Chicago and between New York and London. Trains, which will be traveling twice or three times as fast as they do now, will have film theatres on board. Almost every home of good taste will have its private projection room where miniatures, perhaps, of the greater films will be shown to the family, and, of course, families will make their albums in motion pictures instead of in tintypes and "stills." Steamships will boast of first runs, which will be brought to them in mid-ocean by the airplanes, and I may add that almost all subjects in our schools will be taught largely with the use of picture play and the educational animated picture.

By the time these things come to pass, there will be no such thing as a flicker in your film. Your characters and objects in pictures will come upon the screen (which by then may not even be white, and certainly may not be square, or look anything like what it does now), and they will appear to the onlookers precisely as these persons and objects appear in real life. That much-discussed "depth" in pictures, which no one as yet has been able to employ successfully, will long since have been discovered and adopted. The moving canvas will not appear flat, but if a character moves before a fireplace you will recognize the distance as between the character and the fireplace. Likewise, in landscapes, you will feel the proper sense of distance. Your mountain peaks will not appear to rise one on top of other other, but will appear exactly as if you stood and looked at them. Of course these are merely details that will require long and intense study and experiment, but they will come. In other words, from the standpoint of naturalness, motion pictures one hundred years from now will be so nearly like the living person or the existing object pictured that you will be unable, sitting in your orchestra seat, to determine whether they are pictures or the real thing.

By a perfection of the studio lighting system, film will be as smooth before the eye as if it were a stationary lighted picture. By that time the studios will have changed greatly, and instead of actors being forced to work before great blinding lights, which now at times register 117 degrees of heat, we shall have "cold" lights. We are experimenting in these already. Our studios will be great spreading institutions, as large as many of the cities surrounding New York. I think that one hundred years from now there will be no concentrated motion-picture production such as our Hollywood of today. Films will be made in various cities, most of which will be located near to New York.

It nettles me at times when I am asked if I do not think that in time the popularity of the motion pictures will subside. It seems to me ridiculous. As ridiculous as to assume that the popularity of music, or painting, or acting on our spoken stage will go out.

No. I not only do not think the popularity of motion pictures will decrease; I am already on record as predicting that the popularity of pictures will increase and keep on increasing. Consider my own *Birth of a Nation*. It was revived two years ago, after having been off for ten years, and it was as great a success in revival as in the original. The popularity of motion pictures (which are a natural form of dramatic expression) will ride higher and higher as the quality of motion pictures rises higher and higher. One hundred years from today we shall have novelists devoting all their energies toward creating motion-picture originals. By this I mean that the novelists giving their exclusive time to the films will create characters and situations and dramatic plots in terms of pictures. Motion-picture historians will have been developed, and they will be a great help to production. Motion-picture artists of all kinds will have grown up. It will all make for a more natural, dignified, sincere result because we shall have all our different branches devoting their time and efforts toward the completion of a single object—a motion picture.

I have no hesitancy in saying that the radio has claimed its share of amusement audiences. Unquestionably it has kept many persons away from both the films and the spoken stage. It is a great, useful discovery—a glorious medium. One hundred years from now there will be no confusion as between the radio and the motion picture. There cannot possibly be a connection nor a conflict. It is just possible there may be a conflict as between radio and spoken stage, but never between radio and film. Each occupies its own exclusive place in our lives.

Now let us prepare for a small-sized shock. One hundred years from today it will cost perhaps twice as much as it costs today to see the really first-class cinema. It is perfectly proper that it should. Time, effort, energy, and preparation put into pictures at that time will have advanced greatly. I am just honest enough to say that I do not at the moment understand how more time, effort, energy, and preparation could have been put into my own pictures; but, then, for the average large picture play this will hold true. The average supposedly high-class film play in 2024 will be on view at not less than $5 a seat.

In looking into the crystal I have seen many things which I have not touched upon here. Perhaps they would be too tedious to bring out and discuss. But of one thing I may place myself on record plainly and without qualification. The motion picture is a child that has been given life in our generation. As it grows older it will develop marvelously. We poor souls can scarcely visualize or dream of its possibilities. We ought to be kind with it in its youth, so that in its maturity it may look back upon its childhood without regrets.

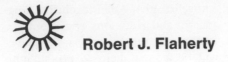

Robert J. Flaherty

*

H O W   I

F I L M E D

" N A N O O K

O F

T H E

N O R T H "

IN AUGUST 1910, Sir William MacKenzie whose transconti-
nental railway, the Canadian Northern, was then in the initial
stages of construction, commissioned the writer to undertake an
expedition to the East Coast of Hudson Bay to examine certain
islands upon which deposits of iron ore were supposed to be
located.

All told I made four expeditions on Sir William's behalf, during
a period of six years, along the East Coast of Hudson Bay, through
the barren lands of the hitherto unexplored peninsula of Ungava,
along the west coast of Ungava Bay and along the southern coast
of Baffin Land. This work culminated in the discovery of the
Belcher Island archipelago in Hudson Bay—a land mass which
occupies 5,000 square miles—upon this land mass were discovered extensive deposits of iron ore but all of too low a grade, however, to be of economic importance. As a part of my exploration
equipment, on these expeditions, a motion-picture outfit was
included. It was hoped to secure films of the North and Eskimo

From *The World's Work, XLIV* (September, 1922), pp. 553-60.

life, which might prove to be of enough value to help in some way to defray some of the costs of the explorations. While wintering in Baffin Land during 1913-14, films of the country and the natives were made, as was also done on the succeeding expedition to the Belcher Islands. The film, in all about 30,000 feet, was brought out safely, at the conclusion of the explorations, to Toronto, where, while editing the material, I had the misfortune of losing it all by fire. Though it seemed to be a tragedy at the time, I am not sure but what it was a bit of fortune that it did burn, for it was amateurish enough.

My interest in films, from then on, grew.

New forms of travel film was coming out and the Johnson South Sea Island film particularly seemed to me to be an earnest of what might be done in the North. I began to believe that a good film depicting the Eskimo and his fight for existence in the dramatically barren North might be well worth while. To make a long story short, I decided to go north again—this time wholly for the purpose of making films.

Mr. John Revillon and Captain Thierry Mallet of Revillon Frères became interested and decided to finance my project. It proved to be a happy arrangement, for among the Revillon Frères' vast system of fur posts which lie scattered through northern Canada I was enabled to use one of these posts as the nucleus for my work. This post was on Cape Dufferin on northeastern Hudson Bay and about 800 miles north of the rail frontier in northern Ontario. The journey thither began on the eighteenth of June, 1920. With Indians by canoe, I followed the Moose River to Moose Factory on James Bay. From thence northward a small schooner was taken to my destination, where I arrived in the middle of August. The resources of the Revillon Frères fur trade post at Cape Dufferin were at my disposal. One of the two living quarters which comprised the Post was mine as living quarters and film laboratory combined.

My equipment included 75,000 feet of film, a Haulberg electric light plant and projector and two Akeley cameras and a printing machine so that I could make prints of film as it was exposed and project the pictures on the screen so that thereby the Eskimo would be able to see and understand wherever mistakes were made.

Of the Eskimo who were known to the Post, a dozen all told I selected for the film. Of these, Nanook, a character famous in the country, was my chief man. Besides him and much to his approval, I selected three younger men as helpers. This also meant their wives and families, dogs to the number of about twenty-five, their sledges, kayacks, and hunting impedimenta.

As luck would have it, the first film to be made was the walrus hunt. From Nanook, I first heard of the "Walrus Island," which is a small island far out at sea and inaccessible to the Eskimo during the open water season since it is far out enough so as not to be seen from land.

On the island's south end, a surf-bound beach, there were, in summer, Nanook said, many walrus, judging from signs that had been seen by a winter sealing crowd of Eskimo who, caught by a breakup of the ice, had been forced to live there until late spring, when, by building an umiak of driftwood and sealskins and by digging out the open water lands of ice which had not yet cleared from the coast, they succeeded in getting on to the mainland. Nanook was very keen about my going, for, as he said, "It is many moons since I have hunted the summer walrus."

When I had decided upon taking the trip the whole countryside was interested. There was no lack of applicants for the trip. Everyone gave me some particular reason why he should be included in the expedition. With an open-seas boat twenty-five feet long rigged with a leg-o'-mutton sail we started, a throng of Eskimo, their wives, children and dogs assembled on the beach to see us off.

A few miles from the Post we reached the open sea when for three days we waited on the coast for easy weather in order to undertake the crossing. We finally reached the island one day at nightfall, and landed on what was nothing but a low waste of bed rock and boulders a mile and a half long and the whole of its shoreland ringed with booming surf. Around the luxury of a driftwood fire (driftwood is rare on the mainland) we lounged far into the night, speculating mainly on what chances there might be for walrus. As luck would have it just as we were turning in, from Nanook suddenly came an exclamation "Iviuk! Iviuk!" and the bark of a school of walrus resounded through the air. When early the next morning we went over, we found much to our disappointment that the walrus herd had gone into the sea again but presently one after another and near the shore the heads of a big school of walrus shot up above the sea, their wicked tusks gleaming in the sun. As long as they were in the water no films could be made and we returned again to the camp. For the next two days we made almost hourly trips to that beach before finally we found them—a herd of twenty—asleep and basking in the sand on the shore. Most fortunately they lay at a point where in approaching, we could be screened from their view by a slight rise in the ground. Behind the rise, I mounted the camera and Nanook, stringing his harpoon, began slowly snaking over the crest. From the crest to where they lay was less than fifty feet and until Nanook crawled to within half that distance toward them none took any alarm. For the rest of the way, whenever the sentinel of the herd slowly raised his head to look around, Nanook lay motionless on the ground. Then when his head drooped in sleep, once more Nanook wormed his way slowly on. I might mention here that the walrus has little range of vision on land. For protection he depends upon his nose and so long as the wind is favorable one can stalk right in to them. When almost right in amongst them, Nanook picked out the biggest bull, rose quickly and with all his strength landed his harpoon. The wounded bull, bellowing in rage, his enormous bulk diving and thrashing the sea (he weighed more than 2,000 pounds), the yells of the men straining for their lives in their attempt to hold him, the battle cry of the herd that hovered near, the wounded bull's mate which swam in, locked tusks, in an attempt to rescue—was the greatest fight I have ever seen. For a long time it was nip and tuck—repeatedly the crew called to me to use the gun—but the camera crank was my only interest then and I pretended not to understand. Finally Nanook worked the quarry toward the surf where he was pounded by the heavy seas and unable to get a purchase in the water. For at least twenty minutes that tug-o'-war kept on. I say twenty minutes advisedly for I ground out 1,200 feet of film.

Our boat, laden with walrus meat and ivory—it was a happy crew that took me back to the Post, where Nanook and his fellows were hailed with much acclaim. I lost no time in developing and printing the film. That walrus fight was the first film these Eskimo had ever seen and, in the language of the trade, it was a "knock-out."

The audience—they thronged the post kitchen to the point of suffocation, completely forgot the picture—to them the walrus was real and living. The women and children in their high shrill voices joined with the men in shouting admonitions, warnings and advice to Nanook and his crew as the picture unfolded on the screen. The fame of that picture spread through all the country. And all through the year that I remained there every family who came wandering into the Post begged of me that they be shown the "Iviuk Aggie." After this it did not take my Eskimo long to see the practical side of films and they soon abandoned their former attitude of laughter and good-natured ridicule toward the Angercak, i e., the White Master who wanted pictures of them—the commonest objects in all the world! From that time on they were all with me. When in December the snow lay heavy on the ground the Eskimo abandoned their topecks of sealskin and the village of snow igloos sprung up around my wintering post. They snow-walled my little hut up to the eaves with thick blocks of snow. It was as thick-walled as a fortress. My kitchen was their rendezvous—there was always a five-gallon pail of tea steeping on the stove and sea biscuit in the barrel. My little gramophone, too, was common property. Caruso, Farrar, Ricardo-Martin, McCormick served their turns with Harry Lauder, Al Jolson and Jazz King orchestras. Caruso in the Pagliacci prologue with its tragic ending was to them the most comic record of the lot. It sent them into peals of laughter and to rolling on the floor.

The difficulties of film development and printing during the winter were many. That convenience of civilization which I most missed was running water. For instance, in the film washing, three barrels of water for every hundred feet was required. The water hole, then eight feet of ice, had to be kept open all winter long and water clotted with particles of ice had to be taken, a barrel at a time, from a distance of more than a quarter of a mile away. When I mention that over 50,000 feet of film was developed over the winter with no assistance save from my Eskimo and at the slow rate of eight hundred feet a day, one can understand somewhat the amount of time and labor involved.

The walrus hunt having proved so successful, Nanook aspired to bigger things. The first of the bigger things was to be a bear hunt at Cape Sir Thomas Smith, which lay some two hundred miles northward of us. "Here," said Nanook, "is where the she-bear den in the winter. I know, for I have hunted them there, and it seems to me that there we might get the big, big aggie [picture]."

He went on to describe how in early December the she-bear dens in huge drift banks of snow. There is nothing to mark the den save the tiny vent or air hole which is melted open by the animal's body heat. He went on with a warning that one should not walk there for one would fall in, in which case the she-bear might be angry! His companions would remain at either side of me, rifles in hand, whilst I filmed (he was going to make sure of my safety in the affair at least). He, with his snow knife, would open up the den block by block. The dogs, in the meantime, would all be unleashed and like a circle of wolves would gather around him howling to the skies. Mrs. Bear's den door opened, Nanook, with nothing but his harpoon, would be poised and waiting.

The dogs baiting the quarry—some of them with her lightning paws the bear would send hurtling through the air—Nanook dancing here and there (he pantomimed the scene on my cabin floor using my fiddle bow for harpoon) waiting to dart in for a close-up throw—this, he felt sure, would be a big, big picture (aggie peerualluk). I agreed with him.

After two weeks' preparation, we started. Nanook with three male companions, two sledges heavily laden, and two 12-dog teams. My food outfit comprised one hundred pounds of pork and beans which had been cooked in huge kettles at my post and then put into a canvas bag and frozen. These beans chopped out with an axe from the frozen mass along with dried fruit, sea biscuit, and tea comprised my food supply.

Nanook and his companions' diet was seal and walrus augmented by tea and sugar from my supply and, most important of all, tobacco, that most valued of the white man's treasure.

We departed on a bitterly cold day—the 17th day of January— every profile of the landscape blurred with drifting snow. For two days we made good progress, for the traveling ground was hard and well packed by the wind. After that time, however, a heavy gale with falling snow wrecked our good going. Day after day we slowly made our way along. Ten miles or less was an average day's travel. We had hoped to cover the 200 miles to Cape Smith in eight days but, when twelve days had elapsed, found we were only half way. We were discouraged, the dogs all but worn out, and to make matters worse the supply of seal and dog food was near the point of exhaustion.

The low coastline off which we traveled for days on end was the confusing mirage hanging in the sky, so that Nanook could not locate himself and our position in relation to Cape Smith. Constantly as we traveled along in that monotony of days, our nearness to Cape Smith became the subject uppermost in our minds. "How near are we?" was the hourly question that became the plague of poor Nanook's existence. The few times he tried to predict, he was invariably wrong. Finally, we had traveled to a point where the Cape, Nanook was sure, was no more than two days on, for he was certain that he had spied through the haze and rime old hunting country of former years. Within the day, his companions found that he again was wrong. They could not contain their impatience and irritation. Poor Nanook became disgusted, and as we continued he kept his head averted and steadfastly refused to ever look upon that confounding mainland again.

We were on our beam ends the day we finally reached Cape Smith. Our brown leader dog, that for the last three days we had been carrying on the top of the sledge in the attempt to save her, was dying of starvation. Nanook ended it all with his harpoon and as he held aloft the carcass said: "There is not enough left for dog food."

Well, anyway there were seals at the Cape, that we were sure of, and moreover we would be there within the day, so we continued cheerfully enough. The great land mass of the Cape rising a sheer 1,800 feet stood out boldly before us. By nightfall we reached our treasure land of bear and seals and plenty. We halted before the rise of an old campground of Nanook's, and, abandoning sledge and dogs, climbed eagerly to a vantage for the welcome sight of the seal grounds. We gazed there a moment or so before we realized that the seal ground we looked out upon was like all the barren ground we had traveled—a solid white field and not a seal-hunting lane of open water anywhere. We forgot about bear hunting; for two and a half weeks we tried for seals, wandering from day to day along the broken ice foot of the Cape. In that interval two small seals were killed and they were just enough to keep the dogs alive. For four days, at one time, we had no seal oil and our igloo was in darkness. The dogs were utterly weak and slept in the igloo tunnel. Whenever I had to crawl out of doors, I would have to lift them to one side like sacks of flour, for they were too weak and indifferent to move away. The irony of it all was that bears there were everywhere; four of them had passed within a thousand feet of our igloo one night, but the dogs were too weak to bay them or bring them to a stand. My own food supply was nearing its fag ends. For days past I had been sharing it with the men.

I will never forget one bitter morning when Nanook and his men were starting off for a hunting day on the ice fields at sea. I suddenly discovered that none of them had touched my food at breakfast time. When I remonstrated with Nanook he answered that he was afraid I might be short!

Our luck turned that day at nightfall, however, when Nanook crawled into the igloo wearing a smile from ear to ear, and shouting the welcomed words "Ojuk! Ojuk!" (the big seal). He had killed a big seal that was "very, very large" and enough for us and dogs for all the long trail south to home again.

What a feast those men had through that memorable night! When it was over, said Nanook in deep content, "Now we are strong again and warm. The white man's food has made us much too weak and cold." The flesh of seal is certainly warmth-giving to the greatest degree. When I awakened the next morning, all of them were still asleep, their bodies were covered with hoar frost and vapor lay floating over them in the cold igloo air.

Though the problem of our food supply was now solved, we were still not able to travel, for the dogs needed feeding up. During this interval we hunted along the gigantic flanks of the cape for signs of bear dens. Tracks there were everywhere, but of dens only one and that one had been abandoned. Had we had the time to spare, it would have been only a matter of days before we would have found one, but I had a great amount of filming to do at my winter post and more time could not be spared, so reluctantly enough we left the Cape and started off on the down trail for home.

We arrived there on the tenth day of March, and so ended the six hundred miles and fifty-five days of our Nanook's "big picture" journey. But it was not all loss: I was richer by a fuller knowledge of the fine qualities of my sterling friends, the Eskimos.

Charles Chaplin

*

DIRECTING

MY

FIRST

FILM

I MADE ABOUT five pictures* and in some of them I had managed to put over one or two bits of comedy business of my own, in
spite of the butchers in the cutting room. Familiar with their
method of cutting films, I would contrive business and gags just
for entering and exiting from a scene, knowing that they would
have difficulty in cutting them out. I took every opportunity I
could to learn the business. I was in and out of the developing
plant and cutting room, watching the cutter piece the films
together.

Now I was anxious to write and direct my own comedies, so I
talked to Sennett about it. But he would not hear of it; instead he
assigned me to Mabel Normand, who had just started directing
her own pictures. This nettled me, for, charming as Mabel was, I
doubted her competence as a director; so the first day there came
the inevitable blowup. We were on location in the suburbs of
Los Angeles, and in one scene Mabel wanted me to stand with a
hose and water down the road so that the villain's car would skid
over it. I suggested standing on the hose so that the water can't
come out, and when I look down the nozzle I unconsciously step

From Charles Chaplin, *My Autobiography* (The Bodley Head, Ltd.,
1964).

* Chaplin's first films—for the Keystone Company—made during 1914.

off the hose and the water squirts in my face. But she shut me up quickly: "We have no time! We have no time! Do what you're told."

That was enough, I could not take it—and from such a pretty girl. "I'm sorry, Miss Normand, I will not do what I'm told. I don't think you are competent to tell me what to do."

The scene was in the center of the road, and I left it and sat down on the curb. Sweet Mabel—at that time she was only twenty, pretty and charming, everybody's favorite; everybody loved her. Now she sat by the camera bewildered; nobody had ever spoken to her so directly before. I also was susceptible to her charm and beauty and secretly had a soft spot in my heart for her, but this was my work. Immediately the staff and the cast surrounded Mabel and went into conference. One or two extras, Mabel told me afterwards, wanted to slug me, but she stopped them from doing so. Then she sent the assistant over to find out if I was going to continue working. I crossed the road to where she was sitting. "I'm sorry," I said apologetically, "I just don't think it's funny or amusing. But if you'll allow me to offer a few comedy suggestions. . . ."

She did not argue. "Very well," she said. "If you won't do what you're told, we'll go back to the studio." Although the situation was desperate, I was resigned, so I shrugged. We had not lost much of the day's work, for we had been shooting since nine in the morning. It was now past five in the afternoon and the sun was sinking fast.

At the studio, while I was taking off my grease paint, Sennett came bursting into the dressing room. "What the hell's the idea?" he said.

I tried to explain. "The story needs gagging up," I said, "but Miss Normand will not listen to any suggestions."

"You'll do what you're told or get out, contract or no contract," he said.

I was very calm. "Mr. Sennett," I answered, "I earned my bread and cheese before I came here, and if I'm fired—well, I'm fired. But I'm conscientious and just as keen to make a good picture as you are."

Without saying anything further he slammed the door.

That night, going home on the streetcar with my friend, I told him what had happened.

"Too bad. You were going great there for a while," he said.

"Do you think they'll fire me?" I said cheerfully, in order to hide my anxiety.

"I wouldn't be at all surprised. When I saw him leaving your dressing room he looked pretty mad."

"Well, it's O.K. with me. I've got fifteen hundred dollars in my belt and that will more than pay my fare back to England. However, I'll show up tomorrow and if they don't want me— *c'est la vie.*"

There was an eight o'clock call the following morning and I was not sure what to do, so I sat in the dressing room without making up. About ten minutes to eight Sennett poked his head in the door. "Charlie, I want to talk to you. Let's go into Mabel's dressing room." His tone was surprisingly friendly.

"Yes, Mr. Sennett," I said, following him.

Mabel was not there. She was in the projection room looking at rushes.

"Listen," said Mack, "Mabel's very fond of you, we all are fond of you and think you're a fine artist."

I was surprised at this sudden change and I immediately began to melt. "I certainly have the greatest respect and admiration for Miss Normand," I said, "but I don't think she is competent to direct—after all, she's very young."

"Whatever you think, just swallow your pride and help out," said Sennett, patting me on the shoulder.

"That's precisely what I've been trying to do."

"Well, do your best to get along with her."

"Listen, if you'll let me direct myself, you'll have no trouble," I said.

Mack paused a moment. "Who's going to pay for the film if we can't release it?"

"I will," I answered. "I'll deposit fifteen hundred dollars in any bank and if you can't release the picture you can keep the money."

Mack thought a moment. "Have you a story?"

"Of course, as many as you want."

"All right," said Mack. "Finish the picture with Mabel, then

I'll see." We shook hands in a most friendly manner. Later I went to see Mabel and apologized, and that evening Sennett took us both out to dinner. The next day Mabel could not have been sweeter. She even came to me for suggestions and ideas. Thus, to the bewilderment of the camera crew and the rest of the cast, we happily completed the picture. Sennett's sudden change of attitude baffled me. It was months later, however, that I found out the reason: it appears that Sennett intended firing me at the end of the week, but the morning after I had quarreled with Mabel, Mack received a telegram from the New York office telling him to hurry up with more Chaplin pictures as there was a terrific demand for them.

The average number of prints for a Keystone Comedy release was twenty. Thirty was considered quite successful. The last picture, which was the fourth one, reached forty-five copies, and demands for further copies were increasing. Hence Mack's friendliness after the telegram.

The mechanics of directing were simple in those days. I had only to know my left from my right for entrances and exits. If one exited right from a scene, one came in left in the next scene; if one exited towards the camera, one entered with one's back to the camera in the next scene. These, of course, were primary rules.

But with more experience I found that the placing of a camera was not only psychological but articulated a scene; in fact, it was the basis of cinematic style. If the camera is a little too near, or too far, it can enhance or spoil an effect. Because economy of movement is important, you don't want an actor to walk any unnecessary distance unless there is a special reason, for walking is not dramatic. Therefore, placement of camera should effect composition and a graceful entrance for the actor. Placement of camera is cinematic inflection. There is no set rule that a close-up gives more emphasis than a long shot. A close-up is a question of feeling; in some instances a long shot can effect a greater emphasis.

An example of this is in one of my early comedies, *Skating*.*

* There is no Chaplin film with this title. Chaplin is presumably referring to *The Rink* (1916), which he made for Mutual.

The tramp enters the rink and skates with one foot up, gliding and twirling, tripping and bumping into people and getting into all sorts of mischief, eventually leaving everyone piled up on their backs in the foreground of the camera, while he skates to the rear of the rink, becoming a very small figure in the background, and sits among the spectators innocently reviewing the havoc he has just created. Yet the small figure of the tramp in the distance was funnier than he would have been in a close-up.

When I started directing my first picture, I was not as confident as I thought I would be; in fact, I had a slight attack of panic. But after Sennett saw the first day's work, I was reassured. The picture was called *Caught in the Rain*. It was not a world-beater, but it was funny and quite a success. When I finished it, I was anxious to know Sennett's reaction. I waited for him as he came out of the projection room.

"Well, are you ready to start another?" he said. From then on I wrote and directed all my own comedies. As an inducement, Sennett gave me a twenty-five-dollar bonus for each picture.

He now practically adopted me, and took me to dinner every night. He would discuss stories for the other companies with me and I would suggest crazy ideas which I felt were too personal to be understood by the public. But Sennett would laugh and accept them.

Now, when I saw my films with an audience, their reaction was different. The stir and excitement at the announcement of a Keystone Comedy, those joyful little screams that my first appearance evoked even before I had done anything, were most gratifying. I was a great favorite with the audience: if I could just continue this way of life, I could be satisfied. With my bonus I was making two hundred dollars a week.

Since I was engrossed in work, I had little time for the Alexandria Bar or my sarcastic friend, Elmer Ellsworth. I met him, however, weeks later, on the street. "Say, listen," said he, "I've been seeing your pictures lately, and, by God, you're good! You have a quality entirely different from all the rest. And I'm not kidding. You're funny! Why the hell didn't you say so in the first place?" Of course, we became very good friends after that.

There was a lot Keystone taught me and a lot I taught Keystone. In those days they knew little about technique, stagecraft or movement, which I brought to them from the theatre. They also knew little about natural pantomime. In blocking a scene, a director would have three or four actors blatantly standing in a straight line facing the camera, and, with the broadest gestures, one would pantomime "I-want-to-marry-your-daughter" by pointing to himself, then to his ring finger, then to the girl. Their mimeing dealt little with subtlety or effectiveness, so I stood out in contrast. In those early movies, I knew I had many advantages, and that, like a geologist, I was entering a rich, unexplored field. I suppose that was the most exciting period of my career, for I was on the threshold of something wonderful.

Success makes one endearing and I became the familiar friend of everyone in the studio. I was "Charlie" to the extras, to the stagehands, the wardrobe department, and the cameramen. Although I am not a fraternizer, this pleased me indeed, for I knew that this familiarity meant I was a success.

Now I had confidence in my ideas, and I can thank Sennett for that, for although unlettered like myself, he had belief in his own taste, and such belief he instilled in me. His manner of working had given me confidence; it seemed right. His remark that first day at the studio: "We have no scenario—we get an idea then follow the natural sequence of events . . ." had stimulated my imagination.

Creating this way made films exciting. In the theatre I had been confined to a rigid, nondeviating routine of repeating the same thing night after night; once stage business had been tried out and set, one rarely attempted to invent new business. The only motivating thing about acting in the theatre was a good performance or a bad one. But films were freer. They gave me a sense of adventure. "What do you think of this for an idea?" Sennett would say, or "There's a flood downtown on Main Street." Such remarks launched a Keystone Comedy. It was this charming alfresco spirit that was a delight—a challenge to one's creativeness. It was so free and easy—no literature, no writers—we just had a notion around which we built gags, then made up the story as we went along.

For instance, in *His Prehistoric Past* I started with one gag, which was my first entrance. I appeared dressed as a prehistoric man wearing a bearskin, and, as I scanned the landscape, I began pulling the hair from the bearskin to fill my pipe. This was enough of an idea to stimulate a prehistoric story, introducing love, rivalry, combat, and chase. This was the method by which we all worked at Keystone.

I can trace the first prompting of desire to add another dimension to my films besides that of comedy. I was playing in a picture called *The New Janitor,* in a scene in which the manager of the office fires me. In pleading with him to take pity on me and let me retain my job, I started to pantomime appealingly that I had a large family of little children. While I was enacting mock sentiment, Dorothy Davenport, an old actress, was on the sidelines watching the scene, and during rehearsal I looked up and to my surprise found her in tears. "I know it's supposed to be funny," she said, "but you just make me weep." She confirmed something I already felt: I had the ability to evoke tears as well as laughter. . . .

This discursive autobiography should not preclude essaying a few remarks about film-making. Although many worthwhile books have been written on the subject, the trouble is that most of them impose the cinematic taste of the author. Such a book should be nothing more than a technical primer which teaches one to know the tools of the trade. Beyond that, the imaginative student should use his own art sense about dramatic effects. If the amateur is creative, he needs only the barest technical essentials. To an artist complete freedom to do the unorthodox is usually most exciting, and that is why many a director's first picture has freshness and originality.

The intellectualizing of line and space, composition, tempo, etc., is all very well, but it has little to do with acting, and is liable to fall into arid dogma. Simplicity of approach is always best.

Personally, I loathe tricky effects, photographing through the fireplace from the viewpoint of a piece of coal, or traveling with an actor through a hotel lobby as though escorting him on a bicycle; to me they are facile and obvious. As long as an audience is famliar with the set, it does not want the tedium of a traveling smear across the screen to see an actor move from one place to another. Such pompous effects slow up action, are boring and unpleasant, and have been mistaken for that tiresome word "art."

My own camera setup is based on facilitating choreography for the actor's movements. When a camera is placed on the floor or moves about the player's nostrils, it is the camera that is giving the performance and not the actor. The camera should not obtrude.

Time-saving in films is still the basic virtue. Both Eisenstein and Griffith knew it. Quick cutting and dissolving from one scene to another are the dynamics of film technique.

I am surprised that some critics say that my camera technique is old-fashioned, that I have not kept up with the times. What times? My technique is the outcome of thinking for myself, of my own logic and approach; it is not borrowed from what others are doing. If in art one must keep up with the times, then Rembrandt would be a back number compared to Van Gogh.

While on the subject of films, a few brief words may be profitable for those contemplating making a super-duper special—which, as a matter of fact, is the easiest picture to make. It requires little imagination or talent in acting or directing. All one needs is ten million dollars, multitudinous crowds, costumes, elaborate sets and scenery. With a glorification of glue and canvas one can float the languorous Cleopatra down the Nile, march twenty thousand extras into the Red Sea, or blow down the walls of Jericho—all of which is nothing but the virtuosity of building contractors. And while the field marshal sits in his directorial chair with script and table chart, his drill sergeants sweat and grunt over the landscape, bawling out order to the divisions: one whistle meaning "ten thousand from the left," two whistles "ten thousand from the right," and three, "all on and go to it."

The theme of most of these spectacles is Superman. The hero can outjump, outclimb, outshoot, outfight, and outlove anyone in the picture. In fact, every human problem is solved by these methods—except thinking.

Also a brief word about directing. In handling actors in a scene, psychology is most helpful. For instance, a member of the cast may join the company in the middle of a production. Although an excellent actor, he may be nervous in his new surroundings. This is where a director's humility can be very helpful, as I have often found under these circumstances. Although knowing what I wanted, I would take the new member aside and confide in him that I was tired, worried, and at a loss to know what to do with the scene. Very soon he would forget his own nervousness and try to help me and I would get a good performance out of him. . . .

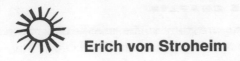

Erich von Stroheim

*

INTRODUCING

"THE

MERRY

WIDOW"

... I WOULD LIKE to introduce to you my friend, my collaborator, Denise Vernac . . . [applause]. . . . It is always a very bad sign when a director has to speak before one of his own films . . . [laughter] . . . because he will be making excuses . . . and that is exactly what I want to do. I have many reasons for it and for asking your patience. In the first place, because I speak very poor French. Secondly, because this film, *The Merry Widow,* was made thirty years ago. It is a very long time. In those days we did not have the techniques and equipment we have today, for instance, lighting, color, sound. . . . And then, this film that you are going to see, this copy is a . . . [Denise Vernac: "contretype" . . .] a contretype from a completely different version. This is a 16mm. copy and it will be projected on a regular-size screen and for that reason the images will not have the sharpness of focus. . . . Also, we don't have music. It was necessary, this very afternoon, to arrange something during the last two hours. In the old days, the M.G.M. company had experienced composers who prepared scores for the theatres which had orchestras. The smaller theatres, naturally,

The text is a translation of Erich von Stroheim's introductory remarks to the showing of *The Merry Widow* (1925) at the Palais des Beaux-Arts, Brussels, November 28, 1955. Originally published in *Hommage à Erich von Stroheim,* February 1966.

had only pianos—that's all. Tonight we have a very intelligent, extremely . . . [Denise Vernac: "able" . . .] able musician who will do his best.

Naturally, I like drama . . . tragedy. . . . But the producers do not like it. . . . They like only what brings money, and in my youth I hated money, although today . . . [laughter and applause]. Therefore I never wanted to direct stories for infantiles like that . . . [laughter] . . . but because, before I embarked on *The Merry Widow,* I had made a great tragedy . . . when I say "great," I mean in length . . . [laughter] . . . and a great story. . . . It was not my story this time—it was one of the greatest stories written by an American, Frank Norris, a student of Zola. And this film was, as the company said, a complete, a complete . . . [Denise Vernac: "fiasco" . . .] fiasco . . . [laughter] . . . because it was not this company that gave me money to make the film but another one, which had supervised me during the shooting but which did not have a money interest in the film! It is very simple—the company did not give the film enough publicity and made it also into a financial fiasco, probably. However, for me, it was a great success artistically. I had always wanted to make a great film, a good film and a long one, too, with an intermission—at a psychologically suitable moment—to give the audience time for dinner as the great Eugene O'Neill did in . . . [Denise Vernac: *"Strange Interlude"* . . .] *Strange Interlude.* He did it several years after me. I wanted to do it in *Greed.* . . . And I made the film. But it was too long for the producer, because he did not think about screening it in two sittings, as I did. So, the company hired a man who had never read Norris's book, did not know anything about my editing ideas, and was ordered to edit it . . . so he edited it . . . [laughter] . . he edited it. . . . When, ten years later, I saw the film myself, for the first time, it was like seeing a corpse in a graveyard. I found it in its narrow casket among plenty of dust and a terrible stink . . . [laughter]. . . . I found a thin part of the backbone and a little bone of the shoulder. And, naturally, I became sick, it made me very sick, because I had worked on this film for two years of my life without any salary. Try to play this on your piano . . . [laughter] . . . two years with a sick woman, with a sick child, very sick, with polio—and me, working without a salary on this film, for two years! At the end of the two years, I thought: if this film comes out the way I made it, I will be the greatest film director living. . . . But, when it was edited like this. . . . And, after all this fiasco, imagine, a producer coming to me and asking me to direct for him a film called *The Merry Widow!* He bought the rights to it for a great sum of money, dollars, not Belgian francs . . . and he had nothing for his money but the title, since the success of *The Merry Widow* was in its music. The story itself was ridiculous, or almost ridiculous. Naturally, I did not want to make it. And, besides, I had never had stars, because I don't like stars—both men and women stars. Particularly women . . . [laughter] . . . because they have ideas. . . . When I direct, it is me who has the ideas. It is me who directs. So, to please me, the Company forced me to accept two stars, not one. Two! . . . [laughter]. . . . Mae Murray, who always played under the direction of her husband, a very great man, very great, six-feet-three, and a very gentle man. I could make a comparison between a Saint Bernard dog . . . [laughter]. . . . She, herself, if I may say so . . . was very active, very agile, too active . . . [laughter]. . . . So this grand man and this little woman . . . you know very well who won the battle . . . [laughter]. . . . It was always Mae Murray, it was always she who won and the big Saint Bernard did exactly what his wife told him to do. But it was very different with me, since I was not married to this woman . . . [laughter]. . . . No. She was very gentle, but she had ideas . . . [laughter] . . . and, as I said before, I have ideas myself. So these two ideas . . . [laughter] . . . clashed. One time we had a terrible battle, during the embassy ball scene, and it was terrible because I had 350 extras in it who loved me very much . . . it was always the workers who liked me, not the producers— the workers . . . do you see the difference? . . . [laughter and applause]. So this woman thought . . . it was after the First World War . . . and she called me "dirty Hun." . . . Naturally, I did not like it, since I was born in Austria, in Vienna, and since she was born in Vienna, too . . . [laughter]. . . . As a matter of fact, she was born in Czechoslovakia, but then I did not see much difference

. . . [laughter] . . . and since my workers, my extras understood that this meant the end, they took off their uniforms and threw them on the floor. . . .

I want to tell you a very, very strange story. You will permit me to sit down [he sits down on the podium]. Thank you. Because this is a very strange story . . . [laughter]. . . . I am very superstitious, also religious, and in many cases that goes together, as you know. I had troubles with Mae Murray, as I said already, and also troubles with electricity, lamps, with the helpers, with everybody. And it was strange, because it had never happened that way before. So, after the duel with Mae Murray, I was discharged by the company, but really . . . [laughter]. . . . But I almost forget to tell you my story. . . . Since I am very superstitious and a mystic, I used to visit a certain voyeuse [Denise Vernac: "voyante" . . .] voyante . . . [laughter] . . . so, before I started workng on *The Merry Widow,* at the time when the company approached me, I naturally went first to my friend Madame Ora . . . [laughter]. . . . She was an old woman, only an EAR, so I asked her what would be the outcome, should I make the film or not? She waited a little while, just enough to give the necessary weight, and said that I should "absolutely do it" because it will be a great feather in my hat . . . [laughter]. . . . In California nobody wears a hat, and I did not have a hat—but she assured me of great success, a large feather, a beautiful plume in my hat, *bon! S*o I started the film, I was discharged, and I came immediately, the first thing I did, to my adviser, Madame Ora. I told her that I was discharged and that the president of the company had shown me the doors himself and that, in my turn, I'd given him a few words which he will never forget, and that I am in the street now. What should I do? And you have assured me that this will be a large feather in my hat! The Madame said to me: "Monsieur von Stroheim, I can't change my idea. You will continue tomorrow on *The Merry Widow,* you will direct it tomorrow, and it will be a great success and it will be a feather in your hat." I said, "Madame, you have not understood me correctly. I am in the street. . . . [laughter] . . . No, Monsieur, it is you who does not understand. You will be continuing tomorrow morning." And this was six o'clock in the afternoon. And she says to me, further, that now, this very moment, there are four or five men in my Los Angeles home waiting to see me . . . regarding tomorrow's work. I said, "But this is ridiculous, isn't it?" And she says, "They are in uniforms . . ." [laughter]. . . . And it was the time of prohibition in California, and I, like a good citizen, had plenty of whiskey in my house . . . [laughter] . . . and a few whiskeys in my car, just like that . . . [laughter]. . . . That meant this . . . [laughter] . . . years not in a private prison but on the island of Alcatraz. . . . So I hurried home, and, believe it or not, there were four men waiting and they were in uniforms. But they were not policemen but from the staff of the company, sent by the president himself to speak with me, to ask me to continue work on the film the next morning! That was too much . . . too strange. During the night the president sent his men twice more, just to be sure that I would definitely be at work the next morning, at 8:30 . . . counting thirty minutes for peace talks. . . . *Oui!* Madame Ora was right. I continued directing, it was one of the great successes of its time, and it was chosen by the critics of America as the best film of 1926. That, perhaps, is not such a great credit in itself, since, probably, the other films were very bad . . . [laughter]. . . . At any rate, this film has made for its company four and a half million . . . though not for me. I had twenty-five per cent of it. How much do you think I received? . . .

I thank you once more and ask you to have patience because the film is thirty years old; this print is only a 16mm. version projected on too large a screen, and I don't have the sound or the color or the cinerama. . . . I have nothing. And so I have made all the possible excuses that I could think of. All the good things in this film were made by me. The things that are no good in it were made by others.

Dziga Vertov

"KINOKS-
REVOLUTION,"
SELECTIONS

KINOKS-REVOLUTION

". . . . I would just like to establish that all we have been doing in cinematography up till now was a 100% muddle and diametrically opposed to what we should have been doing . . ."

DZIGA VERTOV

From the Manifesto of the Beginning of 1922

You—cinematographers:

directors without occupation and artists without occupation, flustered cameramen

and scenario writers scattered the world over,

You—the patient public of the movie-houses with the tolerance of mules under the load of served emotions,

You—the impatient owners of the not-yet-bankrupt movie theatres, greedily snapping up the scraps off the German table, and to a lesser extent the American table—

You wait,

Selections from "The Writings of Dziga Vertov," *Film Culture* no. 25, Summer 1962, pp. 45-61. "Kinoks-Revolution," translated by Val Telberg, first appeared in *LEF* magazine, no. 3, 1922. "From the Notebooks of Dziga Vertov," translated by Val Telberg, is taken from *Iskusstvo Kino,* no. 3, 1957. "Dziga Vertov on Kino-Eye, Lecture I" and "Dziga Vertov on Kino-Eye, Lecture II," excerpts from lectures given in Paris in 1929, are translated by S. Brody and appeared first in *Filmfront, 1935.*

Debilitated by memories, you day-dream and pine for the
MOON of the new six-reel feature . . .
(nervous persons are asked not to close their eyes),
You wait for what will not happen and what you should
not expect.
My friendly warning:
Don't bury your heads like ostriches.
Raise your eyes,
Look around—
There!
Seen by me and by every child's eye:
Insides falling out.
Intestines of experience
Out of the belly of cinematography
slashed
By the reef of the revolution,
there they drag,
leaving a bloody trace on the ground,
shuddering from terror and repulsion.
                    All is ended.

                                        Dziga Vertov

From a Stenograph

. . . A psychological, detective, satirical, or any other picture.
Cut out all scenes and just leave titles. We will get a literary
skeleton of the picture. To this literary skeleton we can add new
footage—realistic, symbolical, expressionist—any kind. Things
are not changed. Neither is the interrelationship: literary skeleton
plus cinematic illustration.

Such are all our and foreign pictures, without exception. . .

From the Manifesto of January 23, 1920, Council of Three to the Cinematographers

. . . Five fullblooded world-daring years have entered you and
left, leaving no mark. Samples of pre-revolutionary art hang like

icons and still attract your prayerful entrails. Foreign lands support you in your confusion, sending into the renovated Russia the uncremated remains of movie dramas dressed with an excellent technological sauce.

Spring is coming. Studios are expected to start work. The Council of Three does not hide its regret as it watches how the producers leaf through literature looking for pieces suitable for conversion into scenarios. The names of theatre dramas and poems slated for possible production are floating through the air. In the Ukraine, and here in Moscow, several pictures have already been made bearing witness to all qualities of impotence.

Pronounced technical backwardness, the loss of ability to think actively as a result of the doldrums, the orientation on the six-reel psycho-drama, i.e., the orientation on one's own behind—condemns in advance all their attempts.

The organism of cinematography is poisoned by the frightful venom of habit. We demand being given an opportunity to experiment with this dying organism, with an objective of finding an antitoxin.

We offer the unbelievers to be convinced: we agree to try out our medicine first on the "rabbits," on the movie études.

Council of Three

Resolution of the Council of Three, April 10, 1923

Resolution on the cine-front: consider not in favor.

First Russian productions shown us, as expected, are reminiscent of the old "artistic" models in the same way that the NEP-men remind us of the old bourgeoisie.

Projected production schedules for the summer, here and in Ukraine, inspire no confidence.

Possibilities of wide experimental work is in the background.

All efforts, all sighs, tears and hopes, all prayers are to her—the six-reel cine-drama.

Therefore, be it resolved, that the Council of Three, not waiting for the admission of Kinoks to production and, in spite of the desire of Kinoks to realize by themselves their own projects, foregoes for the moment the right of authorship and decrees;

publish immediately for broad distribution the general basis and credos of the impending revolution through the Movie newsreel, for which purpose Dziga Vertov is hereby directed, along the lines of party discipline, to publish these passages from the book, *Kinoks-Revolution,* which describe the substance of the revolution.

Council of Three

Carrying out the resolution of the Council of Three of April 10, 1923, the following excerpts are published:

1.

Watching the pictures which came from the West and from America, taking into account the information which we have on the work and searchings abroad here—I come to the following conclusion:

Verdict of death, decreed by Kinoks in 1919, to all motion pictures without exception, is in effect to this day.

Legalized Myopia

The most careful inspection does not reveal a single picture, a single searching, which tries correctly to unserfage the camera, now in pitiful slavery, under orders of an imperfect shallow eye.

We do not object if cinematography tunnels under literature, under theatre; we fully approve the utilization of cinema for all branches of science, but we recognize these functions as accessory, as off-shoots and branches.

The fundamental and the most important: Cinema—the feel of the world.

Way for the Machine

The initial point: The utilization of the camera as a cinema eye—more perfect than a human eye for purposes of research into the chaos of visual phenomena filling the universe.

the camera is posited as the way out of 'subjectivism'

Down with 16 Photographs per Second

The eye lives and moves in time and space, perceiving and re-cording impressions in a way quite different from the human eye. It is not necessary for it to have a particular stance or to be limited in the number of moments to be observed per second. The movie camera is better.

We cannot make our eyes better than they have been made, but the movie camera we can perfect forever.

Accidental Synthesis and Concentration of Motion

To this day the cameraman is criticized if a running horse moves unnaturally slowly on the screen (quick turn of the camera) or, conversely, if a tractor ploughs too fast (the slow manipulation of the camera crank).

These of course are incidental, but we are preparing a thought-out system of these incidents, a system of apparent abnormalities which organize and explore phenomena.

Do Not Copy from the Eyes

To this day we raped the movie camera and forced it to copy he work of our eye. And the better the copy, the better the shot vas considered. As of today we will unshackle the camera and vill make it work in the opposite direction, further from copying.

Machine and Its Career

Out with all the weaknesses of the human eye.

We hereby ratify the eye, which is groping in the chaos of mo-ons for a movement of its own and in its own right; we validate ne eye with its own measurement of strength and in potentiality :fore the self-ratification.

2.

. . . to induce the viewer to see in a way that is best for me to show. The eye obeys the will of the camera and is directed by it to that sequence of moments of action which best brings out a cinema-phrase, the sequence that raises and lowers denouement with the greatest brilliance and speed.

System of the Continuity of Actions

Example: Shooting a boxing bout not from the point of view of a member of the audience, but on the basis of showing off as best as possible the sequence of holds of the boxers.

Example: Shooting a group of dancers—but not from the point of view of the audience, sitting in an auditorium and having in front of it scenes of a ballet.

The Most Inefficient, the Most Uneconomical Rendition of a Scene Is the Theatrical Rendition

For the viewer of a ballet haphazardly follows the whole group or incidental performers, or some legs—a series of scattered observations, different for everyone in the audience.

The movie viewer cannot be presented with this. The system of consecutive actions demands filming the dancers or the boxer in a way which would account for consecutive events with certain details and actions forced upon the viewer, so that there is no chance for him to miss these.

The camera drags the eyes of the viewer from hands to legs, from legs to eyes, in a way that is the most efficient. It organizes the parts into an edited orderly study.

3.

Montage in Time and Space

. . . You are walking on a Chicago street today in 1923, but make you nod to comrade Volodarsky, who is, in 1918, walking down a street in Petrograd; he acknowledges your greeting.

Another example: They are lowering the coffins of national heroes (shot in Astrakhan in 1918), they fill in the graves (Kronstadt 1921), cannon salute (Petrograd 1920), memorial service—hats come off (Moscow 1922). These actions go together even in the ungrateful, not specially filmed, material (see Kino-Pravda #13). Crowds greeting Lenin in different places, in different times are also in this category (see Kino-Pravda #14).

Human Race of Kinoks Council of Three. Moscow, Hall of Intervals
Today—Today April 3. Report by DZV on the Theme Chambre
Cinema-Phase Beginning 8:30 P.M.

. . . I am eye. I am builder.

I implanted you, a most remarkable chamber which did not exist until I created it today. In this chamber there are 12 walls, photographed by me in various parts of the world. Manipulating shots of walls and details, I have succeeded in arranging them in an order which pleases you and in constructing correctly a cinematic phrase, which is the room.

Electric Young Man

I am eye. I have created a man more perfect than Adam; I create thousands of different people in accordance with previously prepared plans and charts.

I am eye.

I take the most agile hands of one, the fastest and the most graceful legs of another, from a third person I take the handsomest and the most expressive head, and by editing I create an entirely new perfect man.

4.

. . I am eye. I am a mechanical eye.

I, a machine, am showing you a word, the likes of which only I can see.

I free myself from today and forever from human immobility, I am in constant movement, I approach and draw away from objects, I crawl under them, I move alongside the mouth of a running horse, I cut into a crowd at full speed, I run in front of running soldiers, I turn on my back, I rise with an airplane, I fall and soar together with falling and rising bodies.

This is I, apparatus, maneuvring in the chaos of movements, recording one movement after another in the most complex combinations.

Freed from the obligation of shooting 16-17 shots [i.e., frames] per second, freed from the frame of time and space, I coordinate any and all points of the universe, wherever I may plot them.

My road is towards the creation of a fresh perception of the world. Thus I decipher in a new way the world unknown to you.

5.

. . . Let us agree once more: the eye and the ear. The ear peeks, the eye eavesdrops.

Distribution of functions.

Radio-ear-edited "hear!"

Cinema-eye-edited "see!"

There it is, citizens, in the first place instead of music, painting, theatre, cinematography and other castrated outpourings.

Organization of Observations by a Human Eye

In a chaos of movements running past, streaking away, running up and colliding—only the eye enters life simply. The day of visual impressions is past. How to convert the impressions of the day into a functional whole—into a visual study? To film everything that an eye has seen will result in a jumble. To edit artfully what had been photographs would result in greater clarity. It would be better yet to scrap the annoying rubbish. Thus we get organized memoirs of impressions of a simple eye.

Decomposition and Concentration of Visual Phenomena

A mechanical eye—that's the movie camera. It refuses to use the human eye, as if the latter were a crib-sheet; it is attracted and repelled by motion, feeling through the chaos of observed events for a roadway for its own mobility and modulation; it experiments, extending time, dissecting movement, or on the contrary absorbing into itself the time, swallowing years and thus diagramming some processes unattainable to the normal eye . . .

Brain

. . . In aid to the eye machine is the Kinok, the pilot, who not only steers the apparatus, but also trusts it in experiments in space and in whatever may follow. Kinok, the engineer, directs the apparatus by remote control.

This concerted action by the liberated and perfected apparatus and the strategy-making brain of man—directing, observing, compensating, will result in an unusual freshness, and even the most commonplace will become interesting.

. . . They are many who, hungering for spectacles, lost their pants in theatres.

They run from weekdays, run from the "prose" of life.

And yet the theatre is almost always only a scabby surrogate of this very life plus an idiotic conglomerate from balletic contortions, musical squeaks, clever lighting effects, stage sets (from those smeared on to those constructed) and sometimes good work from literary masters perverted by all this hog-wash.

Some theatre overseers enlist help: bio-mechanics (a good pursuit by itself), cinema (bestow it honor and glory), literatures (not bad by themselves), constructions (some are not bad), automobiles (how can we not respect them), rifle shooting (dangerous and impressive thing in the front lines). But on the whole not a goddam thing comes out of it.

Theatre and nothing else.

Not only no synthesis but no orderly mixture either.

Could not be otherwise.

We, Kinoks, resolute opponents of premature synthesis ("To synthesis at the zenith of accomplishment"), understand that to mix the crumbs of achievements is to have the infants perish from crowding and disorder.

In general—

Arena Is Small

Please come into life.

Here we work—craftsmen of seeing—organizers of visible life, armed all over with the maturing eye. Here work the master-craftsmen of words and sounds, the most skillful editor-cutters of the heard life. To them I also dare slip over a mechanical ever-present ear and megaphone—radio telephone.

This is

Newsreel Radio News

I promise to wangle a parade of Kinoks in Red Square in case the futurists come out with No. 1 of their edited newsreel.

Neither the newsreel of "Pathé" nor of "Gaumont" (newspaper chronicle) nor even the Kino-Truth (political chronicle), but a real Kinok-type of a chronicle—a dashing survey of visual events deciphered by the movie-camera, fragments of actual energy (as against theatrical energy), with their intervals condensed into a cumulative whole by the great mastery of an editing technique.

Such structure of a cinematic thing allows a development of any theme—be it comical, tragic, or anything else.

It is all a matter of juxtaposition of one visual moment with another, all a matter of intervals.

This unusual flexibility of edited structure allows to introduce into a movie continuity, any political, economic, or any other motif.

Therefore

As of today cinema needs no psychological, no detective dramas,

As of today—no theatrical productions shot on film,

As of today—no scenariozation of either Dostoyevsky, or Nat Pinkerton.

Everything is included in the new concept of the newsreel.

Into the confusion of life, hereby decisively enter:

1) The Eye, disputing the visual concept of the world by the human eye and offering its own "I see" and

2) Kinok-editor, who organizes for the first time what had been so perceived into minutes of life-structure.

FROM THE NOTEBOOKS OF DZIGA VERTOV

I began early. By writing various fantastic novels *(The Iron Hand),* by writing brief sketches ("Whale Hunting," "Fishing"), poems ("Masha"), epigrams and satirical verse ("Purishkevich," "The Girl With Freckles").

Later all this was transformed into a fascination with a montage of stenographic notes and sound recording—in particular, a fascination with the possibility of documenting sounds in writing, in attempts to depict in words and letters the sound of a waterfall, the noise of a sawmill, in musical-thematic creations of word-montage, "Laboratory of Hearing."

Later, in the fall of 1918, came the shift to film, life on 7 Gnezdnikovsky Street, and work on the magazine, *Cinema Weekly.* Ideas on the "armed eye," on the role of the camera in the study of the living world. Early experiments with high speed shooting, the concept of the "cinematic-eye" as a rapid eye (in the sense of a rapid thought) . . .

The early 16 frames per second became obsolete. Not just rapid filming, but multiplication filming, microfilming, macro-filming, reverse filming, filming with a moving camera—all became commonplace.

The "Kino-eye" is in the realm of "that which the naked eye does not see," a microscope and telescope of time, an x-ray eye, the "candid" eye, the remote control of a camera.

All these various definitions mutually complement each other; the "Kino-eye" includes:
all film methods
all cinematic images
all methods and means by which the truth can be shown.

Not the "Kino-eye" for its own sake, but the truth by the means of the "Kino-Eye." Cinematic truth.

The "candid camera," not for its own sake, but to show people without their make-up on; to catch them through the camera's eye at some moment when they are not acting; to capture their thoughts by means of the camera.

The "Kino-eye" as a means of making the invisible visible, the obscure clear, the hidden obvious, the disguised exposed, and acting not acting.

But it is not enough to show bits of truth on the screen, separate frames of truth. These frames must be thematically organized so that the whole is also truth. This is an even more difficult task. There is little theoretical study of this problem. Hundreds, thousands of experiments must be conducted, in order to master this new field of cinematographic work.

The "Kino-eye," which has set for itself the task: "To combine science with cinematic depiction in the struggle to reveal truth . . . to decipher reality," was born in dozens and hundreds of experiments. These experiments which aided the overall development of descriptive and scientific filming, continued month after month, year after year. During all this time it was necessary to overcome great difficulties, not only of an organizational and technical nature, but for the main part difficulties caused by our inability to demonstrate the inevitability and necessity of this work. In this experimental work we can distinguish three periods.

The first period began in 1918. These experiments took place during the Civil War, when *Cinema Weekly* was being published, and filming was being conducted under battle conditions on all fronts. To this period belong such films as *Battle at Tsaritsyn, The Action at Mirnov, Discovery of Sergei Radonezhsky's Remains, The VTIK Train,* etc. This period closes with a long film in thirteen parts: *History of the Civil War* (1921).

The second period begins in 1922. This period could be called the period of *Kino-Pravda (Cinema Truth)*. Review films, sketch films, verse films, film poems, and preview films made their appearance. Each release of *Kino-Pravda* brought something new. Considerable work was also being done in the utilization of new methods for subtitling, transforming them into pictorial units equal to those of the images.

Long, experimental films, like *The Kino-Eye* (1924), *Forward, Soviet!, The Sixth Part of the World* (1926) were released.

The third period—*The Kino-Eye in the Ukraine, The October March, The Eleventh Year, Man with a Movie Camera,* a film without words, and *Enthusiasm,* a symphony of noises, were released in rapid succession.

With *Three Songs of Lenin* (1934), that "symphony of thought" began the third period of experiments. *Three Songs of Lenin* was already a many-sided experimental synthesis which, with its far-reaching roots, delved into the unwritten creative folklore of the Soviet people.   1940, February

Early Thoughts

Nineteen-eighteen. I moved to Gnezdnikovsky #7. Did a risky jump for a slow-motion camera.

Didn't recognize my face on the screen.

My thoughts were revealed on my face—irresolution, vacillation, and firmness (a struggle within myself), and again the joy of victory.

First thought of the Kino-eye as a world perceived without a mask, as a world of naked truth (truth cannot be hidden).

ABC of Cinema

Ilya Ehrenburg, apparently impressed by the first series of the *Kino-eye,* once wrote:

"The work of Vertov is a laboratory analysis of the world-complex, painstaking. Kino-eye takes reality and transforms it into several basic elements—if you will—into a cinematic alphabet."

Nowadays we all know that those who worked on *Kino-Pravda* and *Kino-eye* created a cinematic alphabet, not for its own sake, but to show the truth.

My Views

In 1918 I switched to film. At that time I was working on a film journal (*Cinema Weekly*), on historical films (*History of the Civil War*), film sketches, film verse (see No. 23 of *Kino-Pravda*), film caricatures (*Today, Chervonets, Grimaces of Paris, Soviet Toys*),

films of various war campaigns and actions, experimental studies
(*Battle at Tsaritsyn*), and longer film poems (*Kino-eye, Forward,
Soviet!, The Sixth Part of the World, The Eleventh Year;* songs
without words (*Man with a Movie Camera*), sound symphonies
(*Enthusiasm*), and finally, the recently finished *Three Songs
About Lenin.* All totaled, counting the smaller works, not less
than 150 works.

My attitude towards these films is that of an inventor towards
his invention. Much is outdated and seems to be a little farcical to
me, like a Buster Keaton comedy; but in their own time, these
funny experiments did not evoke laughter, but a storm of controversy, ideas and plans.

These films were less of "widespread demand," than "films
precursing other films."   April, 1934

"Three Songs About Lenin"

I've managed to make *Three Songs About Lenin* (at least to
some degree) accessible and comprehensible to millions. But not
at the price of cinematographic language; and not by abandoning
the principles which had been formulated earlier. No one would
demand this of us.

The important thing is not separate form from content. The
secret lies in unity of form and content. In refraining from shocking the spectator by introducing objects or devices which are
unnatural or extraneous to the work. In 1933 while thinking about
Lenin, I decided to draw from the source of the people's creative
folklore about Lenin. I would like to keep on working in this
direction.

> If he saw darkness, he created light
> From the desert he made orchards
> From death—life

or

> A million sand grains make a dune
> A million peas make a bushel
> A million weak—a great strength

Are these images and songs of nameless poets of the people any poorer than images of the most refined formal works?

This subject in which I am working is the least studied, the most highly experimental subject of cinematography.

The road along which I am going, in an organizational, technical, down-to-earth manner, and in all other senses, demands superhuman efforts. It is a thankless and, believe me, a very difficult road.

But I am hopeful that in my field I will be able to defeat formalism, to defeat naturalism, to become a poet not for the few, but for the ever-increasing millions.

It is far from simple to show the truth.

But truth itself is simple.

Mayakovsky

Mayakovsky—his work is a Kino-eye. He sees what the eye does not.

I liked Mayakovsky from the start, without reserve, from the first book I read. The book was called "Simple as a Bellow." I knew it by heart. I defended him from vilification as well as I knew how; I explained. I did not know Mayakovsky personally at the time. When I first met the poet at the Polytechnic Museum in Moscow, I was not disappointed. He was just as I had imagined him. Mayakovsky noticed me in a group of excited young people. Of course, I looked at him with admiring eyes. He came up to us. "We're awaiting your next book," I said. "Then get your friends together," he answered, "and demand that it gets published more quickly."

My meetings with Mayakovsky were always brief. Sometimes in the street, or at a club, or at a station, or at a cinema. He didn't call me Vertov, but Dziga. I liked that. "Well, how's the Kino-Eye doing, Dziga?" he once asked me. This was somewhere on the road, in a railroad station. Our trains met. "The Kino-Eye is learning," I replied. He thought awhile and said: "The Kino-Eye is a lighthouse of the film world."

The last time I met Mayakovsky was in Leningrad, in the lobby of the Europa Hotel.

Mayakovsky asked the waiter, in a gloomy voice, "Is there going to be a cabaret tonight?" He noticed me and said: "We should have a leisurely talk together. A serious talk. Let's have a 'feature length' creative discussion today."

I waited for Mayakovsky in my room.

It seemed to me that I found the key to filming documentary sounds.

I walked back and forth in my room, waiting for Mayakovsky and rejoicing at having met him again.

I wanted to tell him about my attempts to create a film poem in which montage phrases would rhyme one with the other.

I waited for him till midnight.

I don't know what happened to him, he did not come.

And in a few weeks he was gone.

Some More About Mayakovsky

My love of Mayakovsky's works did not in any way contradict my ideas about creativity of the common people.

I never considered Mayakovsky to be obscure and unpopular.

There is a difference between popularity and popularization.

Mayakovsky is understandable to all who want to think. He does not write for the man who does not think. His work is far from being a popularization, but he is popular.

Unity of form and content—that's what strikes one in the works of the people, and that's what strikes in Mayakovsky.

I work in the field of the poetic documentary film. That's why I feel so close to both the folk songs and the poetry of Mayakovsky.

I am striving in my future works for greater unity of form and content than in *Three Songs About Lenin,* because unity of form and content guarantees success.

On Scenarios for Documentary Films

If we want to achieve continuity and coherence in our scenes not at the cutting table, but much earlier, during filming,

DZIGA VERTOV

95

if we want

this continuity and correspondence of scenes to result in an irresistible movement forward, from the old towards the new quality, by overcoming difficulties, obstacles, contradictions, by the struggle between the old and the new,

if we want

to genuinely solve this most difficult problem of all, then we have to rely on the small scenario. Or even the micro-scenario. Or even the minutest of directions. The smaller it is, the more accurate and complete it should be. And the more accurate and complete we make it, the more difficult it is to make it. Nonetheless it is vital to complete such scenarios.

Because once they are completed,

then the cameramen themselves (each in his own way) attempt to take down in their notes preliminary schemes of the subject, sometimes making notes in the text of the subject, sometimes in film directions, sometimes in accurate scenario plans.

One may say:

Not every cameraman is a specialist. Many of our comrades need assistance. But can they not be helped by our young, energetic specialists?

We have a new group of young men and women, blooming, strong, fiery and talented.

there are many specialists among them.

Why shouldn't they, with their fiery vigor, kindle the flames of enthusiasm in our old specialists?

Why shouldn't our young scenario writers (arm in arm with the cameramen) discover the secrets of small scenario writing for film subjects?

Why shouldn't they become authors of small film-novels?

Why shouldn't they take up this basic task, if it really *is* basic?

Maybe only young people have the right to make the first steps in this direction?

Maybe my thoughts on this are not very clear. My comrades should correct me, and make my ideas clearer.

The point of this whole thing is this: is there in all that I've said a useful grain of truth?

Is there within it even some noticeable approximation of truth? Use of these ideas in practice will give us the answer.

Thus if the small scenario actually does become the key which will open doors to a new quality of subject, then I will have the right to say to myself:

Practice has shown that my assumptions were not wrong or useless.

And practice is the criterion of truth.

Creative Plans, Testimonials, Ideas

1. If "Kino-Pravda" is truth shown by means of the cinematic eye, then a shot of the banker will only be true if we can tear the mask from him, if behind his mask we can see the thief.

2. The only way we can divest him of his mask is by concealed observation, by concealed photography: i.e., by means of hidden cameras, supersensitive film and light sensitive lenses, infra-red film for night and evening shooting, noiseless cameras. Constant readiness of the camera for filming. Immediate shooting of a perceived object.

Not in the theatre, but in life, the thief plays the role of the cashier in order to rob the cash register. Or else the confidence man plays the role of a doting suitor to seduce, and then rob a woman. Or else the hustler plays the simpleton in order to fool his victim. Or else the prostitute plays the-girl-with-a-bow to make a fool of the nincompoop. Or else the hypocrite, the flatterer, bureaucrat, the spy, the bigot, the blackmailer, the contriver, etc., who hide their thoughts while playing one role or another, take their masks off only when no one can see them or hear them. To show them without their masks on—what a difficult task that is, but how rewarding.

3. All this when a man plays someone else's role in life. But if we take a professional actor, playing a role in the theatre, to film him through the "Kino-eye" would be to show the agreement or disagreement between the man and the actor, the correspondence or lack of correspondence between his words and his thoughts, etc. I am reminded of one actor who was playing in one of the old silent films. Dying from wounds in front of the camera, showing

suffering on his body and face, he was at the same time telling an anecdote which was amusing everyone—apparently showing off his ability to act while not feeling the emotions he was portraying. If the convulsions of the wounded man could have been recorded for sound, then in place of moans we would hear, to our astonishment, something directly opposite to what we were seeing on the screen: words with double meaning, jokes, giggling . . .

Apparently, the actor had had to die so many times before the camera that it had become automatic; he did not have to use his mind to act. His mind was free to tell jokes. This—the ability to dissimulate, to affect two identities—seemed quite disgusting to me at the time.

To show Ivanov in the role of Petrov, as seen through the "Kino-eye," would be to show him as a man in life and as an actor on the stage; not trying to pass off acting on the stage as life, and vice versa. Complete clarity. Not Petrov in front of you, but Ivanov playing the role of Petrov.

4. If a fake apple and a real apple are filmed so that one cannot be distinguished from the other on the screen, this is not ability, but incompetence—inability to photograph.

The real apple has to be filmed in such a way that no counterfeit can be possible. The real apple can be tasted and eaten, while the artificial one cannot—a good cameraman can understand this easily.

Films About Women

I am a film writer. A cinepoet. I do not write on paper, but on film. As with every writer, I have to make work notes. Observations. Not on paper, however, but on film. Together with longer poems I write short novels, sketches, verse. Many writers took their heroes from real life. For instance, *Anna Karenina* was based on the life of one of Pushkin's daughters. I thought about recording on film the history of Marya Demchenko from the life of Marya Demchenko. The difference was that I could not write on film events that had already occurred. I can only write simultaneously, as the events are occurring. I cannot write about the meeting of the Komsomol after it has taken place. And I cannot, like some correspondents, write an article on events, on spectacles, on carnivals several days after they have taken place. I do not demand that the cameraman be at the scene of a fire two hours before it breaks out. But I cannot permit that he go to film a fire a week after the fire has gone out. I received permission to film a Kolkhoz meeting, to film Demchenko, etc., from the directors when there was already nothing to film. This we used to call "directorial permission."

Now I am working on films about the Woman. This is not one subject, but a series of themes. These films will be both long and short. They will be about a schoolgirl, about a girl at home, about a mother and child, about abortion, about the creative female youth, about the differences between our girls and those abroad, about recreation and work, about the first steps and first words of a child, about the infant girl, about the teen-age girl, about the mature woman and the old woman . . .

I will also write about specific people, living and working. My selection of people may be planned. I will film the development of the man from diapers to old age. All this will be possible only with organization of the endless research, filming and editing work. The endless process of taking creative notes on film. The endless process of observation with camera in hand.

Some sort of workshop or laboratory should be started where one could work under special conditions—conditions where creative thoughts and organizational forms would not conflict and nullify each other.

DZIGA VERTOV ON KINO-EYE, LECTURE I

The history of Kino-Eye has been a relentless struggle to modify the course of world cinema, to place in cinematic production a new emphasis of the "unplayed" film over the played film, to substitute the document for mise-en-scene, to break out of the proscenium of the theatre and to enter the arena of life itself.

Let me attempt to sum up the results obtained in this direction by the Kino-Eye:

The manifesto of the "kinoks" on the cinema, free from the actors, was published and later developed and popularized in a number of articles and in several public discussions.

2. In order to confirm the contents of the manifesto, there were produced and exhibited about one hundred films without actors. These were of a wide variety, from primitive newsreels to extremely complex documentary films of the "cine-things." We can cite for example the *Weekly Reels, History of the Civil War, Calendars of Goskinof,* and the *Cine-Translations.* Outstanding among those films, which were responsible for heavy blows at the theatrical cinema, must be mentioned : *The Struggle Under Tzarism, Life Caught Unaware, Lenin's Truth, Forward, Soviets, The Sixth Part of the World, The Eleventh Year,* and, finally, *The Man with the Movie Camera.* Among the films produced by some of my pupils may be mentioned: *Moscow Nursery, For the Harvest, A Holiday of Millions.*

3. We have developed a language, proper to the cinema, special methods of shooting and montage which are not those of the enacted film. The language of the film has become absolutely distinct from that of the theatre and literature. We have created the conception of *documentary cinematography.*

4. We have established an experimental studio for the recording of facts, and later *Pravda* on the 24th of July, 1926, published plans for a "factory of unplayed film," a "factory of facts," that is to say, pure documentary.

5. At an open meeting which took place in Moscow in 1924, followers of Kino-Eye revealed the existence of a directive by Lenin which pointed out the necessity of changing the proportion of fact-films on film programmes. Finding support in this directive, the followers of Kino-Eye declared that they demanded an immediate reorganization of all Soviet film production and exhibition; they requested an internal apportionment, that is to say, a certain proportion between the theatrical cinema, the enacted film, the cine-plaything on the one hand, and on the other the cinema which is not played, the cine-eye, the fact-film.

This proposal was boldly called the "Leninist Film Proportion." Attempts were made to publish the proposal in the cinematographic press. N. Lebedev, the editor-in-chief of the only movie magazine appearing at that time, *Kino-Journal,* returned the manuscript to me, declaring that he protested the term "Leninist Film Proportion" and that he was against this attempt to utilize an

"accidental" phrase by Lenin, and to present it as a sort of testi-
monial directive. The proposal of the "kinoks," rejected by the
cinema press, was nevertheless published later by *Pravda* on the
16th of August, 1925. The very term itself, "Leninist Film
Proportion," was not current for very long, and it is only today, in
1929, that it has been taken up again.

6. Kino-Eye has exerted considerable influence on the theatrical film, the language of which it has modified. More and more
our cinema has borrowed the methods of Kino-Eye, superficially
at least, to create what is known as the "art" film. We cite as
examples *Strike, Potemkin,* etc. These borrowings have been
sufficient to arouse attention and have created quite a stir at home
as well as abroad in the domain of the theatrical enacted film.

Nevertheless, these directed films, the methods of which were
superficially taken from Kino-Eye, present only a particular and
incidental facet of the Kino-Eye movement, the spread of which
continues uninterrupted.

7. Kino-Eye has exerted a considerable influence on almost all
arts, notably in the sphere of music and literature. We will recall
here that in their manifesto of the unplayed film, the exponents
of Kino-Eye asked workers in the word, workers in letters, to
initiate the oral chronicle, radio chronicle. We recall that following this, in *Pravda* in 1925, N. Ossinski asked that literature
engage itself upon the road traced by Kino-Eye, that is to say,
that it attempt to present facts—documentary elements—in an
organic form.

"Vertov is right," wrote O. Brik in *Soviet Cinema* No. 2, 1926,
and he demanded of photography that it follow the example set
by Kino-Eye. "It is necessary to get out of the circle of ordinary
human vision; reality must be recorded not by imitating it, but by
broadening the circle ordinarily encompassed by the human eye."

In their earliest declarations on the subject of the sound film,
which was not yet even invented then but which was soon to
come, the "kinoks," who now call themselves the "radioks," that
is, followers of radio-eye, traced their path as leading from the
Kino-Eye to the Radio-Eye; in other words, leading to the sound
Kino-Eye transmitted by radio.

A few years ago I wrote an article entitled "The Radio-Eye" which appeared in *Pravda* under the general heading "Kino-Pravda and Radio-Pravda." I stated in that article that Radio-Eye was a means of abolishing distances between men, that it offered an opportunity for the workers of the world not only to see themselves, but to hear themselves SYNCHRONOUSLY.

The declaration of the "kinoks" provoked at the time most passionate discussions in the press. I remember a long article by Fevralski, "Tendencies in Art and Radio-Eye." I recall a special publication, *Radio,* which devoted one of its issues exclusively to Radio-Eye.

The followers of Kino-Eye, not confining themselves solely to the development of the unplayed film, were preparing themselves to work on the Radio-Eye, the talking and sound film without the play of actors.

Already in *The Sixth Part of the World,* the subtitles are replaced by an oral theme, by a radio theme, contrapuntally adapted to the film. *Eleventh Year* is already constructed like a *visual* and *sonal* cine-thing, that is to say, that the montage was done *in relation not only to the eye, but also to the ear.*

It is in the same direction, in passing from Kino-Eye to Radio-Eye, that our film *The Man with the Movie Camera* was mounted.

The theoretical and practical work of the *kinoks-radioks* (differing in this respect from theatrical cinematography which has found itself caught off guard) have run ahead of their technical possibilities and for a long time have been awaiting a technical basis the advent of which will be late, in relation to Kino-Eye; they await the Sound-Cine and Television.

Recent technical acquisitions in this area lend powerful arms to the partisans and workers of *documentary sound cinegraphy* in their struggle for a revolution in the cinema, for the abolition of play, for an October of Kino-Eye.

From the montage of visual facts recorded on film (Kino-Eye) we pass to the montage of visual and acoustic facts transmitted by radio (Radio-Eye).

We shall go from there to the simultaneous montage of visual-acoustic-tactile-olfactory facts, etc.

We shall then reach the stage where we will surprise and record *human thoughts,* and, finally, we shall reach to the greatest experiments of direct organization of thoughts (and consequently of actions) of all mankind.

Such are the technical perspectives of Kino-Eye, born of the October Revolution.

DZIGA VERTOV ON KINO-EYE, LECTURE II

Kino-Eye is a victory against time. It is a visual link between phenomena separated from one another in time. Kino-Eye gives a condensation of time, and also its decomposition.

Kino-Eye offers the possibility of seeing the living processes in a temporally arbitrary order and following a chosen rhythm, the speed of which the human eye would not otherwise be able to follow.

Kino-Eye avails itself of all the current means of recording ultra-rapid motion, microcinematography, reverse motion, multiple exposure, foreshortening, etc., and does not consider these as tricks, but as normal processes of which wide use must be made.

Kino-Eye makes use of all the resources of montage, drawing together and linking the various points of the universe in a chronological or anachronistic order as one wills, by breaking, if necessary, with the laws and customs of the construction of cine-thing.

In introducing itself into the apparent chaos of life, the Kino-Eye tries to find in life itself an answer to the question it poses: To find the correct and necessary line among the millions of phenomena which relate to the theme.

Montage and a Few Principles of Kino-Eye

To make a montage is to organize pieces of film, which we call the frames, into a cine-thing. It means to write something cinegraphic with the recorded shots. It does not mean to select pieces to make "scenes" (deviations of a theatrical character), nor does it mean to arrange pieces according to subtitles (deviations of a literary character).

Every Kino-Eye production is mounted on the very day that the subject (theme) is chosen, and this work ends only with the launching of the film into circulation in its definitive form. In other words, montage takes place from the beginning to the end of production.

Montage being thus understood, we can distinguish three periods:

First Period

The "Montage Evaluation" of all the documents which are directly or indirectly related to the chosen theme (manuscripts, various objects, film clippings, photographs, newspaper clippings, books, etc.). As a result of this montage which consists in picking and grouping the most precious documents or those simply useful, *the plan indicated by the theme* becomes crystalized, appears more evident, more distinct, more defined.

Second Period

"Montage Synthesis" of the human eye concerning the selected theme (montage of personal observation or of reports by the information-gatherers and scouts of the film). *Plan of shots,* as a result of the selection and classification of the observations of the "human eye." At the moment when this selection is made, the author takes into account the indications of the thematic plan as well as peculiarities of the "machine-eye" of Kino-Eye.

Third Period

"General Montage," synthesis of the observations noted on the film under the direction of the "machine-eye." Calculation in figures of the montage groupings. Unification of homogeneous pieces; constantly, one displaces the pieces, the frames, until all shall have entered a rhythm, where all the ties dictated by the meaning shall be those which coincide with the visual ties. As a result of all these mixtures, of all these displacements and of all these reductions, we have a kind of visual equation, a visual formula. This formula, this equation, which is the result of the general montage of the cine-documents recorded on the film, is 100 percent the cine-thing: I see, I cine-see.

Kino-Eye is:

montage, when I select a theme (to pick a theme among a possible thousand);

montage, when I keep watch over the execution of the theme (of a thousand observations, to make a proper choice);

montage, when I establish the order of exposition of what has been shot according to the theme (of a thousand possible combinations to select the most adequate, basing one's self as much upon the qualities of the filmed documents as upon the requirements of the chosen theme).

The school of Kino-Eye requires that the cine-thing be built upon "intervals," that is, upon a movement between the pieces, the frames; upon the proportions of these pieces between themselves, upon the transitions from one visual impulse to the one following it.

Movement between the pieces—spectacular interval—spectacular relations between the pieces. According to Kino-Eye: a great complexity, formed by the sum total of the various relations of which the chief ones are: (1) relations of planes (small and large); (2) relations of foreshortenings; (3) relations of movements within the frame of each piece; (4) relations of lights and shades; (5) relations of speeds of recording.

Starting with this or that combination of relations, the author of the montage determines: the duration of each piece in meters for each of the images, the duration of projection of each distinct image. Moreover, at the same time that we perceive the movement which determines the relation between images, we also take into consideration, between two adjoining images, the spectacular value of each distinct image in its relations to all the others engaged in the "montage battle" which begins.

To find the most convenient itinerary for the eyes of the spectator in the midst of all these mutual reactions, of these mutual attractions, of these mutual repulsions of images among themselves, to reduce this whole multiplicity of intervals (of movements from one image to the other) to a simple spectacular equation: to a spectacular formula expressing in the best possible manner the essential theme of the cine-thing, such is the most difficult and important task of the author of montage.

This theory which has been called the "theory of intervals" was launched by the "kinoks" in their manifesto "WE" written as early as 1919. In practice, this theory was most brilliantly illustrated in *The Eleventh Year* and especially in *The Man with the Movie Camera*.

S. M. Eisenstein

*

ABOUT

STEREOSCOPIC

CINEMA

NOWADAYS ONE meets very many people who ask: "Do you
believe in stereoscopic cinema?"

To me this question sounds as absurd as if I were asked: "Do
you believe that in nought hours it will be night, that the snow will
disappear from the streets of Moscow, that there will be green
trees in the summer and apples in the autumn?"

To doubt that stereoscopic cinema has its tomorrow is as naïve
as doubting whether there will be tomorrows at all.

However, what makes us so certain of this?

After all, what we see on the screen at present are no more
than single "Robinsonades."*

And it is almost symbolical that the best of what we have seen
is precisely the screen description of Robinson Crusoe's life.

But what we have seen here is, in its turn, still no more than that
raft of Robinson's, in the film itself, trying to slip through the
overgrowth (one of the most convincing stereoscopic shots in
Andreevsky's film) which represents the myriad difficulties that
still have to be surmounted in the destiny of stereoscopic cinema.

This essay, translated by Catherine de la Roche, is the last written by
Eisenstein and was originally published in *Penguin Film Review*, no. 8,
January 1949, pp. 35-44.

* Eisenstein is referring to Semyon Ivanov's *Robinson Crusoe,* the first
feature-length stereoscopic movie made in the Soviet Union.

Yet the day is not far distant when not only rafts, but galleys, frigates, galleons, cruisers, battleships and dreadnoughts will sail into the harbors of stereoscopic cinema.

But why are we so certain of this?

Because, in my view, the only vital varieties of art are those which, of their very nature, are an embodiment of the hidden urges existing in the depths of human nature itself. What matters is not only which subject is incorporated in a work of art, but also which of the means peculiar to a given art form are employed.

In the problems connected with the extinction of one or another art form, there probably exists the same law of natural selection as in everything else.

And the forms which survive are those which are so composed as to embody the deep, inner, organic tendencies and needs of both the spectator and the creator.

The deeper the questions and the fuller the answers, the greater is the reason for an art form to become realized, the firmer the foundation for its development.

Is not the so-called aimless art perishing inexorably and hopelessly before our eyes because it does not contain an answer to the latent need for enlightenment existing in every progressive-minded person?

It came into being and could linger on for awhile, as a reflection of the sterility of the expiring class which gave it birth.

But it could not, of course, become an independent branch or variation capable of standing on its own among the other arts, capable of developing in its own way, of changing and growing.

At the same time, has not there existed through the centuries, and hardly evolving at all, a branch of art equally barren of content—the circus?

And the reason for this is that without touching the sphere of enlightenment (which is much more perfect and expressive in the other arts), the perfection of skill, strength, self-control, will-power and daring which gives brilliance to the circus will always be an expression of the natural urge for the fullest development of the qualities which are the essence of our physical nature.

For the same reason sport is unchangingly popular—both as an occupation and as a spectacle—for here the powers inherent in us are given the possibility to develop in the most perfect forms and on the widest scale, not only as a commonly shared intuitive experience, but in our own actions and behavior.

Can it be said that the principle of three-dimensional cinematography responds as fully and as consistently to certain of our deeper needs, to some kind of latent urges?

Further, can it be affirmed that, in its striving for the realization of these latent needs, mankind has for centuries been moving towards stereoscopic cinema, as to one of the most complete and immediate expressions of such strivings—strivings which, at different stages of social development and of the developments in the means of artistic expression, in different and incomplete ways, yet invariably and persistently—were attempts to realize some such latent need?

It seems to me that it was precisely so.

And I should like to try to reveal the nature of this striving, glancing at the historical modifications through which the arts of former times realized these tendencies, before discovering the most admirable and complete form for its incarnation in the technical wonder of stereoscopic cinema.

Let us try to define for which of the spectator's latent urges the technical phenomenon of steoroscopic cinematography can serve as an expression, just as the phenomenon of cinematography has in its very nature the independent, absolute attraction of the fundamental sign of developing vitality in the universe, mankind and progress—movement!

In order to do this, let us first establish the nature of the phenomenon itself.

Let us note in a few words what it is that strikes the spectator on his first acquaintance with stereoscopic cinema.

Stereoscopic cinema gives a complete illusion of the three-dimensional character of the object represented.

And this illusion is completely convincing, as free from the slightest shadow of a doubt, as is the fact in ordinary cinematography that the objects depicted on the screen are actually moving. And the illusion of space in one instance and of movement in the other is as unfailing for those who know perfectly well that, in one case, we are looking at a rapid succession of separate, motionless phases which represent a complete process of movement, and in the other, at nothing more than a cunningly devised process of superimposing one upon the other of two normal flat photographic records of the same object, which were taken simultaneously at two slightly different, independent angles.

In each case the space and the movement is compellingly convincing, just as the personages in a film seem undeniably authentic and living, though we know quite well that they are no more than pale shadows, affixed by photochemical means on to kilometers of gelatine ribbon which, rolled on to separate reels, and packed into flat tins, travels from one end of the globe to another, giving spectators everywhere the same compelling illusion of their vitality.

The stereoscopic effect can be of three kinds:

Either the image remains within the limitations of the ordinary cinema—resembling a flat alto-relievo, balanced somewhere in the plane of the mirror-screen.

Or else it pierces through to the depth of the screen, taking the spectator into previously unseen distance.

Or, finally (and this is its most devastating effect), the image, palpably three-dimensional, "pours" out of the screen into the auditorium.

A cobweb with a gigantic spider hangs somewhere between the screen and the spectator.

Birds fly out of the auditorium into the depths of the screen, or perch submissively over the very heads of the spectators on a wire palpably extending from the area which used once to be the surface of the screen up to . . . the projection booth.

Branches of trees are suspended all around, overhanging the auditorium.

Panthers and pumas leap out of the screen into the arms of the spectators, and so on.

Different calculations during the filming force the image either into Space, endlessly extended to the sides and in depth, or into three-dimensional Volume, moving in materially towards the spectator and positively palpable.

And that which we have been accustomed to see as an image on the flat screen suddenly "swallows" us into a formerly invisible distance beyond the screen, or "pierces" into us, with a drive never before so powerfully experienced.

As in color—this new stage of color expressiveness in relation to the former pictures restricted by the white-gray-black palette—so here, in the first instance, there only occurs a more perfect, continuing development of the tendencies towards the realization of which cinematography was striving already in the "two-dimensional" period of its existence.

Incidentally, one of my favorite types of exterior (in particular) shots was composed quite distinctly in the spirit of these tendencies.

It used to be composed (and continues to be) by means of exceedingly sharp emphasis on the foreground, very much enlarged, while keeping the background almost completely in focus, and toning it down only to the extent required by the air perspective in order to obtain the maximum distinction between depth and foreground.

By creating a feeling of a vast interval in scale between the foreground and the background, the maximum illusion of space was achieved.

The distorting powers of the 28-lens contributed in creating this effect, sharply accentuating the perspective, diminishing in depth —the only lens which is technically capable of giving clarity to the enlarged detail in the foreground and depth to the entire background in the same composition by retaining one and the other in distinct focus.

The attraction of such a composition is equally great both in the case of a thematic juxtaposition of both these planes, and in the case of blending them according to the unity of the material.

In the first instance, such a construction, juxtaposing volume—space, creates the maximum conflict imaginable within a single composition.

In the second case, it creates the most plastic and distinctly expressed feeling of unity between the general and the particular.

But such a composition is most expressive dramatically in those cases where it combines both these possibilities, and the thematic unity, say, both planes is achieved concurrently with their sharply accentuated plastic (scale and color) incommensurability.

That is how, for instance, one of the final scenes in *Ivan the Terrible,* Part I, was treated. The most memorable montage piece in this scene shows the boundless snow-covered space in the background of the composition, the general view of the Moscow peasants' procession moving across it, and, in the foreground, the greatly enlarged profile of the Czar's head bowing to them.

This shot, establishing the thematic unity between the people, imploring the Czar to return, and the Czar himself giving his consent, was composed with the maximum plastic "disunity" imaginable between these two "objects."

. . . It is interesting to note that all these examples from "flat" cinematography are, so far, superior by virtue of the power of their pictorial composition to that which is being achieved by purely technical means in stereoscopic cinema.

And the simple reason for this is that the technical possibilities of stereoscopic filming are at present restricted by the necessity to use only one lens, and the least expressive one at that—the 50.

But at the same time, from the anticipated potentialties of stereoscopic cinema, we can foresee developments that will enable us to achieve a hitherto undreamed-of quality, using the selfsame means.

One way or the other, though not yet creating a complete impression, these, precisely, are the two equal possibilities for depicting space as a physically palpable reality that the stereoscopic cinema has given us. The capability to "draw" the spectators with unprecedented intensity towards that which was once the plane of the screen, and, with no less reality, to "hurl" at the spectators that which formerly remained flattened out on its mirrored surface.

Well, what of it? you may ask. And why should these two "astounding possibilities" of the stereoscopic screen have something so hugely attractive for the spectator?

. . . Of course, not in any other art—throughout the whole of its history—can there be an instance so dynamic and so perfect of volume being transfused into space, and space into volume, both penetrating into each other, existing simultaneously, and this within the process of real movement.

In this sense stereoscopic cinema is superior also to architecture where, at times, the mighty symphony of the interplay between massives and the delineations of space is hampered in its dynamics and alternations by the tempo and sequence in which the architectural ensemble may chance to be traversed by the spectator, who has no other means of "penetrating" this architectural ensemble—dynamically.

. . . Belonging to the category histrionic arts, stereoscopic cinema should, of course, be regarded not only as the grand-nephew of Edison's and Lumière's inventions, but also as something like the great-grandson of theatre, appearing, in its present form, as the youngest and newest stage in the theatre's development.

And the riddle concerning the validity of the principle of stereoscopic cinema (if one exists) must, of course, be sought here, in theatrical history, in one of its fundamental tendencies which threaded its way through practically every stage of this history.

But of all the diverse questions concerning theatre, the one which interests me most at the moment is this same problem of analyzing the relationships and connections between the spectator and the spectacle.

. . . And the remarkable thing is that, almost at once, from the moment there's a "parting of the ways" between the spectator and a participant, a "longing" sets in for the two severed halves to be rejoined.

Not only in the intelligent writings which flourished in the epoch coinciding with the most extreme and acute individualism, not only in the countless practical experiments which were particularly characteristic of the newest times—not only in these endeavors to realize the tendency towards the renaissance of the original collective "entity" of a spectacle, but also during the entire course of theatrical history, which, in the innumerable examples of past theatrical techniques, through the centuries, at practically every step, unfailingly and consistently reveals the self same tendency—distinct in its forms, yet single in purpose—to "cover" the breach, to "throw a bridge" across the gulf separating the spectators and the actor.

These attempts fall into various categories, from the most "crudely material" external devices, such as the layout of the auditorium and of the area of action and the stage manners of the actors, to the most subtle forms of a "metaphorical" incarnation of this dream of unity between spectator and actor.

Furthermore, the tendency to "penetrate" into the midst of the spectators, no less than the tendency to draw them towards the actors, invariably and of equal right, either compete, take turns, or try to move hand in hand, as if to presage those two peculiar possibilities which represent the essential signs of the technical nature of that which we have noted as the fundamental plastic characteristic (the fundamental optical phenomenon) of stereoscopic cinema!

. . . The bourgeois West is either indifferent or even hostilely ironical towards the problems of stereoscopic cinema—problems to which the researching and inventive thought of the country of Soviets, its Government, and the directorate of its cinematography devote so much attention.

Does not the musty conservatism, with which news of work on the stereoscopic front is met in the West, sound absurd and, in its way, insulting to the eternally developing tendencies of a genuinely vital art?

Do not these lines about stereoscopic cinema, for instance, written by Louis Chavance in 1946 (!), sound like sacrilege and obscurantism:

". . . In what is the dramatism of a situation enriched by means of this new technical discovery?

"Does a three-dimensionally represented comedian find some additional means of expressiveness in this stereoscopy?

"A physical roundness?

"Will this be the triumph of fat people?

"What can anger, jealousy, hatred gain from the fact that they will occur in three dimensions?

"And laughter. . . . I cannot believe that one could induce more laughter than is induced by a custard pie hitting Mack Sennett's flat personages. And intrigue? Comedy? . . .

"Is there any need of further proof that stereoscopic cinema is a fruitless, sterile instrument?

"Of course, other hypotheses could be put forward, and I could speak of the purely visual aspect. But we should not become analogous with the plastic arts, and quote the sculptors after having talked of painters. Of course, Michelangelo's life could be filmed in relief and Titian's in color. . . . Charming result! But what pleasure for the eye? Sculpture evokes the idea of tactility, but, in any event, we do not touch the screen. . . ."

In what is Chavance mistaken?

His mistake, of course, lies in the fact that while making a pose of his contempt for the analogies, he is entirely their captive, completely encircled by the limits and conceptions of former arts, the norms of theatrical drama, the actors' functions and "sculpture evoking the idea of tactility."

But is it possible that Chavance does not think with us that there is bound to be an explosion and a complete revision of the relationships between the traditional arts in their encounter with the new ideologies of new times, the new possibilities of new people, the new means of controlling nature possessed by these people?

Is not the eye capable of seeing in the dark with the aid of the infra-red spectacles of "night-sight"?

The hand capable of directing shells and aeroplanes in the distant spheres of other skies by means of radio?

The brain, by means of electronic calculating machines, capable of completing within a few seconds calculations on which, formerly, armies of accountants worked for months on end?

Is not consciousness, in the tireless, postwar struggle, hammering out a more distinct and concrete form of a genuinely democratic international ideal?

Will all this not call for absolutely new arts, unheard-of forms and dimensions ranging far beyond the scope of the traditional theatre, traditional sculpture and traditional . . . cinema, which in the course of such development, must needs become mere palliatives?

And will not the new dynamic stereoscopic sculpture cast out beyond the confines of dimensions and peculiarities the former, static sculpture, according to which Chavance would set his standards?

There is no need to fear the advance of this new era.

Still less—to laugh in its face, as our ancestors laughed, throwing lumps of mud at the first umbrellas.

A place must be prepared in consciousness for the arrival of new themes which, multiplied by the possibilities of new techniques, will demand new esthetics for the expression of these new themes in the marvelous creations of the future.

To open the way for them is a great and sacred task, and all those who dare to designate themselves as artists are called upon to contribute to its accomplishment.

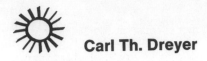

Carl Th. Dreyer

*

C O L O R

A N D

C O L O R

F I L M S

COLOR FILMS have now been on the screens of the world for twenty years. How many of them do we remember for the esthetic pleasure they gave us? Two—three—four—five?

Possibly five—but probably not more.

Romeo and Juliet just manages to be among these—after Olivier's *Henry V* and Kinugasa's *Gate of Hell*. Olivier got his ideas for his color schemes from the illumined manuscripts of the period. Kinugasa got his from the classical wood-engravings of his people.

Except for these three films there have been only attempts to accomplish things with color. These attempts are best exemplified by *Moulin Rouge,* where the smoke-filled room, right at the beginning, compelled admiration. The rest of the film, so far as color is concerned, was mediocre. Why? In the other scenes the director did not have Toulouse-Lautrec to hold on to. Huston is a great director, but as a painter Toulouse-Lautrec was greater.

So, in twenty years' time there have been three or four esthetically satisfying color films. A modest yield.

Apart from the amusing and surprising color effects that are to be found in filmusicals, a rather plain taste has dominated the use of color in motion pictures. This may be due to a fear to depart

Reprinted by permission from the April 1955 issue of *Films in Review* from the firm fundament of naturalism—firm, but boring. There can be poetry, of course, in the colors of daily life, but color film does not become art by even a sincere imitation of nature's own colors. When a film colorist is merely imitating nature, the audience is merely appraising how well or ill the colors come out.

Indeed, we have so often seen the grass green, and the sky blue, that sometimes we wish we could see a green sky and blue grass— just for a change. Also, there might be an intention of an artist behind it. Let us not forget that color in film can never look exactly like the colors of nature. The reason is simple: in nature, color nuances are endless, and the human eye cannot distinguish them all from one another.

The tiny color differences, the semi-tones, all those nuances the eye receives without discrimination, are missing in color films. To demand that color in color films should be *natural* is to misunderstand all that is involved. Indeed, the spectator can have a much greater esthetic experience *because* color in film differs from that in nature.

Color is a valuable help to the director. When colors are chosen with due regard to their emotional effect, and selected to match each other, they can add an artistic quality to a film that black-and-white lacks. But it must always be borne in mind that color composition is as important in color film as composition is in black-and-white.

In black-and-white films light is set against darkness, and line against line. In color films surface is set against surface, form against form, color against color. What the black-and-white film expresses in changing light and shade, in the breaking of lines, must, in color films, be expressed by *color constellations*.

There is also the matter of rhythm. To the many other rhythms in films, it is necessary now to add the color rhythm.

While a color film is being made the problem of how it will be cut—i.e., edited—must be a constant concern. The slightest shift can change the balance between the color planes and cause disharmony.

It must never be forgotten that because persons and objects constantly move in motion pictures, the colors in color films constantly slide from one place to another in changing rhythms, and, when the colors collide, or melt together, very surprising effects can occur. The general rule about this is: use the smallest possible number of colors, and use them in conjunction with black and white. Black and white are too little used in color films. They have been forgotten in the childish rapture over the many bright colors in the paint-box.

All this makes the director's task more difficult—and more attractive too. Creating a scene in black and white is a fight, as every director of integrity knows. Colors do not make this fight easier, but they do make the victory, when won, sweeter. And the victory will be much bigger when the director succeeds in breaking the vicious circle which confines color films to naturalistic ideas. The color film can be a really great esthetic experience—in regard to colors—when it has been freed from the embrace of naturalism. Only then will the colors have a chance of expressing the inexpressible, i.e., of expressing that which can only be perceived. Only then can the motion picture encompass the world of the abstract, which, hitherto, has been closed to it.

The director must not see his pictures in black and white first and *then* think of color. The colors for the scenes must be in his mind's eye from the beginning. The director must *create* in colors. However, color feeling is not something one can learn. Color is an optical experience, and the capacity to see, think and feel in colors, is a natural gift. We may presume that painters, in general, have that gift.

If there are to be more than just four or five artistic color films in the next 20 years, it will be necessary for the film industry to get assistance from those who can help—that is to say, from painters, just as the film industry has had to get help from authors composers and ballet-masters. The director of a color film will have to add a painter to his already large staff, and the painter, in cooperation with, and responsible to, the director, must create the color effects of the film. A "color script" should parallel the actual script, and the painter's drawings in this "color script" should abound with details.

People may object: the director has his color technicians. These advisers are, and will undoubtedly remain, immensely useful to the director, for their knowledge of chromatology and color theories can save him from many traps. But, with all due respect to their efficiency and sense of responsibility, a good painter has one important quality they do not: he himself is a creative artist and fetches impulses from his own artistic mind. Incidentally, it will help the color technicians also to have a professional painter at hand.

Let us take a purely suppositious case. Suppose Toulouse-Lautrec were alive and had worked on *Moulin Rouge* from the beginning to the end, not merely during the opening scene, but in all the scenes. Wouldn't these then have been at the same high level as the opening scene, which was based on an actual color composition by Toulouse-Lautrec? And would not *Moulin Rouge,* instead of being a promising attempt, have turned out to be a really great color film? The director would not have been lessened thereby. It is not his job to do everything himself, but to guide everything, and keep it all together and force the parts into an artistic whole.

The wish underlying what I have written here is for the color film to get out of the backwater in which it is and sail forth on its own. As it is now, the color film seems to aim no further than to "look like" something—it is not. *Henry V* tried to resemble a medieval illuminated manuscript, and *Gate of Hell,* a Japanese print.

It would be ever so beneficial for there to be a color film which bore throughout the hallmark of a colorist of today. Then the color film would no longer be mere film with colors, but an alive art.

**FILM
MASTERS**

AND

**FILM
MENTORS**

*

Part

Two

Alfred Hitchcock

ALFRED HITCHCOCK'S office was on the first floor of the Paramount Studio. As I walked in, it all came back to me. I had been in that office before, to talk to Frank Capra or to Willie Wyler. I couldn't remember which. It had been a long time ago and both Capra and Wyler had been gone from Paramount for years. For all I knew, they might be on their way back. Things happen that way in Hollywood.

The small round man who occupied that office now had a long pink nose and a slow voice that wheezed as he talked. He was neither Capra nor Wyler. Instead, he was his own highly individual self, but a number of intelligent people believe that in his own bailiwick Alfred Hitchcock has no remote rival as a directorial genius.

I'd been trying to see him for a week, but he'd been very ill. Then he was reported convalescent. At last I got the word if I'd be at Paramount at three o'clock the following afternoon, he'd be happy to talk to me. When I saw him he looked amazingly well. I was surprised. I'd met him once before while covering the Hollywood beat and he looked better now than he had then.

Originally published in *The Saturday Evening Post,* July 27, 1957, pp. 36-37, 71-73.

123

"I hear you had more than one operation," I said. "Coming one on top of the other, they must have been quite a shock. . . ."

"A New York doctor once told me that I'm an adrenal type," he said. "That apparently means that I'm all body and only vestigial legs. But since I'm neither a mile runner nor a dancer and my present interest in my body is almost altogether from the waist up, that didn't bother me much."

"Who drew that cartoon of you I see on my TV screen?" I said. "The one composed of two or three lines that gradually turns into you."

"I drew it myself," he said. "I began to draw it years ago, when I was a movie art director. With one exception, there's been little change in it since then. At one time I had more hair. All three of them were wavy."

"TV viewers are funny," I said. "I've noticed that one of the things about you which seems to appeal to them is the fact that when they stare at you on a TV screen, you stare right back at them contemptuously. But what seems to fascinate your viewing audience even more than your superciliousness is your lack of reverence for your sponsor."

"Remember the old saying, 'A knock is as good as a boost,' " he said. "My guess is that my sponsor enjoys my lack of obsequiousness, but in the beginning they had difficulty in getting used to my approach and they took umbrage at my less worshipful remarks. However, the moment they became aware of the commercial effects of my belittling—they took a look at their sales chart—they stopped questioning the propriety of my cracks. But there's no getting around it, I did take getting used to. The tradition is that the sponsor must be coddled. In such an atmosphere I was a novelty.

"The type of humor I wanted to use on TV was the type I employed in my film, *The Trouble With Harry*. In that film, Harry was a dead body who was a botheration to those who were alive. The awkward question, 'What'll we do with Harry?' was always popping up. There were those who found the notion gruesomely amusing, so I told myself that if no reverence for a dead body is amusing, no reverence for a live sponsor might be amusing too.

"In selecting the stories for my television shows, I try to make them as meaty as the sponsor and the network will stand for. I hope to offset any tendency toward the macabre with humor. As I see it, that is a typically English form of humor; even a typically London type of humor. It's of a piece with such jokes as the one about the man who was being led to the gallows to be hanged. He looked at the trap door in the gallows, which was flimsily constructed, and he asked in some alarm, 'I say, is that thing safe?'

"A story about the comedian Charles Coborn is cut from the same bolt of cloth," Hitchcock said. "I mean the original Charles Coborn, not the Hollywood one, whose name is spelled slightly different. The first Charles Coborn, who was famed for singing "The Man That Broke the Bank at Monte Carlo," attended the wartime funeral of another comedian named Harry Tate, who'd been hit by some antiaircraft-shell fragments. A large assembly of comedians was gathering at the graveside. Old Charles was so ancient that he was retired, and as the coffin was being lowered into the grave, one curious young sprout leaned over and whispered, 'How old are you, Charlie?'

" 'Eighty-nine,' Coborn said.

" 'Hardly seems worth while you going home,' the young 'un said.

"That's an example of the kind of humor I'm talking about," Hitchcock said. "But in case you've already heard that one, here's another story about two charwomen having a day off at a fair. They were in a sideshow watching a man whose quaint notion of entertaining the public was to bite the heads from live rats and chickens. In carnival lingo, parties who purvey such entertainment are called 'gooks.' The two chars stared at the gook, horrified, but one of them couldn't help trying to make a bit of a joke. 'Wouldn't you like a piece of bread with it?' she called out."

Hitchcock looked at me with a pleased expression, as if he'd just unburdened himself of a fragile and delicious witticism, but I was glad that I'd already had my lunch. However, his mention of hens triggered my next remark.

"I hear your father was a poulterer," I said.

"He was," Hitchcock told me. "And there's a theory that I've never liked eggs because of my father's occupation. It's true that I do regard eggs as loathsome, and to me, the most repulsive smell in the world is that which reeks up from a hard-boiled egg, but my father's occupation has nothing to do with my reaction. I hate the whole idea of eggs so much that when I can, I drop one of them negatively, shall we say, into my pictures to cover them with the obloquy they so richly deserve. For example, in *To Catch a Thief* I had a woman stub out her cigarette in an egg yolk."

"I do remember that," I said, "but it's the only one of your egg scenes I do remember."

"In a picture made years ago, *Shadow of a Doubt*," he said, "there was a moment in which I wanted a man to be shocked by something someone had said. His knife was headed straight for a fried egg, and the instant the remark was made, the knife punctured the yolk and immediately yellow goo spread all over his plate. To me, it was much more effective than oozing blood.

"People constantly ask me, 'Why are you so interested in crime?'" Hitchcock went on. "The truth is I'm not. I'm only interested in it as it affects my profession. Actually I'm quite terrified of policemen; so much so that in 1939, when I first came to America, I refused to drive a car, for fear a policeman would stop me and give me a ticket. The thought that if I drove I would face that possibility day after day frightened me horribly, for I can't bear suspense."

My face must have registered amazement, for he hastily explained, "I mean I hate it when I'm on the receiving end. People told me, 'Maybe if you will open a door in your subconscious, behind which you are concealing a psychosis acquired in your childhood, you'll lose your fear of policemen.'

"I grubbed back into my memory and opened the following door: when I was a small lad my father sent me to the local chief constable with a note. The constable read the note, laughed and locked me into a cell for a minute or two while he said, 'That's what we do to naughty boys.' It was my father's idea of teaching me an object lesson. When they hear that, everyone says, 'Of course! That's why you're afraid of police.' Unhappily, however, the fact that I have exposed that incident to the light has not allayed my fears. Cops still give me goose pimples."

I told him that one of my favorite Hitchcock touches was the sequence in the film *The Lady Vanishes,* in which the two Englishmen discuss news of the latest cricket scores.

"You mean Basil Radford and Naunton Wayne," he said. "When I discovered Wayne, he was a compère at a cabaret in the Dorchester Hotel in London. A compère is a man who is not really in the show at all. He can be the anonymous flunky who hands the illusionist the silk hat stuffed with rabbits. In Wayne's case, his compèring meant that he announced each act and said a few words between turns. Radford was the leading man in the original company of *Night Must Fall*—he is also known for his portrayal of the commander of the Home Guard in the film *Tight Little Island*—but I'm proud of the fact that, having found those two, I put them together. They formed a combination that complemented each other as happily as arf and arf or fish and chips."

"To me," I said, "one of the all-time classic motion picture scenes was that pair, sitting in a small station in a European city with all hell breaking loose in the world around them while their only concern was to find out what the cricket scores were back in England. As an American," I went on, "it was the quintessence of Britishness. Did the British think it thoroughly British too?"

"No," Hitchcock said. "They knew that it was merely a humorous exaggeration. Such things have been called the Hitchcock touch, but they're really examples of English humor based on carrying understatement to an absurd extreme.

"I suppose you might call it the oblique approach to melodrama. Melodrama is the most highly colored form of storytelling. Its villains, heroes and heroines are usually played heavy-handedly and bumblefootedly. I approach it somewhat differently. I've never gone in for the creaking-door type of suspense. To me, murder by a babbling brook drenched in sunshine is more interesting than murder in a dark and noisome alley littered with dead cats and offal.

"My hero is always the average man to whom bizarre things happen, rather than vice versa. By the same token, I always make my villains charming and polite. It's a mistake to think that if you put a villain on the screen, he must sneer nastily, stroke his black mustache or kick a dog in the stomach. Some of the most famous murderers in criminology—men for whom arsenic was so disgustingly gentle that they did women in with blunt instruments—had to be charmers to get acquainted with the females they murdered. The really frightening thing about villains is their surface likableness.

"Not long ago I did a piece for *The New York Times Sunday Magazine* describing the appeal of the true murder tale as opposed to the fictional variety. Once more I made the point that part of the fascination of the true murder lies in the fact that most real-life murderers are very ordinary, very polite, even engaging. I've heard the complaint that a true murder lacks mystery. I don't agree that that's a weakness. To me, suspense is immeasurably more potent than mystery, and having to read a fiction murder story through in order to find out what happened bores me.

"I've never used the whodunit technique, since it is concerned altogether with mystification, which diffuses and unfocuses suspense. It is possible to build up almost unbearable tension in a play or film in which the audience knows who the murderer is all the time, and from the very start they want to scream out to all the other characters in the plot, 'Watch out for So-and-So! He's a killer!' There you have real tenseness and an irresistible desire to know what happens, instead of a group of characters deployed in a human chess problem. For that reason I believe in giving the audience all the facts as early as possible."

I could hardly wait for him to finish, to tell him that I couldn't agree with him more; that one of my hobbies—in fact, my principal hobby—is the collecting, reading and rereading of accounts of true crimes, with a special leaning for those which took place against a British background. "Someday," I said, "I hope to find an editor interested in persuading me to compile an anthology of such diverting writings. I would have cheerfully paid my own way over to England to cover the trial of Doctor Adams, the Eastbourne physician with the strange appeal for elderly and generous English gentlewomen." Reluctantly I stopped riding my hobby and returned to a discussion of the Hitchcockian technique.

I asked, "How would you handle a potential bomb explosion in one of your stories?"

"The point is to let the audience know where the bomb is, but not let the characters in my story know," he said. "For example, you and I are sitting here chatting. We needn't talk about death or anything of serious consequence, but if the audience knows that there's a bomb under my desk, set to go off, the suspense will be harrowing to them. But if we don't tell our audience about the bomb ticking away under my desk, and it goes off and blows us to smithereens, the only thing the audience will get is a shock, and a one-second shock at that, as opposed to sixty to ninety minutes of breath-holding waiting."

"The thing you do that really wrings me out," I said, "is that sometimes you have a device like a basket or a box slowly opening while I'm sitting on the edge of my seat, waiting to see what name-less horror will emerge from it. Then something as dangerous as a small black kitten wanders out. You've prepared me for some-thing catastrophic, but what happens is something harmless."

"By judicious hinting it is possible to persuade an audience to put a shattering interpretation on the most innocuous things," he explained. "But you must be careful not to disappoint them completely. They'll react with a gratifying crawling of the flesh to things that turn out not to be so bad as they thought, but only if you ultimately come through with a real marrow chiller. Other-wise they'll feel let down and they'll leave your show resenting you as a cheat."

"I've noticed that you let the public supply its own conclusion for some of your TV half-hour shows," I said. "That's a new technique to me. At least I've never seen it done before."

"It's quite a trick to find thirty-nine shows a year, each with a twist at the end," he told me. "So we sometimes let you supply your own twist after you switch your set off, based, of course, on what you've just seen and heard."

"They tell me you'll be doing something different on TV this fall," I said. "But I'm not quite sure just what it is."

"In addition to our weekly half-hour show, I'll do ten one-hour shows," he said. "I'll have more time to develop character in them. For that matter, some stories deserve a longer telling than others. One of the first stories I'll do is the Cornell Woolrich story, *Three O'Clock*. It's about a man who makes a homemade bomb because he suspects his wife of having a lover and he's determined to blow them both up, even if it means blowing up his own home. However, immediately after he's started his bomb's timing device going, two burglars break into his house, truss him up and put him in the cellar while they rob the house. Then they leave. There he is, helpless, facing his own ticking bomb and not finding the situation all that it might be. In fact, he feels that it's extremely doubtful if there's any future in it."

I waited; then asked, "Well?"

Hitchcock blinked large, oyster-shaped eyes at me and said, "If you think I'm going to tell you what happens, you're quite wrong. I suggest that you tune in this fall and find out.

"I've never thought of the motion pictures I've made as being primarily commercial," he said thoughtfully. "Nevertheless, I've usually encountered a firm insistence from the front offices of the studios for which I've worked that I attach a satisfactory ending. In this community, to have what is known as an unhappy ending is to commit the unforgivable Hollywood sin called 'being downbeat.' And while you'll find heated denial in film circles that the average movie audience is only of teen-age intelligence, and whereas a number of people in motion pictures take it for granted that TV is only for morons, the truth is that we who make TV films are allowed to end our stories on a downbeat note as often as not. So, in spite of bleats from some TV writers, we have more freedom on TV than we do in motion pictures. Perhaps all that this proves is that people will accept more mature entertainment if they don't have to pay for it. It may be that when they pay to go to a movie they feel they have bought the right to come out with a satisfied feeling.

"It has been said of me that if I made *Cinderella,* the audience would start looking for a body in the pumpkin coach," Hitchcock went on. "That's true. Although my product hasn't been wholly melodramatic—I once tried an ill-starred comedy with Carole Lombard—there's no point in denying that I'm thoroughly typed. If an audience sees one of my productions with no spine-tingling, they're disappointed."

"Do you remember Robert Vogeler?" I asked. "He was the

American businessman who was mysteriously snatched on a journey between Budapest and Vienna, disappeared as if a crack in the earth had swallowed him, although he finally showed up in an Iron Curtain prison and eventually was released. As I read about him I thought, *How can Alfred Hitchcock make any more motion pictures, now that things are happening in real life which once only happened in his films?"*

"That question has presented a problem," he said. "After all, I couldn't dream up a more bizarre episode than Rudolf Hess's flight to Scotland during World War Two. The fact is, if I had put that into a movie before it happened, nobody would have believed it. Not only that, things have reached a point where those who live a life of wild and improbable adventure are copying devices from my movies."

"Such as?" I asked.

"Such as my picture *Foreign Correspondent*," he replied. "In it, a man was assassinated by a pistol concealed in a camera. In my film a photographer said, 'Just a moment,' to a diplomat on the steps of a large building; then pointed his camera at him and shot him dead. It gave me a turn when, a year later, the same thing occurred in real life in Teheran."

"I can see how it might rock you," I said.

"At first I thought I had suggested a *modus operandi* to the real-life assassins," he admitted, "but eventually I comforted myself with the thought that the whole thing was a coincidence. But I have to be careful that the pressure of real-life competition doesn't make me go too far with the bizarreness of my film situations, for the key to effective suspense is believability. The simpler and more homely the peril, the more real that peril."

"You've edited a book called *Stories They Won't Let Me Do On TV,*" I said. "I've noticed it in the bookstores. Why were those stories turned down?"

"Too macabre," he said. "I won't try to outline the plot of the short story called "Two Bottles of Relish," by Lord Dunsany, for you, because I'm sure your editor would be stuffy about it and find it distasteful, but there's another one in that book of mine that he may not find unpalatable. In it, a man murders his wife, then transforms her into chicken feed. Afterwards he serves a pair of his chickens to the local police inspector when he has him in for dinner."

I gulped and fished a piece of paper from my wallet. From it I read aloud this statement written about him by Ernest Havemann for *Theater Arts:*

> Almost any director can come up with a good, rousing historical epic or he can translate a first-rate Broadway play to the screen, but it's something else to take a simple little idea for a melodrama and use it in such a way that it keeps the audience half swooning with fear and half falling out of their seats with laughter.

"It *is* something else," Hitchcock said. "The secret is the way in which the story is pieced together. With me, all the little bits of business and the situations must be planted and established before a camera rolls. Sometimes I plan as many as six hundred camera setups before I begin to shoot. If I ever tried to improvise a plot structure on the set, I couldn't get the effects or the reactions I want to get."

"There must be very little wastage when you're done," I said.

"There's practically no spare footage," he told me. "It's been said of my stories that they are so tightly knit that everything depends on everything else, and that if I ever made a change before the camera I might as well unravel the whole sweater. That's true too. Take a ready-made stage play like *Dial M For Murder.* As the director of that play in its filmed form, there was almost no work for me to do. The various bits and pieces had already been put together on the stage. I've often wondered why so many successful stage plays fail as movies. I think the reason is this: someone has decided to 'open up' the stage play with added exteriors and turn it into a movie and, as a result, the tightness and tautness of the stage play is lost."

One of the questions I wanted to ask him was: "In one of your stories is one of your problems the job of offering an explanation for all the hush-hush stuff; the mayhem and the villains still pursuing? In other words, don't the baddies have to be after something?"

"That is what I call the McGuffin," he told me. "It's the gim-

mick; it's what the excitement is all about. In a spy story the
McGuffin is what the spies are after. In *The 39 Steps* the spies
were after an airplane-engine formula, but the odd part of it is
that the McGuffin never matters very much. In a film called
Notorious I had Ingrid Bergman go to South America and get
mixed up with some German spies. The question arose, What
were the spies after? In other words, what was the McGuffin?

"Although it was a full year before Hiroshima, I said, 'Let's
make it uranium samples.' I had a hunch that somewhere some
spies from some country or other must be after an atom bomb
or the knowledge of how to make one. So with Ben Hecht, the
writer of my film story, I went to see Doctor Millikan of Cal
Tech, to ask him what was to us a natural and not startling
question: 'How big is an atom bomb?'

"Doctor Millikan almost dropped his teeth. 'Do you want to be
arrested?' he blurted. 'Do you want me to be arrested too?' But
after those anguished questions, he pulled himself together and
spent an hour telling us how impossible it was to make an atom
bomb. We didn't know it, but the Manhattan Project had already
been launched, and Doctor Millikan was one of the big wheels in
it. It must have given him quite an odd feeling when we walked in
with our question, but, as I say, he did his best to keep his knowledge top secret by telling us how ridiculous our notion was. However, when we left, I said to Hecht, 'I'm going ahead with the
uranium McGuffin anyhow.' We made the picture and it grossed
seven millions. Today, it would gross two or three times that
much."

I asked him to explain the origin of the term "McGuffin."

"Using the McGuffin to mean the papers, jewelry, whatever the
spies are after, is my own adaptation of the word," he said. "It
comes from an old English music-hall joke about two men on a
train. One of the men says to the other, 'What's that package on
the rack above your head?' and the other man says, 'Oh, that's a
McGuffin.' The first man asks, 'What's a McGuffin? and the
second man replies, 'A McGuffin is an apparatus for trapping
lions in the Adirondacks.'

" 'But there are no lions in the Adirondacks,' the first man says.
'Then that's no McGuffin,' the second man says."

I said I had heard that he had a reputation as an outstanding practical joker. "I have pretty much outgrown that now," he said. "And I'm afraid that if I tried to describe them to you, they'd seem pretty flat and contrived, but I still have a little fun in elevators. Sometimes in a crowded elevator I turn to someone with me and say, 'Of course, I didn't know the gun was loaded, but when it went off it blasted a great hole in his neck. A flap of his flesh fell down, and I could see the white ligaments uncovered. Presently I felt wetness around my feet. I was standing in a pool of blood.' Everyone in the elevator stiffens; then I get out and leave them standing there. Once when I described that imaginary shooting one woman begged the operator, 'Let me out of here, please.' and she got out at the next floor."

I asked him where he got such Hitchcock touches as people losing themselves in funeral processions or ducking into amusement parks or into halls where political speeches were being made to hide from their pursuers.

"I simply look around and ask myself what background I can use next," he explained. "Someday I'll have a character dash into a hospital, pretend to be a patient, lie down on one of those litters on which they wheel you into the operating room, and before it's over, I'll have him operated on."

I had heard that he'd once told one nervous young actor who was jittering around in front of a camera, "I can't understand why you are all of a twitter. There's nothing depending upon your performance except your whole career."

I wanted to ask him what had happened to that young man. Had his career taken him on to become an Academy nominee? But I didn't get a chance to ask.

He stood up and said, "I know you'll forgive me, but I'm fifteen minutes late to look at screenings of various actresses I am considering for my next film. It turns out that the girl I had selected for the part has made a previous engagement with a bird who has a nose even longer than mine—a stork."

There are some things that even a great director, who anticipates every move before he turns a camera, can do nothing about.

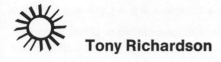

Tony Richardson

   *
THE
TWO
WORLDS
OF
THE CINEMA

THERE IS NO DOUBT that *Saturday Night and Sunday Morning** has been a big financial success. And I believe it has been a notable *creative* success, too. Ordinary audiences recognized themselves on the screen for the first time, and that they were not going to see some kind of unreal, overly comic or overglamorized world. Instead they were seeing people whom they could recognize on every street corner. This film expressed something that was close to a whole working-class section of England, and therefore people went to see and enjoy it because of this; because the film was no longer remote, but was something that they lived with every day.

I have been asked if I think that British audiences are ready for films in this vein which don't have any easily recognized dramatic or sensational ingredients. New things can always be done. Antonioni's *L'Avventura* was a success. Maybe this kind of film will be done in England some day, exactly when and how I don't know. It is just that some particular mood and expression captures the public imagination.

Obviously, if you have a strong story and a certain amount of

From *Films and Filming,* June 1961, pp. 7, 41.

* Directed by Karel Reisz.

  135

violence and sex this will have a more immediate popular appeal; but on the other hand if there was an English film like either *L'Avventura* or *Moderato Contabile* which had a big critical success to launch it, I think it would catch on with a wider audience. I don't say that necessarily the success would be on the same scale, any more than the commercial success of a film like *Saturday Night* could ultimately compare with the commercial success of *Ben-Hur*. But there could be a big enough audience for the thing to work economically.

What is wrong with the policy of the major studios in America is that they are not content to make films for a small audience; to recognize that certain films only have a limited audience and that once you've worked within those terms you can do all sorts of things and have much greater freedom: but if you think of the greatest possible amount all the time, then obviously you are going to sacrifice the minority picture.

Unfortunately, in the business as it is at present the success of films like *Saturday Night* will lead to copies. Anything that is immediately successful is copied. There may be good copies which are influenced by them which produce something new and interesting, something similar but which generally has its own truth and vitality: but there will also be many bad copies. It is exactly the same situation as we encountered at the Royal Court Theatre after we had a success. We started receiving plays like *Look Back in Anger,* which dealt with the color problem. Already Warwick has filed the title *Every Night and Every Morning,* and somebody else is making a film called *A Taste of Money.*

For myself, in future I would like to do *original work.* I don't really think of *A Taste of Honey* as being from a play I directed, because I prepared the script and conceived the film before I directed the play. In fact when I was first going to do the film I didn't intend to direct the play and it was only because of problems in setting the production up that I did the play on Broadway. I hope that it is not influenced as much by the theatre as the other films I've done. I don't really want to do another film which uses a play as basic material because the theatre and the film work quite differently. Once you've done a thing in the theatre it is terribly difficult to look at it as freshly as one should.

I don't think back on work I've done, and I'm not particularly interested in critically assessing it. I feel that you either achieve or do not achieve things at the time. On the whole I think that I achieved more things in *The Entertainer* than in anything else I've done. Probably from an overall audience viewpoint, and from at any rate what is accepted as a sort of professional and technical standard, *Look Back in Anger* is a more complete film. I think in this way they reflect the play. *The Entertainer,* I think, is a much greater play, and a greater conception than *Look Back in Anger,* which was better shaped dramatically.

I don't consider that I am going to make films in this neo-realistic pattern all the time, and I think that although, again, it is to a certain extent realistic in approach, *A Taste of Honey* will in itself have a slightly different style than any other film I have made. I shall eventually make films that are not quite in the same mold. I would like to do some historical films, but not Shake-speare. I have an idea for an epic film about India which I want to do in about four years' time.

Art is not to sell any sort of message; it is to pick a certain experience and a certain pattern of life and show the effect it has on people at a particular time in history. I don't think an artist has any job to try and preach any kind of social or political doctrine, although he should not deliberately try to avoid these. Obviously as a human being he has certain attitudes to society, politics and to all the big issues of his day. If he is successful, I don't mean in a commercial sense but in that he is able in the whole of his work to present himself, his attitudes are going to be in what he does; and implicit in it will be all sorts of political and social moralities. But they are not things that are pushed on to the films; they are the very fabric of the guy who is doing it.

I came to do *Sanctuary* through directing on Broadway. I had also been discussing making a film for Darryl Zanuck for some while. I went to Hollywood for a number of reasons. The diffi-culties of the production setup in England was one. Another was

that I liked the idea of certain things in the script and the avoca-
tion of a certain period. I thought at the time that by going to
Hollywood I would be much freer and be able to work in a more
interesting way than in fact it turned out. Partly I went there, quite
frankly, because one is always tempted in every direction . . . at
least I am.

I'm thrilled I went there because I know that I never want to
make a film in Hollywood again. It is impossible to make anything
that is interesting or good under the conditions imposed by the
major studios in America. It is a totally impossible creative setup:
even after the film is made, so much mutilation goes on, and it
becomes the product of many different people.

When one enters the Hollywood setup, one is always promised
the earth, and you think that you can beat them at their own game
and that you can handle these people. But you can't, because the
underlining is not big and dramatic. It is not as though there are
great issues in which one refuses in a black and white way not to
compromise, it's in every tiny detail that the whole quality of the
picture is eroded away leaving nothing. At no time can you win
on a particular issue. Everything slides away, and everyone who
works on the film is in that atmosphere. The production starts as a
mirage which gradually slips away as the reality takes over.

There are signs of a new movement within America. British
films are influencing this. A number of small-budget films, like
Shadows and *The Connection,* have been made in New York, to
a large extent financed rather like a theatre production. I'm sure
this is the way film production is not merely going to go, but *has*
to go in America. If you can make films cheaply then you can
have a certain kind of freedom, and as Broadway is getting more
expensive it is becoming in fact cheaper to make a film than to do
a Broadway musical, which means that more people will start
putting money into films. Once you have one or two really good
and successful films made in this way outside the major studio
setup, it will encourage a whole new form of production. The
major studios are just an anachronism; they are really as extinct as
the dodo.

John Cassavetes is now directing a film for Paramount because of the success of *Shadows,* and the company offered him complete freedom. This is how it all starts. He may succeed in making an interesting and original film, but I'm very skeptical of anything to do with a major studio because they make promises but in the end they really want to fit people into the mold that they have found successful in the past.

I believe the future of American films lies with these small independent companies who are completely independent of finance from major companies, and where the control is in the hands of the people who actually make the film. Films of this type don't have to be shown in every single cinema in the country. If anyone makes a really successful film and the public takes to it, they'll have no problem in getting any cinema in the country because cinemas are dying for films that will bring people in.

It was my decision to do *A Taste of Honey* independent of a studio because I think you get an authenticity that you can never get in a studio, because there you tend to become more conventional in every way: the film looks more conventional, is more conventionally lit, and I think the actors act more conventionally. This suits a certain type of professional star actor, but I'm not terribly interested in them.

In *A Taste of Honey* I wanted to force a much rougher style on the film, and to force myself to shoot in, I hope, a freer way. I strongly believe actors are much better when they have to work in the conditions of location. If ever I did an interior set for a realistic film in a studio again, I would never allow them to take walls out or anything like that. I would force everyone to work within the limitations of the room because I think anything else is a sort of theatrical viewpoint and that this is the really cinematic way.

I would like to have a theatre company of my own and naturally I would like to use these actors in films as well, almost on the pattern that Ingmar Bergman does. But not exclusively so, because casting films needs more careful decision. It's not just a matter of having a good actor; you have to have exactly the right actor, and sometimes within a theatre company you haven't quite the person you want for a particular part. I like working with people who are doing their first film and with people who haven't been used thousands of times, because I think they are like old worn coins that the public doesn't respond to freshly and so doesn't believe in the character they are playing. You cannot obtain from them the total believability that you can from someone the public has never seen before. Newcomers are more spontaneous and fresh, and I don't think they are necessarily unprofessional. For instance, Rita Tushingham is thoroughly professional and picked up what professional technique you need to know in the first few days.

Working as a producer is something I don't like because I am really interested in being a director. Producing films absorbs much of one's energy. Eventually there will, I hope, be a series of other directors, and maybe producers, in Woodfall working on their own films under the general banner of Woodfall.

Jean Cocteau

*

D I A L O G U E S
W I T H
C O C T E A U

André Fraigneau

I

A.F.: I'D LIKE this dialogue of ours to bear exclusively upon your activity in films, my dear Jean Cocteau. Would you be willing to approach our conversation from that angle?

J.C.: I can't do that, because for me the cinematograph is only one medium of expression among others. Speaking about it will inevitably lead me into other paths. I use the word *cinematograph* deliberately, in order to avoid any confusion between the medium it expresses and that which is commonly called the *cinema,* a somewhat dubious Muse in that it is incapable of waiting, whilst all the other Muses wait, and should be painted and sculpted in waiting poses.

Whenever people see a film for the first time, they complain about some passages being too long or too slow. But quite apart from the fact that this is often due to the weakness of their own perception and to their missing the deep underlying design of the work, they forget that the classics, too, are full of passages that are long-winded and slow, but are accepted because they

From Jean Cocteau and André Fraigneau, *Cocteau on the Film* (London: Dobson, 1954), translated by Vera Traill.

are classics. The classics must have faced the same reproaches in their lifetime. The tragedy of the cinematograph lies in its having to be successful immediately. It takes such a vast sum of money to make a film that it is necessary to get that money back as soon as possible by massive takings. That is a terrible, almost insurmountable handicap. I have just said that Muses should be represented in attitudes of waiting. All Arts can and must wait. They often have to wait for the death of their makers before they are able to live. Can, then, the cinematograph rank as a Muse? Besides, Muses are poor. Their money is invested. But the cinema Muse is too rich, too easy to ruin at one go.

To this we must add that, for the public, films are just a pastime, a form of entertainment which they have been accustomed, alas, to view out of the corners of their eyes. Whereas for me the image-making machine has been a means of saying certain things in visual terms instead of saying them with ink on paper.

A.F.: Can you give me a more explicit definition of the *cinema* as a form of mass entertainment, and also tell me what you understand, in contrast, by the *cinematograph* as a medium of self-expression? I think that this would help readers to grasp the distinction you so persistently draw between the two terms.

J.C.: What is commonly called "cinema" has not been, up till now, a pretext for thought. People walk in, look (a little), listen (a little), walk out, and forget. Whereas the cinematograph, as I understand it, is a powerful weapon for the projection of thought, even into a crowd unwilling to accept it. *Orphée,* for instance, irritates, intrigues and shocks, but forces people to discussions with others and with their own selves. A book has to be read and reread before it comes to occupy its rightful place. And cinema managers have noticed that some spectators of *Orphée* returned to see it several times and brought other spectators with them. Besides, however inert and hostile an audience may be, it enables a few attentive individuals to see the film. Without such audiences, my message couldn't have reached the few unknown spectators for whom it was destined. You might say that if a film falls flat the message dies. Of course. And with *Orphée* I took enormous risks. But I was convinced that in the case of an unusual and difficult film, the curiosity that brings people to see it is stronger than the laziness that keeps them away. Every day I receive letters which show that I was right. Their authors usually complain about the audience with which they found themselves locked in for the duration of the performance. But they forget that it's that very audience that enabled them to see the film at all.

A.F.: I was struck by an expression you used earlier on: "the image-making machine." Do you mean that you use cinematic images just as a writer uses literary images?

J.C.: No. The cinematograph requires a syntax. This syntax is obtained through the connection and the clash between images. No wonder that the peculiarity of such a syntax (our style) expressed in visual terms seems disconcerting to spectators accustomed to slap-dash translations and to the articles in their morning paper. If the wonderful language of Montaigne were transposed into images, it would be as difficult for such spectators to watch as it is difficult for them to read his writings.

My primary concern in a film is to prevent the images from flowing, to oppose them to each other, to anchor them and join them without destroying their relief. But it is precisely that deplorable flow that is called "cinema" by the critics, who mistake it for style. It is commonly said that such and such a film is perhaps good, but that it is "not cinema," or that a film lacks beauty but is "cinema," and so on. This is forcing the cinematograph to be mere entertainment instead of a vehicle for thought. And this is what leads our judges to condemn in two hours and fifty lines a film epitomizing twenty years of work and experience.

A.F.: Now I understand how much it meant for you, at a given moment in your career, to discover the cinematograph as a vehicle for thought—thought which you had previously expressed in so many different ways. But did you find a greater freedom in that new medium?

J.C.: No. Even if one is free to do as one pleases, there are, alas, too many heavy burdens (capital, censorship, responsibility towards the actors who agree to being paid later) to be what I would call completely free.

I am not thinking of actual concessions, but of a sense of responsibility which directs and restricts us without our even being fully aware of it. I've been completely free only with *Le Sang d'un Poète* because it was privately commissioned (by the Vicomte de Noailles, just as Buñuel's *L'Age d'or*), and because I didn't know anything about film art. I invented it for myself as I went along, and used it like a draftsman dipping his finger for the first time in Indian ink and smudging a sheet of paper with it. Originally Charles de Noailles commissioned me to make an animated cartoon, but I soon realized that a cartoon would require a technique and a team nonexistent at that time in France. Therefore I suggested making a film as free as a cartoon, by choosing faces and locations that would correspond to the freedom of a designer who invents his own works. Moreover, I've often been helped by chance (or at least by what is commonly called chance but never is for one who lets himself be hypnotized by a task), including even the petty vexations of the studio, where everybody thought I was mad. Once, for example, as I was nearly at the end of *Le Sang d'un Poète,* the sweepers were told to clear up the studio just as we had started on our last shots. But as I was about to protest, my cameraman (Périnal) asked me to do nothing of the kind: he had just realized what beautiful images he would be able to take through the dust raised by the sweepers in the light of the arc lamps.

Another example: as I didn't know any film technicians, I sent out postcards to all the cameramen in Paris, giving them an appointment for the next morning. I decided to take the one who would come first. It happened to be Périnal, thanks to whom many images of *Le Sang d'un Poète* can vie with the loveliest shots of our time. Unfortunately, in those days a silver salt was used in film printing, which was done at a pace impossible today. This is why cinematic Art is so fragile. A very old copy of *Le Sang d'un Poète* is as bright and shows as much contrast as any modern American film, whereas more recent copies look like old copies and weaken the whole effect of the film.

Although this too is arguable. To quote an instance: a friend of mine, whose intelligence I respect, detested *La Belle et la Bête.* One day I met him at the corner of the Champs Elysées and Rue la Boétie. He asked me where I was going and whether he could come with me. I said, "I'm going to work on the subtitling of *La Belle et la Bête,* and I'd hate to subject you to such an ordeal." He came along nevertheless, and I forgot him in a corner of the little cinema. I was working with my chief editor on a very old strip, almost unpresentable, gray and black and covered with stains and scratches. At the end of the projection I went back to my friend, and he announced that he found the film admirable. I concluded that he had seen it in a new perspective, rather as we do in film societies when we are shown old films in a disastrous condition.

A.F.: It seems to me that such strokes of chance, and all the miseries and splendors of film making, coupled with the difficulty of understanding a film, that is, to see and hear it with sufficient attention in the course of one fleeting projection, make it difficult, if not altogether impossible, for a message expressed in a film to have any *lasting* existence.

J.C.: Yes, indeed. The inevitable *invisibility* of any work of art which doesn't conform to public habits which make things visible —I mean, an invisibility arising from habits which were themselves acquired through contact with things that were not visible originally, but which have become visible through habit—this invisibility is an almost insuperable problem for those who treat the cinematograph as an Art, as a vehicle of thought. It is almost impossible to solve it without resorting to some subterfuge which would make that thought visible in the immediate present, but would condemn it for the future. There is no future for a film. Or, at best (provided the American laws becomes more sensible and one ceases destroying a story told in one manner for the sake of being able to retell it in another) the film will have a future of a sort with film clubs and a handful of amateurs. A film thus takes a reverse course compared to that followed by other works of art, which start on a small scale and reach a big one later, when they have proved their worth. The industrial machine forces films to begin on a large scale; after which they may live to reach a small one, if they survive the thousand perils threatening the existence of a negative: human carelessness, fire, and all the changes that technique is bound to bring into film production.

A film worthy of the name encounters the same obstacles as

does a canvas by Vermeer, Van Gogh or Cézanne. But whilst these paintings land in the public museum only after a long time, a film must begin in it. Then it ascends a slope, gets classed, and from then on can only count on being seen by a few individuals, similar to the few who saw the paintings when they first appeared, before the eye and mind had grown accustomed to them. In short, a painting that isn't worth a penny to begin with will be worth millions later on. Whereas a film that was worth millions at the start will survive, if at all, in dire poverty.

A.F.: After these generalities on cinematography, will you allow me to ask you a more personal question? And will you promise to give me an exhaustive answer? Can you tell me the deep motives that brought you, first among the poets, to an art which most writers despise—even though we observe that they despise it less and less as time goes on?

J.C.: Before I reply to the main part of your question, I will say that these writers have a good excuse. Film making is a manual art, a craftsman's job. A work written by one man and then transposed onto the screen by another is no more than a translation, and can, indeed, be of very little interest for a genuine writer (or be of interest only to his pocket). Before film art can be worthy of a writer, the writer must become worthy of film art. I mean, he should not be content with leaving some left-handed work of his to be interpreted by other people, but should seize hold of it with both his hands and work hard at building an object in a stlye equivalent to his written style. A desk-and-pen man is naturally quite uninterested in films, and doesn't even value them as a means of propagating his ideas.

II

A.F.: Let's come back to *Orphée*. How did you manage to avoid laboratory tricks, which you call "picturesque" and which you loathe? How, for example, do your characters walk in and out of mirrors?

J.C.: In a different way each time. Our subterfuges were based on the fact that in a film a mirror isn't taken into account, but only the void, or, rather, the frame. We built twin rooms and filled them with twin objects, and if you look carefully enough you can easily notice it, for the mirror (which doesn't exist) every image is reversed except the little engravings on the wall and the bust on the chest of drawers. I relied entirely on a card-trick speed. Do you realize that it would have been impossible to take some of the shots if we had been facing a proper mirror reflecting the camera and the camera crew? When Maria Casarès opens a three-leafed mirror, it would have been impossible for her to walk out of a two-dimensional surface. She walked out of the second room. A double, dressed like her and back to back to her, walked off in the opposite direction, playing the part of her reflection. The funny thing was that Maria Casarès changed three times during that scene (a black dress, a gray and a white), and that as my finances forbade me to reproduce all three, when Casarès had a black dress on, her reflection wore a gray one. Nobody noticed anything, and I assure you that I myself was duped when I saw the rushes, which shows to what extent a truth fabricated by us can be convincing, owing to the mere fact that it is *seen*. It has all the persuasiveness of a false witness. Another instance: when Marais goes towards the mirror and raises his rubber-gloved hands, a portable camera is placed on the shoulder of a studio-hand wearing a jacket and wet gloves similar to Marais's. Thus I was able to approach facing the false room, from the back of which Marais in person advanced, playing the part of his own reflection. The gloved hands met. I cut, and passed on to another angle. Such an effect requires all the skill of the camera operator and the focus man, for neither the close up nor the medium shot must be blurred. The new American lenses permit that. Ours do not. All rests, as I have said before, upon the skill of our crafts-men, whose mental agility alone enables them to keep up with the progress of technique.

In some of the shots I made Nicholas Hayer's task easier by substituting (in the Court scene) the real characters for the fictitious ones. This muddled people, presenting both childish difficulties and truly baffling riddles. You see the reflection of the judges: those are the judges themselves. But what is muddling is that Maria Casarès in the foreground, seen from the back, is the real Maria Casarès.

When Jean Marais and François Périer appear in the court room, Marais leaps in slow motion through the empty frame in which we saw (in the same shot) one of the motor cyclists playing the part of the reflection of another motor cyclist (they were two brothers). I cut, and take Marais motionless. After that he moves back and his movement draws the camera with him towards Périer in front of a real mirror (quickly substituted in the meantime) from which he seems to have emerged saying the line, *"Nous sommes faits comme des rats."* I forgot to explain that when Jean Marais jumps, he jumps backwards through an identical frame (since the real judges are supposed to be their reflections in the mirror). The entire mechanism, which oftens remains a riddle even for those who take part in it, falls into place in the projecting room, where the whole unit rushed every evening in order to understand what they had done entirely on trust during the day.

I don't pretend to have invented the method of having the reflection in a mirror acted by another person. I used it as a syntax. You find it in the Delannoy-Sartre film (done with twin sisters). In fact, none of these things is new. They're all the same old dictionary words. Already Méliès used them, and to use different ones would mean to be emphatic, which is as deplorable in the visual language as it is in writing. Besides, even if a film is made without any attempt at tricks, they are still there. They are the secret arsenal of painting and of poetry. A bad film is like a poet without culture, content to tell a story in verse (with nothing of that which makes a poem a poem).

A.F.: I hoped, like many other members of the audience, to have spotted a few of the special effects of *Orphée*. Thus in the dunes, after the scene in the chalet, I thought I noticed a cut in the sound, a deliberate silence.

J.C.: This would have been impossible. A cut in the sound would make a hole that is not silence. What you *heard* was real silence, and I insist on the word "heard" because an attentive ear can detect the thousand and one imperceptible sounds of which that silence is composed. There is deliberate silence, yes. But that silence is derived from the locality itself. And it sometimes happens that the locality resists, refusing to be at our beck and call. The ruins of Saint-Cyr, for instance (which very nearly caused my own, for the night shooting, as I've already mentioned, cost us a fortune in generating equipment) gave me a nasty shock. There were about one hundred and fifty trains passing there every night. The *sous-préfet,* Amade, stood watch in hand announcing the times of the trains and the intervals in the din. But it was very rare, alas, that a shot could be made to coincide with the railway timetable. This is why in *Orphée* you occasionally hear distant whistles and a kind of hollow factory noise. We tried to dub these passages. But in the projecting room I realized that the whistles and the factory noises gave a background of mystery to the dialogue, and that they should on no account be cut.

A.F.: So you made use of accidental noises as though they were a trick? But have you on any other occasion manipulated sound as you manipulate the pictures?

J.C.: I'm quite as interested in the use of sound as in the use of images. When we were making *Le Sang d'un Poète,* as the sound film had just appeared, we kept experimenting till we were quite exhausted. We kept building up walls and then demolishing them, trying in vain to obtain the sound of a crash. At last in desperation I hit upon the discovery that the only way to get that sound was by crumpling up two newspapers simultaneously. It happened to be the *Temps* and the *Intransigeant* (one of which is printed on stiffer paper than the other). In the same film, with the exception of Rachel Berendt's voice, who dubbed for Miss Lee Miller, all the voices are my own, disguised. The chatter in the theatre box consists of various phrases said by me and made to overlap in the mixing.

A.F.: And what about *Orphée?*

J.C.: In *Orphée,* for the coming and going through the mirror we used the entire range of the actual sound, but without the initial shock. I kept only the prolongation of the waves (to be in fashion, I should say the undulatory prolongation). I told you about the drums. After shooting the scene where Cégeste rises up in front of the Princess in reverse and in slow motion, I took the whole scene twice in close-up, once with the camera trained on Maria Casarès and once on Dermithe. As the Casarès shots didn't come out very well, I kept only the Dermithe ones. But as I liked Dermithe's voice better during the Casarès shots, I put the words of the shots we had taken from behind him on to the shots of the close-up of his face, making them coincide with his lip movements. There are so many subterfuges of that kind in *Orphée* that I couldn't enumerate them all now. But since you seem so interested in these secrets of our trade, and since you think that they might interest the reader, I will tell you about the wall of Saint-Cyr at the corner of which Orphée and Heurtebise fly away. It is a trick I had previously used in *Le Sang d'un Poète,* and which I reproduced this time in a corridor of the Folies Dramatiques. We built a model of the arcades of Saint-Cyr erected in a horizontal position on a large scaffolding half way up to the ceiling. On the floor, some photographic devices produced scenes that gave the effect of a distant perspective. We were in a tip-bucket suspended from rails, so that what we saw when we looked through the camera lying flat on our stomachs were the normal arcades.

At the extreme left-hand corner of that vast contraption was a wooden sheet which sloped down almost perpendicularly and ended in a trench filled with straw. An old woman, leaning her back against some railings suspended over the void, with her legs flat against the *décor,* appeared to be sitting in a corner of the arcade and added to the deception. One saw (although, alas, they could be barely distinguished) two children asleep, lying against a plank in front of one of the fake pavements, in such a position that Orphée and Heurtebise could slip between them and the wall. The two actors (Marais and Périer) had to drag themselves towards the slope without allowing their feet to leave the false ground, which was all there was between them and a long fall; or if they did leave it, they did so with a peculiar clumsiness which, once the picture was set upright, assumed the extraordinary ease of movement of a dream. At the end of that journey, Orphée rolled over the edge and fell down the slope. Heurtebise was supposed to follow him. But Jean Marais is a daredevil, whereas François Périer is not accustomed to that kind of sport. I was afraid to put him to such a test. But after four takes with a stand-in I realized that I would have to impose that sacrifice on him. He agreed readily, and sprained his ankle in the straw. His sole comment was to ask if the shot was all right, and as it was good (or at least I told him it was, so as not to make him roll down again), he declared that the thing was well worth a sprained ankle, which didn't matter tuppence anyway. That is the kind of man he is.

A.F.: I don't want to tire you, but all these details are so fascinating that I must try and record as many as I can. Nobody except you is so willing to speak of what happens behind the scenes, which shows to what extent you are free from relying on secrets and surprises for communicating your poetry.

J.C.: Well, here are a few more. The mirror into which Orphée dips his hands required about eight hundredweight of mercury. But there is nothing harder to come by than mercury, and nothing less simple to find than a tank big enough and strong enough to hold it. On top of that, it wouldn't have been safe to keep such a treasure in the Studio. So we had to do the shooting in one day, and we wasted a lot of time because it was almost impossible to get the caps off the drums in which the mercury had been delivered, and because the mercury itself was dirty. It had to be polished with chamois leather, like a silver dish. No sooner had one got that soft heavy surface clean than the impurities rose again and floated on top like oil stains. I thought I might be able to do without Jean Marais by putting the gloves on somebody else of his size. But when I tried I saw that hands were like a person, and we would have to have the actor himself. So he was sent for, an we spent the entire day, from seven in the morning till six in the evening, on that one shot.

A.F.: Why, if it so difficult to handle, did you have to have mercury?

J.C.: Because mercury shows only the reflection and not the part that has penetrated into the mirror, as water would have done. In mercury the hands disappear and the gesture is accompanied by a kind of shiver, whereas water would have produced ripples and circles of waves. On top of that, mercury has resistance.

A.F.: This provides me with an opportunity to ask you about a shot that must have been extremely difficult, namely when Orphée knocks against the mirror immediately after the last motor cyclist has passed through it.

J.C.: You guessed right. As there's only one shot, the motor cyclists couldn't have disappeared if there had been glass. Jean Marais knocked against an empty space and simulated the collision. I added the noise afterwards. The glass was put in only for the following shot, when Marais brushes against it and his cheek is flattened by the pressure. The third shot, in reverse, is taken with a real mirror; the fourth (the one after the room, in the deserted countryside), with a mirror buried in the sand, which plays the part of a glass-like puddle.

Another kind of trick effect, akin to a device used by novelists, is the creation of an unknown deserted little town through a combination of several different districts of Paris. For this, the streets had to be empty of people and extracted from their proper surroundings. The car pulls up at the bottom of the Grenelle steps, at the top of which there is a lamp-post of an unusual shape and some chalky blocks of flats, very much like another unusual lamp-post and some chalky houses in the Square Bolivar (in the Buttes Chaumont district) where Marais enters in the following shot. Maria Casarès disappears in a gateway in the street which runs at the top of that sloping square. Marais dashes in after her, to emerge under the arcades of the Place des Vosges. He turns round the corner and walks into Boulogne, at the covered market where the sequence ends. As to Maria Casarès appearing in the market, it was simply done in two shots and doesn't require any special explanations.

But what I'd find more fascinating than dwelling on the kind of things every film-maker knows, or on the thousand funny incidents which inevitably occur when a crowd that must be hidden persists in trying to be seen, would be to speak about Time and Space. Film art is the only art form that allows us to dominate both. It very seldom happens that adjoining rooms are erected on the same floor, or that an interior set corresponds to the exterior set to which it is supposed to lead. And shooting is very rarely done in the right time order. We are free to manipulate as we please a world in which nothing seems to permit man to overcome his limitations. Not only is our situation similar to that of a painter, who endeavors to transpose the three-dimensional world in which he lives into two dimensions, but what's more, in films these two dimensions express more than three, for we overcome time as well, which is also a dimension, and we can therefore say without any fear of ridicule that we operate in the fourth. In *La Belle et la Bête,* Jean Marais and Michel Auclair walk into the merchant's house (after the archery tournament) in Touraine, and finish the gesture of shutting the door behind them two months later in Paris, having during all the inadmissible lapse of time led their own lives. It is thanks to the magnificent American camera owned by Pathé (there are only two or three of them in existence) that I was able to shoot Orphée and Heurtebise in the ruins of Saint-Cyr. One is walking (Marais), the other standing motionless (Périer). The atmosphere around the one is dead and diffuse, the other is made animate by wind and light. Marais played his part in Saint-Cyr. François Périer played his much later, in the studio on the banks of the Seine. The system of mirrors is well known and in current use. But for a scene of such precision, where the characters speak to each other and aren't content with merely moving across a given locality, it was imperative to use a perfect machine. I ought to have gone even further, and put two Orphées in the picture, one shoulder to shoulder with Heurtebise and the other behind him. "Why," he would have asked, "are there two of us?" and Heurtebise would have said his line, "Why, always why? Don't keep asking me questions," and the rest. Unfortunately a film costs too much money to be corrected after it's been made and, besides, by the time these good ideas come to us it is usually roaming the world over. This is just one more instance of victory over our limitations, and of the kind of work that the laymen who come to visit us don't understand. That's why the visitors in a film studio get bored and cannot follow what's going on, for what they see are only some phenomena of punctuation. They never read a complete sentence.

A.F.: I would be tempted to generalize, and to extend your description of visitors in a film studio to life in general, in which time is a phenomenon of perspective, and where we wait without understanding what we are part of and who the director is whom we are expected to obey.

J.C.: You are quite right. One always comes back to the amusing reply made by Sainte-Beuve (I think), when somebody declared, "At bottom, all is in all," and he said: "And vice versa."

A.F.: The more you speak, the more you enter into details, the more I become aware of the hard work involved in the creation of a film which is designed for public entertainment but at which the public barely looks, speaking at the same time as the actors, commenting on the story or the actresses' dresses throughout the entire performance.

Alain Resnais

THE VENICE 1961 Golden Lion picture, Alain Resnais' *L'Année dernière à Marienbad,* is a "sealed" work of art. Some of its mysteries are unsolved by the director himself. Two young French writers—André S. Labarthe and Jacques Rivette—have been analyzing the film with Resnais. And Resnais, in turn, has been discussing its implications with its author, novelist Alain Robbe-Grillet.

The debate started with a detail that may prove for many the big issue of *Marienbad* . . . a game played throughout by the two men, while the woman waits. What is the mystery of the game?

RESNAIS: The game is the only point about which I am unable to tell you anything. I have never played it. Apparently it is very ancient; the Chinese played it three thousand years before Jesus Christ. It was the game of Nim, of which Robbe-Grillet has invented a variation without even knowing it existed.

QUESTION: But it functions less as a game than as a trap?

RESNAIS: Quite. My personal impression is that when Albertazzi loses it is consciously and deliberately. Perhaps through sheer unconcern. In any case X has a very complex character; he

First published in English in *Films and Filming,* February 1962, pp. 9-10, 41; translated by Raymond Durgnat from *Cahiers du Cinéma.*

has periods of violent willfulness and obstinacy which abruptly give way to discouragement.

Q: What is the hidden relationship between the game and the film?

RESNAIS: It is, I believe, the necessity of making a decision. Of course, the characters, while playing, may be allowing themselves a few moments' reflection while arriving at their decisions. In any case, the whole thing is possibly a part of the woman's stream of consciousness, as, on the point of deciding what to do, she recalls all the various factors in a few seconds. I don't think there are any other meanings, except possibly that there may be a cyclic recurrence of one's problems. This would correspond to the element of musical form and to the obsessive qualities of dreams. But so far as I am concerned *Marienbad* contains no symbols or allegories.

Q: But there *are* things which one may take as symbols.

RESNAIS: Yes, of course, one may be reminded of the legend of the Grail, or anything else. But the film is open to any such myth. If you look for parallels to ten different themes, whether mythological or realistic, you will arrive at a correct interpretation of 60 or 80 percent of the film. But your interpretations will never hold good for the film as a whole.

One of the themes which interests me in the film is that of the parallel universe. It is quite possible that all the characters are speaking the truth. We didn't deliberately organize the film around this possibility, but there is a certain connection with "automatic writing." The possibility of "automatism" can't be dismissed simply on the grounds that Robbe-Grillet's style is extremely precise and his vision very clear-cut. His way of working often reminds me of Le Douanier Rousseau, who used to start his canvas in the left-hand corner, filling in the smallest details, and then work across to finish in the right-hand corner. This is what was so fascinating about the film; we were forced to begin orientating it, I won't say without knowing how it would end, but, all the same, the last pages of the script had hardly been typed when we began shooting. The important thing was a constant fidelity to our intuition. It's the sort of film of which one says, "Once it's shot, there will be twenty-five possible ways of editing it." But on the contrary; we always fell back on our original ideas. This is why Robbe-Grillet and I feel so *excluded* from the film, we look on it as something apart from ourselves. We wanted the film to work quite differently from a conventional entertainment; by a sort of contemplation, of meditation, a series of advances and retreats from the subject. We wanted to feel ourselves in the presence of a sculpture which one studies first from one angle, then from another, from near or farther away.

Q: But there is still a resistance by the cinematic material, which has to be overcome.

RESNAIS: Yes. Personally, I see the film as an exploration of various themes, an attempt to discover which are the blind alleys and which are the real avenues of approach. Both are present in the film. For the time being, I am too close to the film to see it clearly. Every morning I read what has been written about it, and I notice that some critics speak of a work which is as cold as the poems of Mallarmé, while others call it tender and passionate. Which doesn't enlighten me very much. Possibly both reactions are justified, the film may act as something like a mirror for every spectator.

Q: Without setting out to make an exegesis of the film, isn't there a snag in the idea of guiding the spectator towards the past or the future? Seeing it again, we have the impression that the film is not concerned with time so much as with the relationship of the real and the imaginary.

RESNAIS: The film is about *degrees* of reality. There are moments where it is altogether invented, or interior, as at the moments where the picture corresponds to the dialogue. The interior monologue is never in the sound track; it is almost always in the visuals, which, even when they show events in the past, correspond to the *present* thoughts in the mind of the character. So what is presented as the present or the past is simply a reality which exists while the character is speaking. The other day, I was talking to a girl who had just returned from India; and suddenly I visualized her wearing a blue dress and standing in front of the temple of Angkor. Yet she had never been to Angkor and the blue dress was the one she was wearing now.

Q: There are a great many interpretations. When Robbe-Grillet summarizes the film he describes it from the point of view of the man who suggests a past to the woman.

RESNAIS: That's right. If one accepts Truffaut's dictum, "Every film should be summarized in one word," then one can say: *L'Année Dernière à Marienbad*, or, *Persuasion*. That's a solution, but there are others.

Q: One can also take the film as if the past was real, that the woman repudiates it, and that the man plays a rôle analogous to that of a psychoanalyst, forcing her to accept events which she has deliberately repressed.

RESNAIS: It's from this angle that I directed the film. Some psychoanalytic themes were introduced quite consciously, for example, the ostentatiously large rooms, indicating a tendency towards narcissism. They signify impotence; I finally cut them out during the editing, because they didn't conform to my idea of his character. Or perhaps because I was too aware of their psycho-analytical significance?

Q: The moments of tension between Albertazzi and the girl correspond to those arising between analyst and patient?

RESNAIS: I don't know if you remember that scene towards the end, where the man has his hand against the door, just after the hypothetical sequence of death, where she imagines that if she left with him she would be killed, and so on. When she says, as if in despair, "But I have never stayed so long anywhere," I get the impression, particularly from her intonation, of an acquiescence which is total: so that the scene is real. It is also attractive to conceive of her as an invalid. First of all, that hotel has a special air. And I have always been intrigued by Sacha Pitoeff's words to the woman as she lies on the bed: "You must rest, remember that is why we came here." This always reminds me of *Caligari,* where the doctor says, at the end, "Yes, he will be calmed, I shall cure him." There does seem to be a certain similarity. Perhaps the hotel is really a clinic.

Q: There is another interpretation which you sensed: that Albertazzi is death.

RESNAIS: Robbe-Grillet finally hit on the phrase "granite flagstone" and he realized that the description of the garden would fit a cemetery. On pursuing this line of thought, he realized that the film had affinities with the old Breton legends—the story of Death coming to fetch his victim and allowing him a year's respite. But we never attempted to make the film conform to any precise meaning; we always allowed a certain ambiguity.

In the first quarter of the film, things seem to have a fairly high degree of reality; we stray further and further from it as the film proceeds; it is quite conceivable that, at the end, suddenly, everything converges, that the conclusion of the film is the most real part of all.

Q: And there'd be a big climax halfway through when she recognizes the statue.

RESNAIS: Yes, when she discovers the garden and realizes that the garden is, after all, only the place where they happen to be. This poses all the problems of the film's chronology.

Q: There is a moment when she realizes that she is trapped. Is that when she laces her shoe?

RESNAIS: Exactly. From that moment, we can take it that she has *remembered*. If, perhaps, she is sincere at the beginning; if her refusal is not sheer coquetry, or fear, then, from that moment, she remembers. But, of course, we never really know if the scenes are occurring in the man's mind or the woman's. There is a perpetual oscillation between the two. You could even maintain that everything is told from her viewpoint. Several spectators have told me that the woman does exist, that she died long before, that everything is happening between two ghosts. But, one only thinks of these possibilities after the film has been completed— not while shooting, or even editing.

Q: What was your guiding principle in organizing this material, which you were deliberately keeping vague; was it a feeling of affinity between theme and image; internal rhyming?

RESNAIS: Interestingly enough, I was not the only one to be guided as I was. During the whole shooting there was no disagreement, whether among the actors or the technicians. Now and again we discussed various possibilities. We talked about the shots beforehand; we said: "This is in the 'tone' of the film, this isn't." But such discussions never lasted more than a few moments. We were all compelled to follow the one path, from which we were not allowed to stray. It almost became teamwork, of a sort; we were prisoners, not of a logical argument, but of a paralogic, which kept us in constant agreement, from Philippe Brun to Sacha Vierny or Albertazzi. It would be most interesting to draw up a diary of "correspondences" in the selection of locations and actors. There was any number of bizarre coincidences, phenomena which would have delighted André Breton or Jean Cocteau. I have the impression that the form must have pre-existed, I don't know how or where, and that somehow, as one writes, the story automatically takes the mold.

Every time I make a film I discover that one can't allocate gestures or words to the characters just as one pleases. There was a moment, during the preparation of *Marienbad,* where I arrived with my little black notebook and suggested to Robbe-Grillet that we should introduce the real world under the guise of conversations concerning a political problem, which would be insoluble, at least for those who were interested in it. But we realized that the real world would be introduced by the spectators themselves as they watched the film, and that it was impossible to include them in it.

At one point I also wanted the woman to be pregnant; I mentioned it to Robbe-Grillet, but it turned out to be hardly feasible. We were not free. I am convinced that we don't make these films as we choose.

For me the film represents an attempt, still crude and primitive, to approach the complexity of thought and of its mechanisms. But I must stress that it is only a small step forward compared to what we should achieve eventually. I have found that in each descent into the unconscious an emotion is born.

I remember how I felt while watching *Le Jour Se Lève,* with its sudden moments of ambiguity, as when the image of the wardrobe begins to fade out and another scene gradually materializes. In reality we don't think chronologically; our decisions never con-

form to an ordered logic. We all have *clouds,* factors which determine our being but are not successions of logical acts following a
perfect sequence. I am interested in exploring that universe from
the point of view of reality, if not actually of morality.

Q: There is the danger of falling into a trap, rather like that
which Paulhan mentioned in connection with language; what one
thinks of as the height of liberty is liable to be for someone else
totally arbitrary.

RESNAIS: The difficulty is inherent in all communication,
whether between two people or ten million.

One has to know how much of one's subjective reality one can
share with others (for we have sight, hair, thought, and so on).
One arrives naturally at the idea of a "global unconscious." I am
attracted by the idea of applying disciplines rather different from
those of the most contemporary films. It arouses my curiosity. In
the cinema I am drawn to the idea of popularization. A book or a
painting first make contact with a thousand people, while a film
reaches millions straight away.

From this angle, it is interesting to recall the experiences of a
writer in 1880 or a painter to only a few connoisseurs. I dislike
sectarianism; and any attempt to demolish the walls of the *clique*
delights me for its own sake. In any case, even if one wanted to
repeat exactly what others have already done, the chemical composition of the Cinema is too different. When Van Gogh amuses
himself by copying Delacroix, or Picasso Velasquez, the result is a
completely new painting. Of course, the Cinema is rather clumsy,
with its concrete images. Its style is rather pachydermous. We are
still afflicted by the old dichotomy between the realism of Lumière
and the fantasy of Méliès. We wobble between these two alternatives and often fall between two stools. *Lola,* for example: is it
Lumière or Méliès?

When I see a film, I am less interested in the characters than
in the play of feelings. I think we could arrve at a Cinema without
physchologically definite characters, where the pattern of feelings
exists freely, just as, in a modern painting, the play of forms is
more important than the "story."

Q: What alarms us is the position which René Clair pushes to its logical absurdity when he says: "Shooting is just a chore."

RESNAIS: For me, shooting is elucidation. I do make small sketches beforehand, but for the sake of peace.

Q: While shooting, what attitude do you adopt towards your sketches?

RESNAIS: I still study them. It helps in my relationships with the actors and the cameramen. They save the actor from getting panicky eight or ten days before we shoot. If he has read the shooting script and has a clear idea of it, and then, while shooting, I place him in a position or composition which hasn't been foreseen, he is apt to worry. And as I like everyone to be as relaxed as possible on the set, I prefer arguments to be over before shooting. I'm all in favor of rehearsing the entire film before shooting begins.

For *Marienbad* we drew up a complete chronology on squared paper. And before beginning any scene with the actors, we said, "In the editing, this scene follows such and such a scene, but, in actual chronology it follows another scene, which will appear much later in the film." I frequently recorded a fragment of the preceding scene, so as to work from the continuity rather than from the cue. This chronological chart was drawn up after the scenario was finished. Obviously, all the changes of costume correspond to different "layers" of time.

That isn't the "key" to the film, assuming there is one. But one could edit the film so as to restore the chronological order of the scenes. One might see the film as extending over a week, or with all that is shown in the present tense as taking place from Sunday to Sunday inclusive. This doesn't stop Robbe-Grillet from saying: "Maybe it all happens in five minutes." This is consistent with the dilatation of time in dreams, at least as far as we understand the mechanism of dreams.

Q: Your montage is in a sense the modern version of the "montage of attraction." For Pudovkin, the shots were the words of a phrase, whereas for Eisenstein each shot was in itself a living element.

RESNAIS: Eisenstein has more in common with the encounter between "an umbrella and a sewing-machine on a dissecting-table." And insofar as I remain very aware of the Surrealist discipline, I feel much nearer Eisenstein's conceptions. Each shot retains its life.

Q: There is an attitude of great humility before each of the elements, whether in reality or on creative work, which must preserve its organic life and at the same time be part of an organic whole.

RESNAIS: I would be reluctant to transform a setting, even in small details, to suit the camera. It is up to the camera to present the decor in the right way, it's not for the setting to conform to the camera. The same holds good for the actor. I have an immense respect for an actor's work. How rarely we alter the shooting to suit an actor's feelings, whereas we are constantly changing it on account of the weather!

 **Alain Resnais
Alain Robbe-Grillet**

*
L A S T
W O R D S
O N
L A S T
Y E A R

LAST MONTH Alain Resnais commented on the diversity of interpretations with which the viewer can approach his new film,
L'Année dernière à Marienbad. Now we can continue the discussion, with writer Alain Robbe-Grillet, and discover the influences
the winner of the Venice Golden Lion may have on world cinema. The picture itself plays tricks with time. What, to the creator, does the time element mean in a film?

ROBBE-GRILLET: An image is always in the present. I remember an era when the idea of the past was established by a halo—a
halo which often persisted throughout the entire flashback. But
we soon reverted to using the same photographic quality for the
present as for the past. In other words, we admit that everything is
in the present.

RESNAIS: You say we *soon* reverted. It wasn't as soon as all
that. The first real example of the past into the present, with
images of absolute clarity, and without recourse to the dissolve or
a little snatch of indicative music, was, I believe, *Orphée,* when
Roger Blin makes his statement to the police. At that moment we
see a shot of the past, then the conversaton continues exactly as

First published in English in *Films and Filming,* March 1962, pp. 39-41;
translated by Raymond Durgnat from *Cahiers du Cinéma.*

before. I have the idea that it was Cocteau who first used this technique so precisely.

QUESTION: Already in *Hiroshima Mon Amour* I felt that the flashback was no longer being used for strictly dramatic ends. The flux of images which it provoked rather smothered its dramatic function.

ROBBE-GRILLET: Yes, in *Hiroshima* the spectator could still think back on the scenes and mentally replace them in their chronological order. There were certain shots which one didn't at first recognize as belonging to the past. For example, the shot showing the body of the German soldier. Its shock value is total, but, of course, any spectator who wants to be pedantic about it could always say to himself later: "Ah, yes, she was remembering the death of her first lover." But the kind of realism we are seeking is: she sees the Japanese on the bed, suddenly, she sees the dead German. There are two images, one exterior to her, the other interior.

But since she sees them both on the same plane, as it were, the cinema should be able to give them both the same *present* quality.

RESNAIS: All in all, it represents a victory for realism. At least it is a gain for realism. It is not for us to pass judgment on the old-fashioned rhetoric which used symbols to introduce the past, but it certainly has no more justification than any other convention. Try for yourselves. Talk to someone for quarter of an hour, then stop and ask him: "You've seen what's been happening. We are here, in a restaurant, eating. I talked about the sea, holidays. Which would be the most realistic way of showing the scene we have just lived through during the last quarter of an hour? To show the two of us dining in a restaurant, or to show the beach and the waves we have been talking about? Or even to show them, not in the way we spoke of it, but in presenting the mental images in our heads, corresponding, interfering, even contradicting one another?"

ROBBE-GRILLET: Obviously all this is contrary to ingrained habits, to a rhetoric which the public accepts, but which is not functionally linked to the way the human spirit works. It is associated with an artistic style, a certain romanticism, but scarcely to a mental reality. It is not for reasons of human truth that the past was introduced with specific references to the past, that the restaurant was showed in preference to the waves. It is just a convention; I should call it sheer formalism.

RESNAIS: Now, I have certain scruples. We can't say it was never done. I am thinking of *Mongol Train* (*The Blue Express?* —R.E.D.) which I saw seventeen years ago. We see a fat capitalist in a restaurant car, flinging his hand forward into the lens. We are shown his hand with three huge fingers and immediately afterwards a torpedo-boat whose three guns are repeating approximately the movements of his hand.

ROBBE-GRILLET: Yes, of course, but what distinguishes *Marienbad,* and may prove rather disconcerting, is simply the general use of these devices. They are not disguised as exceptions to a rule, but as a consistent style of thinking, completely compatible with realism—perhaps more realistic. When we say that what goes on in our minds is just as real as what goes on in front of our eyes, we are laying the foundations for a cinematic style which can switch to and from between the things around us, like this tape-recorder, and the subject of our conversation, and include images more or less intermediary between the scene around us, your thoughts, my thoughts, and so on. Such a film still employs conventions, but would be rather more realistic than the convention of systematically restricting oneself to any one category of reality.

RESNAIS: In any case, if you study *Marienbad* closely, you see that certain images are ambiguous, that their degree of reality is equivocal. But some images are far more clearly false, and there are images of *lying* whose falsity is, I feel, quite evident. You mustn't think that while shooting we amused ourselves and left the spectator to sort it out.

ROBBE-GRILLET: The use of decor is characteristic. When the room has an extraordinarily complicated baroque decor, or the walls are heavily encrusted with wedding-cake ornamentation, we are probably watching a rather unreliable image. Similarly when the heroine takes 300 identical photographs from a drawer, the image is improbable and must be more imaginary than objective.

Perhaps, if we were speaking in terms of a strictly objective reality, we might say she only took one picture out; but she wished there were 300. Not that we can always give a single and definite interpretation of an image.

Q: What is so striking about *L'Année dernière à Marienbad* is the experience of being confronted by an object requiring all our resources of understanding and interpretation—like a fragment of reality.

ROBBE-GRILLET: The question is whether the uncertainties aroused by the images are more intense than all the uncertainties of everyday encounters or whether they are of the same order. Personally I believe that things really happen as vaguely as this. The theme is of a passionate love affair and it is precisely these relationships which comprise the highest proportion of inconsistencies, doubts and phantasms. *Marienbad* is as opaque as the moments we live through in the climaxes of our feeling, in our loves, in our whole emotional life. So to reproach the film for its lack of clarity is really to reproach human feelings for their obscurity.

Q: There is a risk of misunderstanding here. For if *Marienbad* does seem obscure, it is not because you deliberately conceal certain items which might clarify the film.

ROBBE-GRILLET: Exactly. We show everything even those things which can't be reduced to simple explanations. It is strange how people will quite willingly accept the plethora of irrational or ambiguous factors in everyday life, yet complain bitterly when they come across them in works of art, whether novels or films, they suppose, ought to present something more reassuring than reality. They feel the work of art is made to explain the world to them, to provide them with reassurance. I am quite sure that art is not meant simply to reassure people. If the world is so complex, then we must re-create its complexity. For the sake of realism.

But we should go further. So far we seem to be assuming that reality exists "outside" the work of art; which is far from certain. A work of art is a kind of consciousness. The world of everyday life doesn't exist completely without a consciousness to perceive it; and the same is true of a work of art. The events it recounts have no real existence outside the account which the work of art gives of them.

Q: In this connection, I have sometimes heard of films reproached for "formalism."

ROBBE-GRILLET: It's very strange how the people who reproach *Marienbad* for being "concocted" are those who accept as "spontaneous" works of art which scrupulously observe all the previously formulated rules of construction, all the formulae, all the conventions. And these people are reasoning as if there were a reality which existed before the work of art, and all a work of art did was to find the "form" in which it would be most accessible to the public. For us, on the contrary, the "anecdote" has no existence whatsoever beyond the "form" in which it is told. The genesis of the film is particularly illuminating. When Resnais and I had our first discussion, we found we had both conceived a cinematic "form" of the same kind. I knew that all my ideas on the Cinema would somehow suit whatever Resnais would set out to achieve from then on. It so happened that he wanted to make the kind of film I had been thinking of. I didn't actually produce four outlines in three days for him, but I have written four projects each about a page and a half long, which I have had in mind for a long time.

RESNAIS: When I had finished reading his work I said to myself: we've already made one film together—*Toute La Mémoire du Monde*.

ROBBE-GRILLET: That doesn't stop us from having different ideas about all his films or my novels. But we do seem to have a world in common, which we can both inhabit. There was never any question of compromise between Resnais and myself, but of a common "form" which functioned in the same way for us both, although it's not certain that we both give the same importance to the details.

RESNAIS: We don't have the same tastes, and we sometimes disagree violently about a book, a film, or a way of life . . .

ROBBE-GRILLET: All the same we are constantly having the same intuitions. For example, I was explaining a camera-movement, and Resnais said: "Don't worry, it's the movement I would have chosen in any case." Still, it is quite possible that *Marienbad* isn't exactly the same film for Resnais as it is for me. We must see the world around us rather different, although it's the same world.

Q: This will probably startle you, but *Marienbad* reminded me of Bioy Casares' book *L'Invention de Morel* (*Morel's Invention*).

ROBBE-GRILLET: Not at all. I have nearly always been disappointed by what science-fiction I have read, but *L'Invention de Morel* is an astounding book. Oddly enough, Claude Ollier telephoned me after seeing *Marienbad* to say: "It's just like *L'Invention de Morel!*"

RESNAIS: I'm not in a position to comment as I don't know the book.

Q: It's a novel written in the first person and based on the myth of "total cinema." The narrator disembarks on an island where a machine perfected twenty years previously, reproduces in three dimensions events it has recorded. Naturally these 3-D images merge with the real world so closely that it is impossible to distinguish the two. Just as in some shots of *Marienbad:* the objects are under suspicion, they are there, but what are they really?

RESNAIS: Yes, the similarity to *Marienbad* is quite remarkable. We have had many surprises like this. I remember the first take we saw projected. It was a shot of the young woman, in the sunlight, on the balustrade, behind the statue. When the lights went up I said: "How funny, we're right in the serials of Fantomas."

ROBBE-GRILLET: And I described the shot without knowing the serials. I have hardly read the Fantomas stories.

Q: I thought of Fantomas too, but at the moment when the balustrade crumbles.

ROBBE-GRILLET: Yet that shot is described in detail in the scenario. And of course I could hardly have been influenced.

RESNAIS: It is one of the *lying* images. I remember telling Albertazzi as were shooting to stride over the balustrade in Arsene Lupin style. The feeling was there. And I think it's legitimate, for, insofar as it is an image of the future, probably imagined, under the stress of her anguish, by the young woman, it is quite natural that she should have recourse to popular novels. It's perfectly normal.

ROBBE-GRILLET: And at that moment the young woman says: "Depart, I bescech you, for the sake of the love you bear me!" which gives an idea of the theatricality of the scene.

RESNAIS: Which sharpens my regrets at not having directed *Fantomas!*

Q: These coincidences would tend to confirm the idea so dear to Malraux, that art derives its sustenance from art.

ROBBE-GRILLET: I think that the artist replenishes himself directly from the reality and that art interests us because we find in it ready-made the things to which we feel impelled by the emotions reality has generated in us. I don't think we really derive our inspiration from art, not during our creative moments.

Q: So you would oppose Malraux's theory?

RESNAIS: Personally I'm in favor of it. I think that a longing to belong to the world of art does exist very powerfully. It's not incompatible with what Robbe-Grillet is saying.

ROBBE-GRILLET: The real shock is produced by the world and art is only a reminiscence of it. An illumination, perhaps. If I like, say, the work of Kafka it is really because I rediscover in it the way in which I have been seeing the world around me, it's as if I knew it before I read it. When an image strikes me in the cinema, it is always because I recognize my own experience, otherwise communication would be impossible. Every work of art would be purely subjective and absolutely no contact with anyone else would be possible.

RESNAIS: A few years ago I received a letter from a lady, which said, more or less, "Ah, I have seen your film *Van Gogh,* what a marvelous film, what delightful journeys you must have made going to film all those different places." She seemed to remember a film which showed both canvases by Van Gogh and real landscape!

Q: To return to *Marienbad,* there is one curious phenomenon. One can say equally well: it's a Resnais film, or: it's a Robbe-Grillet film. But it's no secret that there are a few minimal differences between the very detailed shooting script and the finished product.

ROBBE-GRILLET: In the scenario I handed over to Resnais there were already numerous specifications as to editing, composition, and the camera-movement. But I had no notion of the technical terms used in the Cinema nor of its real possibilities. I described a film which I saw in my imagination and in very naive terms.

RESNAIS: Not at all. In any event it was very precise. You even used many of the dodges of an experienced editor!

ROBBE-GRILLET: We didn't use them all. For example towards the end there was a series of dissolves. None of them remains. They weren't intended to indicate the passage of time; quite the reverse. For example there was a dissolve between two sequences in the present; and then a brusque transition between the present and the past.

Q: Yet in your books there is nothing corresponding to a dissolve.

ROBBE-GRILLET: Oh, there is, I think.

RESNAIS: No. I don't feel they are dissolves. They are phrases which transform the images. A dissolve wouldn't give that impression.

Q: At any rate the dissolve, as an indication of the passage of time, would have no place in *Marienbad*. Is it reasonable to assume that the story unfolds in eight days, in 24 hours, or during the running time?

ROBBE-GRILLET: One can say that the only time is the time of the film. There again, there is no reality outside the film. Everything is shown. Nothing is ever hidden and it is a mistake to think that the film's hour and a half represents any longer period whether two hours, two days, or eight. I wouldn't say the same of Clouzot's *La Vérité*, for instance, which does create the impression that there is another time, more real than that of the film. For *Marienbad*, no other temporal order seems possible to me. All others are derived from "interpretations" and only restrict the film. But if we say that the story lasts an hour and a half, we leave it intact.

Q: There is one shot which surprised me and is even more surprising now I know that all the shots and their editing were preconceived on paper by Robbe-Grillet, and that is the long, over-exposed tracking-shot which concludes with a repetition of the last part of the movement. Such a shot is very hard to conceive beforehand.

RESNAIS: That is in fact one of the few shots which weren't anticipated from the outset.

ROBBE-GRILLET: Resnais told me beforehand he wasn't going to shoot what was written in the script. It was *the* point of friction between us. Resnais knew that, there, for a few seconds, there would be something else.

RESNAIS: The idea for the new version came to me a fortnight or more before shooting.

ROBBE-GRILLET: There was another passage which I hadn't anticipated, although I should have thought of it myself, for it strikes me as exactly right; it's the series of shots where we see Delphine Seyrig sitting in various ways on the left and right of her bed, in quick succession: I feel quite upset over not having thought of that!

Q: What were your feelings on seeing the film for the first time?

ROBBE-GRILLET: I found it far more beautiful than I had imagined. I recognized it as my film, but it had become marvelous. Everything had been planned: yet everything was still to be done. One can't describe a shot as it eventually turns out; it is created during the shooting.

RESNAIS: All the same, if the shooting script took me only two and a half days to prepare it was only because Robbe-Grillet had anticipated everything so precisely.

ROBBE-GRILLET: Even so, a composition that has been foreshadowed by a description still has to be *executed*. It is obvious that the film would have been altogether different if it had been assigned to another director, or an electronic robot. It was a question, not of following my descriptions, but of *directing* them.

RESNAIS: Just as we had to *execute* the statue in the park.

ROBBE-GRILLET: One can think of *Marienbad* as a documentary about a statue: with "interpretative" glimpses of gestures and constant returns to the gestures as they endure, "frozen," by the sculpture. Imagine a documentary which centered on a statue with two people, and succeeded in combining a series of shots, taken from different angles and by various camera-movements, so as to tell a complete story. And in the end we realize that we have returned to our starting point, the statue itself.

Q: In this sense, all your books are documentaries and it is because of their documentary quality that they seem to be fantasies. So the father of screen fantasy is not *Méliès* after all, but Lumière.

RESNAIS: In this case fantasy is much the more important of the two. The most fantastic moments of *Nosferatu,* for example, are the "realistic" moments.

ROBBE-GRILLET: Yes, in *Marienbad* the important thing is always a sort of hollow in the heart of the reality. In *Marienbad* it is the "last year" which provides the hollow. What happened then—if anything—produces a constant emptiness in the story. Similarly, the hero of *Jealousy* is only a void; and the main event of *The Voyeur*—the murder—is a void. The narrative covers everything as far as the void, and then everything subsequent to it; and we then try to join the two so as to *dispose* of that disquieting emptiness. But the opposite happens; the emptiness spreads, it fills everything. In *Marienbad* at first we think that there is no last year, then we realize that last year dominates everything: that we are definitely caught up in it. At first we think that *Marienbad* did not exist, only to realize that we have been there from the beginning. The event which the girl repudiates has, by the end of the film, contaminated everything. So much so that she has never ceased to struggle against it, to believe that she was winning, since she has always rejected everything, and, in the end, she realizes it is all too late, she has, after all, accepted everything. As if everything were true—although probably it isn't. But *true* or *false* have been emptied of meaning.

RESNAIS: Of course, there was never any question of faking.

ROBBE-GRILLET: You know the phrase, "Larvatus prodeo," "I advance masked, but revealing my mask." The Cinema is a technique which displays itself. It is the unmasking of that technique which creates a truth. There is no question of a truth preexisting a technique whose job is to trap it. That is why I am

inclined to say that the story lasts for an hour and a half and has
no existence before or afterwards. If the characters leave at the
end, it isn't to go anywhere. They cease to be. There has never
been anything but the film's *here and now*.

Q: An example of the way the film exists is the proverb
whose first words are repeated several times: "From the compass
to the ship . . ."

ROBBE-GRILLET: Yes, if you like. I have invented a half-proverb. Again, we have concealed nothing from anyone. Why invent a whole proverb so as to retain only the first half? Evidently
on the basis of that half-proverb we can imagine many things.

RESNAIS: One doesn't need to know the rest. Say those words
in a drawing room, everyone will seem to know the proverb. No
one will ask what the rest of it is. I know. I've tried it!

Luis Buñuel

*

A

STATEMENT

1. IN NONE OF THE traditional arts is there such a wide gap between possibilities and facts as in the cinema. Motion pictures act directly upon the spectator; they offer him concrete persons and things; they isolate him, through silence and darkness, from the usual psychological atmosphere. Because of all this, the cinema is capable of stirring the spectator as perhaps no other art. But as no other art, it is also capable of stupefying him. Unfortunately, the great majority of today's films seem to have exactly that purpose; they glory in an intellectual and moral vacuum. In this vacuum, movies seem to prosper.

2. Mystery is a basic element of all works of art. It is generally lacking on the screen. Writers, directors and producers take good care in avoiding anything that may upset us. They keep the marvelous window on the liberating world of poetry shut. They prefer stories which seem to continue our ordinary lives, which repeat for the umpteenth time the same drama, which help us forget the hard hours of our daily work. And all this, of course, carefully watched over by traditional morals, government and international censorship, religion, good taste, white humor and other flat dicteria of reality.

3. The screen is a dangerous and wonderful instrument, if a free spirit uses it. It is the superior way of expressing the world of dreams, emotions and instinct. The cinema seems to have

Originally published in *Film Culture*, no. 21, Summer 1960, pp. 41-42.

been invented for the expression of the subconscious, so profoundly is it rooted in poetry. Nevertheless, it almost never pursues these ends.

4. We rarely see good cinema in the mammoth productions, or in the works that have received the praise of critics and audience. The particular story, the private drama of an individual, cannot interest—I believe—anyone worthy of living in our time. If a man in the audience shares the joys and sorrows of a character on the screen, it should be because that character reflects the joys and sorrows of all society and so the personal feelings of that man in the audience. Unemployment, insecurity, the fear of war, social injustice, etc., affect all men of our time, and thus, they also affect the individual spectator. But when the screen tells me that Mr. X is not happy at home and finds amusement with a girl friend whom he finally abandons to reunite himself with his faithful wife, I find it all very moral and edifying, but it leaves me completely indifferent.

5. Octavio Paz has said: "But that a man in chains should shut his eyes, the world would explode." And I could say: But that the white eye-lid of the screen reflect its proper light, the Universe would go up in flames. But for the moment we can sleep in peace: the light of the cinema is conveniently dosified and shackled.

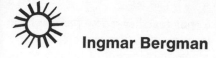

Ingmar Bergman

*

WHAT

IS

"FILM

MAKING"?

"FILM-MAKING" IS for me a necessity of nature, a need comparable to hunger and thirst. For some, self-expression involves writing books, climbing mountains, beating one's children or dancing the samba. In my case, I express myself in making films.

In *The Blood of a Poet,* the great Jean Cocteau shows us his alter ego stumbling down the corridors of a nightmare hotel and gives us a glimpse, behind each one of the doors, of one of the factors of which he is composed and which form his ego.

Without attempting here to equate my personality with Cocteau's, I thought I would take you on a guided tour of my internal studios where, invisibly, my films take form. This visit, I am afraid, will disappoint you; the equipment is always in disorder because the owner is too absorbed in his affairs to have time to straighten it up. Furthermore, the lighting is rather bad in certain spots, and on the door of certain rooms, you will find the word "Private" written in large letters. Finally, the guide himself is not always sure of what is worth the trouble of showing.

Whatever the case may be, we will open a few doors a crack. I won't guarantee that you will find precisely the answer to the questions you are wondering about, but perhaps, in spite of

Originally published in *Cahiers du Cinéma,* XI, no. 61 (July 1956), pp. 10-19; translated from the French by Royal S. Brown.

everything, you will be able to put together a few pieces of the complicated puzzle that the forming of a film represents.

If we consider the most fundamental element of the cinematographic art, the perforated film, we note that it is composed of a number of small, rectangular images—fifty-two per meter—each of which is separated from the other by a thick, black line. Looking more closely, we discover that these tiny rectangles, which at first glance seem to contain exactly the same picture, differ from each other by an almost imperceptible modification of this picture. And when the feeding mechanism of the projector causes the images in question to succeed each other on the screen so that each one is seen only for a twentieth of a second, we have the illusion of movement.

Between each of these small rectangles the shutter closes and plunges us into total darkness, only to return us to full light with the next rectangle. When I was ten years old and working with my first apparatus, a shaky lantern made of sheet metal—with its chimney, its gas lamp and its perpetual films which repeated themselves indefinitely—I used to find the above-mentioned phenomenon exciting and full of mystery. Even today, I feel myself quiver as I did when I was a child when I think of the fact that, in reality, I am creating illusion; for the cinema would not exist but for an imperfection of the human eye, namely its inability to perceive separately a series of images which follow each other rapidly and which are essentially identical.

I have calculated that if I see a film that lasts an hour, I am in fact plunged for twenty minutes in total darkness. In making a film, therefore, I am making myself guilty of a fraud; I am using a device designed to take advantage of a physical imperfection of man, a device by means of which I can transport my audience from a given feeling to the feeling that is diametrically opposed to it, as if each spectator were on a pendulum; I can make an audience laugh, scream with terror, smile, believe in legends, become indignant, take offense, become enthusiastic, lower itself or yawn from boredom. I am, then, either a deceiver or—when the audience is aware of the fraud—an illusionist. I am able to mystify, and I have at my disposal the most precious and the most astounding magical device that has ever, since history began, been put into the hands of a juggler.

There is in all this, or at least there should be, the source of an insoluble moral conflict for all those who create films or work on them.

As for our commercial partners, this is not the place to bring out the mistakes they have made from year to year, but it would certainly be worthwhile someday for a scientist to discover some unit of weight or measure which one could use to "calculate" the quantity of natural gifts, initiatives, genius and creative forces that the film industry has ground through its formidable mills. Obviously, anyone entering into the game must accept the rules in advance, and there is no reason why work in the cinematographic branch should be more respected than anywhere else. The difference is due to the fact that, in our specialty, brutality is manifested more overtly, but this is actually rather an advantage.

Loss of balance offers consequences that are even more grave for the film-maker than for a tightrope walker or an acrobat who performs his tricks beneath a circus tent and without a net. For the film-maker as well as for the equilibrist, the danger is of the same order: falling and being killed. No doubt you think I am exaggerating; making a film isn't as dangerous as all that! I maintain my point, however; the risk is the same. Even if, as I mentioned, one is a bit of a magician, no one can mystify the producers, the bank directors, the movie-theatre owners or the critics when the public abstains from going to see a film and from paying out the obol from which producers, bank directors, movie-theatre owners, critics and magicians must draw their subsistence!

I can give you as an example a very recent experience, the memory of which still makes me shudder—an experience in which I myself risked losing my balance. A singularly bold producer invested money in one of my films which, after a year of intense activity, appeared under the title of *The Naked Night (Gycklarnas afton)*. The reviews were, in general, destructive, the public stayed away, the producer added up his losses, and I had to wait several years before trying again.

If I make two or three more films which fail financially, the producer will quite justifiably consider it a good idea not to bet on my talents.

At that point, I will become, suddenly, a suspect individual, a squanderer, and I will be able to reflect at my leisure on the usefulness of my artistic gifts, for the magician will be deprived of his apparatus.

When I was younger, I didn't have these fears. Work for me was an exciting game and, whether the results succeeded or failed, I was delighted with my work like a child with his castles of sand or clay. The equilibrist was dancing on his rope, oblivious and therefore unconcerned about the abyss beneath him and the hardness of the ground of the circus-ring.

The game has changed into a bitter combat. The walk on the rope is now performed in full awareness of the danger, and the two points where the rope is attached are now called "fear" and "incertitude." Each work to be materialized mobilizes all of the resources of one's energy. The act of creation has become, under the effect of causes that are as much interior as they are exterior and economic, an exacting duty. Failure, criticism, coldness on the part of the public today cause more sensitive wounds. These wounds take longer to heal and their scars are deeper and more lasting.

Before undertaking a work or after having begun it, Jean Anouilh has the habit of playing a little mental game in order to exorcise his fear. He says to himself, "My father is a tailor. He intimately enjoys creating with his hands, and the result is a beautiful pair of pants or an elegant overcoat. This is the joy and the satisfaction of the artisan, the pride of a man who knows his profession."

This is the same practice I follow. I recognize the game, I play it often and I succeed in duping myself—and a few others—even if this game is in fact nothing but a rather poor sedative: "My films are fine pieces of work, I am enthusiastic, conscientious and extremely attentive of details. I create for my contemporaries and not for eternity; my pride is the pride of an artisan."

I know however that, if I speak this way, it is in order to deceive myself, and an irrepressible anxiety cries out to me, "What have you done that can last? Is there in any of your movies a single foot of film worthy of being passed on to posterity, a single line of dialogue, a single situation which is really and indisputably true?"

And to this question I am forced to answer—perhaps still under the effect of a disloyalty which is ineradicable even in the most sincere people—"I don't know, I hope so."

You must excuse me for having described at such length and with so much commentary the dilemma which those who create films are forced to confront. I wanted to try to explain to you why so many of those who are devoted to the realization of cinematographic works give in to a temptation which cannot really be expressed and which is invisible; why we are afraid; why we sometimes lose our enthusiasm for the works we are doing; why we become fools and allow ourselves to be annihilated by colorless and vile compromises.

I would still, however, like to dwell a bit longer on one of the aspects of the problem, the aspect that is the most important and difficult to comprehend—the public.

The creator of films is involved in a means of expression which concerns not only himself but also millions of other people, and more often than not he feels the same desire as other artists: "I want to succeed today. I want celebrity now. I want to please, to delight, to move people immediately."

Midway between this desire and its realization is found the public, who demands but one thing of the film: "I've paid, I want to be distracted, swept off my feet, involved; I want to forget my troubles, my family, my work, I want to get away from myself. Here I am, seated in the darkness, and, like a woman about to give birth, I want deliverance."

The film-maker who is aware of these demands and who lives on the money of the public is placed in a situation which is difficult and which creates obligations for him. In making his film, he must always take the reaction of the public into account. On my part, personally, I am forever asking myself this question: "Can I express myself more simply, more purely, more briefly? Will everybody understand what I want to say now? Will the simplest mind be able to follow the course of these events? And, even more importantly, this question: up to what point do I have the right to admit compromise and where do my obligations to myself begin?"

Any experimentation necessarily involves a great risk, for it always keeps the public at a distance, and keeping the public at a distance can lead to sterility and to isolation in an ivory tower.

It would be quite desirable, then, for producers and other technical directors of the cinema to put laboratories at the disposition of the creators. But this is scarcely the case today. The producers have confidence only in the engineers and stupidly imagine that the salvation of the film industry depends on inventions and technical complications.

Nothing is easier than frightening a spectator. One can literally terrify him, for most people have in some part of their bearing a fear that is all ready to blossom. It is much more difficult to make people laugh, and to *make them laugh* in the right way. It is easy to put a spectator in a state worse than the one he was in when he entered the theatre; it is difficult to put him in a better state; it is precisely this, however, that he desires each time he sits down in the darkness of a movie-theatre. Now, how many times and by what means do we give him this satisfaction?

This is the way I reason; but at the same time I know with an absolute evidence that this reasoning is dangerous, since it involves the risk of condemning all failures, of confusing the ideal with pride, and of considering as absolute the frontiers that the public and the critics establish, whereas you neither recognize these frontiers nor consider them your own, since your personality is perpetually in the process of becoming. On the one hand, I am tempted to adapt myself and to make myself what the public wants me to be; but on the other hand, I feel that this would be the end of everything, and that this would imply a total indifference on my part. Thus, I am delighted to have not been born with exactly as many brains as feelings, and it has never been written

anywhere that a film-maker must be contented, happy, or satisfied. Who says you can't make noise, cross frontiers, battle against
windmills, send robots to the moon, have visions, play with dyna-
mite or tear pieces of flesh from one's self or others? Why not
frighten film producers? It is their job to be afraid, and they are
paid to have stomach ulcers!

But *"film-making"* is not always confronting problems, dilemmas, economic worries, responsibilities and fear. There are also
games, dreams, secret memories.

Often it begins with an image: a face which is suddenly and
strongly illuminated; a hand which rises; a square at dawn where
a few old ladies are seated on a bench, separated from each other
by sacks of apples. Or it may be a few words that are exchanged;
two people who, suddenly, say something to each other in a completely personal tone of voice—their backs are perhaps turned
from me, I can't even see their faces, and yet I am forced to listen
to them, to wait for them to repeat the same words which are
without any particular meaning but which are pregnant with a
secret tension, with a tension of which I am not yet even fully
conscious but which acts like a crafty potion. The illuminated
face, the hand raised as if for an incantation, the old ladies at the
square, the few banal words, all of these images come and attach
themselves like silvery fish to my net, or more precisely, I myself
am trapped in a net, the texture of which I am not aware of—
fortunately!

Quite rapidly, even before the motive has been entirely designed in my mind, I submit the game of my imagination to the
test of reality. I place, as if I'm playing a game, my sketch, which
is still very rough and fragile, on an easel in order to judge it from
the point of view of all the technical resources of the studios. This
imaginary test of "viability" constitutes for the motive an effective ferruginous bath. Will it suffice? Will the motive keep its
value when it is plunged into the daily, murderous routine of the
studios, far from the shadows of sunrises, which are quite pro-
pitious for the games of the imagination?

A few of my films mature very quickly and are finished rapidly.
These are the ones that meet the general expectations, like chil-

dren that are still undisciplined but in good health and about whom one can predict immediately: "They are the ones who will support the family."

And then there are other films, films which come slowly, which take years, which refuse to be imprisoned in a formal or technical solution, and which, in general, refuse any concrete solution. They remain in a shadowy zone; if I want to find them, I have to follow them there and find a context, characters and situation. There, faces that are turned aside begin to speak, the streets are strange, a few, scattered people glance out through window-panes, an eye glistens at dusk or changes into a carbuncle and then bursts with a noise of breaking crystal. The square, this autumn morning, is a sea; the old ladies are transformed into ancient trees and the apples are children building cities of sand and stone near the foam of the waves.

The tension is there, ever present, and it appears again, either in the written word, or in the visions, or in the excess of energy, which bends like the arch of a bridge, ready to rise up by its own forces, by these forces which are the most important element, once the manuscript is finished, in setting in motion the immense wheel which the work required in shooting a film represents.

What is "shooting a film," then? If I were to ask this question of everybody, I would no doubt obtain quite different responses, but perhaps you would all agree on one point: shooting a film is doing what is necessary in order to transport the contents of the manuscript onto a piece of film. In doing so, you would be saying quite a lot and yet not nearly enough. For me, shooting a film represents days of inhumanly relentless work, stiffness of the joints, eyes full of dust, the odors of make-up, sweat and lamps, an indefinite series of tensions and relaxations, an uninterrupted battle between volition and duty, between vision and reality, conscience and laziness. I think of early risings, of nights without sleep, of a feeling keener than life, of a sort of fanaticism centered about a single task, by which I myself become, finally, an integral part of the film, a ridiculously tiny piece of apparatus whose only fault is requiring food and drink.

It sometimes happens—in the middle of all this excitement, when the studios are humming with a life and a labor that seem as if they should make the studios explode—that, suddenly, I find the idea for my next film. You would be wrong, however, if you thought that the activity of a film-maker supposes, at this moment, a kind of ecstatic vertigo, an uncontrolled excitement and a frightening disorganization. To shoot a film is to undertake the taming of a wild beast that is difficult to handle and very valuable; you need a clear mind, meticulousness, stiff and exact calculations. Add to this a temper that is always even and a patience that is not of this world.

Shooting a film is organizing an entire universe, but the essential elements are industry, money, construction, shooting, developing and copying, a schedule to follow but which is rarely followed, a battle plan minutely prepared where the irrational factors occur the most often. The star has too much black around her eyes—a thousand dollars to start the scene over again. One day, the water in the pipes has too much chlorine in it and the negatives get spotted—let's start again! Another day, death plays a dirty trick on you by taking away an actor—let's start with another—and there are several thousand more dollars swallowed up. It starts to thunder, the electric transformer breaks down, and there we are, all made up and waiting in the pale light of the day, the hours flying by and money with them.

Idiotic examples, chosen at random. But they have to be idiotic, since they touch that great and sublime idiocy, the transforming of dreams into shadows, the chopping up of a tragedy into five hundred small pieces, the experimentation with each of these pieces, and finally the putting back together of these pieces so that they constitute again a unity which will once more be the tragedy. It is the idiocy of fabricating a tapeworm 8,000 feet long which will nourish itself on the life and mind of the actors, producers, and creators. Shooting a film is all that, but it is still something else, and it is much worse.

Film-making is also plunging with one's deepest roots back into the world of childhood. Let's descend, if you wish, into this interior studio, located in the most intimate recesses of the life of the creator. Let's open up for a moment the most secret of these rooms so that we can look at a painting of Venice, an old window-blind, and a first apparatus for showing "action films."

At Upsala, my grandmother had a very old apartment. While I was there, I once slipped beneath the dining-room table; I was wearing an apron with a pocket in front of it; from my vantage point I listened to the voice of the sunbeams which entered through the immensely high windows. The rays moved continually; the bells of the cathedral chimed out; the rays moved, and their movement generated a sort of special sound. It was one of those days between winter and spring; I had the measles and I was five years old. In the neighboring apartment, somebody was playing the piano—it was always waltzes—and on the wall hung a big painting of Venice. While the rays of sun and the shadows were passing like waves across the painting, the water of the canal began to flow, the pigeons flew up from the pavement of the square, people spoke to each other noiselessly, making movements with their hands and heads. The sound of the bells wasn't coming from the cathedral but rather from the painting, as were the strains from the piano. There was something very strange about this painting of Venice. Almost as strange as the fact that the sunbeams in my grandmother's living-room were not silent but had a sound. Perhaps it was all those bells—or perhaps the enormous pieces of furniture which were conversing uninterruptedly.

I seem to remember, however, an experience even more distant than the one of the year I had measles: the perception—impossible to date—of the movement of a window-blind.

It was a black window-blind of the most modern variety, which I could see, in my nursery, at dawn or at dusk, when everything becomes living and a bit frightening, when even toys transform into things that are either hostile or simply indifferent and curious. At that moment the world would no longer be the everyday world with my mother present, but a vertiginous and silent solitude. It wasn't that the blind moved; no shadow at all appeared on it. The forms were on the surface itself; they were neither little men, nor animals, nor heads, nor faces, but *things for which no name exists*! In the darkness, which was interrupted here and there by faint rays of light, these forms freed themselves from the blind and moved toward the green folding-screen or toward the bureau, with its pitcher of water. They were pitiless, impassive and terrifying; they disappeared only after it became completely dark or light, or when I fell asleep.

Anyone who, like myself, was born in the family of a pastor, learns at an early age to look behind the scenes in life and death. Whenever Father has a burial, a marriage, a baptism, a mediation, he writes a sermon. You make an early acquaintance with the devil and, like all children, you need to give him a concrete form. Here is where the magic lantern comes in, a little sheet-metal box with a gas lamp (I can still smell the odor of the heated metal) and which projected colored pictures. Among others, there was Little Red Ridinghood and the wolf. The wolf was the devil, a devil without horns but with a tail and vivid red mouth, a curiously palpable and yet elusive devil, the emissary of evil and persecution on the flowered wallpaper of the nursery.

The first film I ever owned was about ten feet long and brown. It pictured a young girl asleep in a prairie; she woke up, stretched, arose and, with outstretched arms, disappeared at the right side of the picture. That was all. Drawn on the box the film was kept in was a glowing picture with the words, "Frau Holle." Nobody around me knew who Frau Holle was, but that didn't matter; the film was quite successful, and we showed it every evening until it got torn so badly we couldn't repair it.

This shaky bit of cinema was my first sorcerer's bag, and, in fact, it was pretty strange. It was a mechanical plaything; the people and things never changed, and I have often wondered what could have fascinated me so much and what, even today, still fascinates me in exactly the same way. This thought comes to me sometimes in the studio, or in the semidarkness of the editing room, while I am holding the tiny picture before my eyes and while the film is passing through my hands; or else during that fantastic childbirth that takes place during the recomposition as the finished film slowly finds its own face. I can't help thinking that I am working with an instrument so refined that with it, it would be possible for us to illuminate the human soul with an infinitely more vivid light, to unmask it even more brutally and to annex to our field of knowledge new domains of reality. Perhaps we would even discover a crack that would allow us to penetrate into the *chiaroscuro* of surreality, to tell tales in a new and overwhelming manner. At the risk of affirming once more something I cannot prove, let me say that, the way I see it, we film-makers utilize only a minute part of a frightening power—we are moving only the little finger of a giant, a giant who is far from not being dangerous.

But it is equally possible that I am wrong. It might be that the cinema has attained the high point of its evolution, that this instrument, by its very nature, can no longer conquer new territory, that we are stuck with our noses to the wall, since the road ends in a dead end. Many people are of this opinion, and it is true that we are treading water in a marsh, our noses just rising above the surface of the water, and paralyzed by economic problems, conventions, stupidity, fear, incertitude and disorder.

I am asked sometimes what I am trying to attain in my films, what my *goal* is. The question is difficult and dangerous, and I usually answer it by lying or hedging: "I am trying to tell the truth about the condition of men, the truth as I see it." This answer always satisfies people, and I often wonder how it happens that nobody notices by bluff, because the true response should be, "I feel an incoercible need to express through film that which, in a completely subjective way, takes form some place in my consciousness. This being the case, I have no other goal but myself, my daily bread, the amusement and respect of the public, a kind of truth that I feel precisely at that moment. And if I try to sum up my second answer, the formula I end up with is not terribly exciting: 'An activity without much meaning.' "

I am not saying that this conclusion doesn't distress me inordinately. I am in the same situation as most artists of my generation; the activity of each one of us doesn't have much meaning. Art for art's sake. My personal truth, or three-quarters of a truth, or no truth at all, except that it has a value for me.

I realize that this way of looking at things is quite unpopular, particularly today. Let me hasten, then, to form the question in a different way: "What would be your goal in making your films?"

The story is told that, a long time ago, the cathedral of Chartres was struck by lightning and burned from top to bottom. It is said that thousands of people rushed there from the four corners of the world, people of all conditions; they crossed Europe like lemmings in migration; together, they began to rebuild the cathedral upon its old foundations. They stayed there until the immense edifice was completed, all of them, architects, workers, artists, jugglers, nobles, priests and the bourgeoisie, but their names were unknown, and, even today, nobody knows the names of those who built the cathedral of Chartres.

Without letting that give you any preconceived ideas about my beliefs or doubts—which, furthermore, have nothing to do with what we are discussing here—I think that any art loses its essential potency the moment it becomes separated from the "cult." It has cut the umbilical cord and it lives its own separate life, a life that is astonishingly sterile, dim, and degenerate. Creative collectivity, humble anonymity are forgotten and buried relics, deprived of any value. Little wounds of the ego and moral colics are examined under a microscope *sub specie aeternitatis*. The fear of the dark which characterizes subjectivism and scrupulous consciences has become quite stylish, and ultimately we are all running around in a big enclosure where we argue with one another about our solitude without listening to each other or even noticing that we are pushing ourselves mutually to the point of dying of suffocation from all this. It is in such a way that individualists look each other in the eye, deny the existence of those they see and invoke omnipotent obscurity without ever having once felt the saving force of the joys of community. We are so poisoned by our own vicious circles, so closed in by our own anguish that we are becoming incapable of distinguishing true from false, the ideality of gangsters and sincere unaffectedness.

To the question concerning the goal of my films, I could therefore answer: "I want to be one of the artists of the cathedral that stands above the plains. I want to occupy myself making from stone a dragon's head, an angel or a devil, or perhaps a saint, it doesn't really matter; I feel the same enjoyment in each case. Whether I am a believer or an unbeliever, a Christian or a pagan, I am working along with everybody else to construct a cathedral, because I am an artist and an artisan, and because I have learned to extract faces, limbs, and bodies from stone. I never have to worry about the judgment of posterity or of my contemporaries; my first and last names are engraved nowhere, and they will disappear with me. But a small part of my self will survive in the anonymous and triumphant totality. A dragon or a devil, or perhaps a saint, what does it matter!"

Federico Fellini

*

THE BITTER
LIFE—
OF
MONEY

YES, *La Dolce Vita* has been very successful. But I hope people will not think it presumptuous of me if I say that happy as I am that the film has been a success, even if it hadn't been, I would still have got my satisfaction out of it. My passion is in the making of a film. Afterwards, it's largely a matter that doesn't concern me.

I have this detached attitude, which I assure you is absolutely sincere, to thank if, as I hope, I am able to resist the lure of success. One has to be strong or just unconscious. I don't want to think about it. Indeed it worries me that everybody has their own interpretation of *La Dolce Vita*. It takes away my freedom if everyone wants me on their pedestal. However, don't think me too much of a cynic if I add that they want me *after* I have made my films. I had to try fifteen producers before I found one willing to make *La Strada*. After *Cabiria* and a second Oscar, I still had great difficulty finding a producer for *La Dolce Vita*.

Now I won't have to look for producers any more because I have at last got my own film company. I have got at least that out of *La Dolce Vita*. Many people think that this film has made me rich; but I didn't have a percentage of the profits it is making all over the world. And my salary went to pay back the producer who had first backed the film but who wanted an American actor to play Marcello [i.e., Mastroianni's rôle]!

From *Films and Filming,* January 1961, pp. 13, 38.

My new company, Federiz, might be called a gift, or bonus, from Angelo Rizzoli, who put up the money for *La Dolce Vita*. I have always had trouble with producers, you see. After my early successes, they always wanted me to make the same film again. After the *Vitelloni* they wanted the *Vitellini*! They'd have paid me anything I asked. (But they hadn't the courage to let me make the *Vitelloni* in the first place.) After *La Strada* I had scores of offers. To make the *Bidone*, which I was then planning? No. To make *Gelsomina on a Bicycle* or anything with Gelsomina in the title. They didn't realize that in *La Strada* I had already said all I wanted to say about Gelsomina. They all wanted Gelsomina. I could have earned a fortune selling her name to doll manufacturers, to sweet firms; even Walt Disney wanted to make an animated cartoon about her. I could have lived on Gelsomina for twenty years!

Why this insistence on sequels? Have they so little imagination? Of course, they wanted a sequel to *Cabiria*. Now, I ask you, what could that be? And now? Oh, yes, they'd all like a sequel to *La Dolce Vita*. They've even tried to make one of the typical Italian pot-boiler comedies with Toto. I have a great admiration for Toto but I don't see why I should let the *Dolce Vita* become a vehicle for a rubbishy parody.

Certainly the *Vitelloni* was the one film which could have had a sequel in the idealistic sense. At one time, I did plan to make *Moraldo in the City*. But in the end, even that idea didn't appeal to me any more. And though some may think *La Dolce Vita* a sort of sequel to *Vitelloni*, insofar as it is the story of a young man from the provinces who has been in Rome for ten years, there is really no connection between Moraldo and Marcello. The only connection is the autobiographical vein that is in all my work.

My new offices in Rome just off the Piazza di Spagna are not intended to be just the headquarters of a production company. When we are working, be it on a film of mine or of one of the young directors that I intend to help, there will be room for the production managers and assistant directors. But all the year round, it will be a "workshop" where my friends can gather to exchange ideas. Our conversation will not be the usual gossip of the cafés with no practical object. Our dreams will be realized;

anyway let's hope so. I want to surround myself with saltimbanks, storytellers and jesters, as in a medieval court. But there will be no despotism.

I know what it means for a young director to fight against the despotism of the producers. Maybe I survived myself because I created a fakir's wall around me. For others it is not so easy. They don't all have my fanaticism and they let themselves be browbeaten. If I had to give a definition of the policy of my company, I would say that it is one that will never make its directors change the endings of their films. Producers always want to change the endings. I shall leave the director to do as he wishes. Rizzoli has had faith in me. I shall have faith in my directors.

Money doesn't count any more. The other day, I saw a man with a briefcase going out of the office. I asked my production manager, Clemente Fracassi, who the man was. "Oh, he is from the Bank," he said. I was worried because usually when men from banks come to see me they want to take away my furniture or my car. "What the devil did he want?" I asked. "Oh, he wanted to invest eight hundred million lire in Federiz, but I told him we didn't want it," said Fracassi. He knew he didn't have to ask me. On the Via Veneto that evening, I confessed I got quite a kick out of telling people we had refused half a million pounds!

Even in Italy, nobody quite understands how I can refuse the fabulous sums that are offered me. In the article I wrote for the last special issue of *Films And Filming*, I told you how I had turned down a quarter of a million dollars offered me by an American company to make a film about horses with an Italian star. I hear it made some people incredulous in England. Perhaps they thought it facetious of me. But, honestly, I can't take these offers seriously.

When I went to the United States, I was given a public relations man to look after me during the month I was there. When he met me at the airport, the first thing he told me was that he had "layed on" a television interview for that evening. "Twenty million people will be watching you," he told me proudly. I looked in the paper and saw it was already announced that at a certain hour, somebody would be telling the American public how to cook *spaghetti alla napoletana* and the famous Italian film director Federico Fellini would show gentlemen how to kiss a lady's hand!

That poor publicity man had a terrible time with me. He just couldn't understand my attitude. He thought I was kidding or else trying to be smart. How could anyone in his senses turn down a quarter of a million dollars? I was left alone in the film producer's office to meditate on that check, with the contract and pen beside it. After ten minutes, when they came back and found I hadn't signed, they couldn't believe their eyes. In the end, the publicity man said, with a hurt look in his eyes, "Maybe in Italy it's being a poet to turn down this sort of money but if you do it in the States you're a ——." He didn't know how to justify it to his boss who was convinced that I was holding out for more money. The publicity man begged me to say that I was ill; that my liver troubled me; and I wanted to get back to Italy as soon as possible. The producer immediately offered me his private plane to take me to some place in Texas where he knew there was a wonderful clinic for curing liver complaints.

When I was leaving New York, the publicity man was by then resigned. I think he was even beginning to sympathize. Certainly he didn't have any more resentment. He just looked at me sorrowfully and said, "You're a strange guy."

I was interested in the idea of making a film about the relationship between a European and just such an American as that publicity man I had known on my previous visit. The idea appealed to me. And I had many other ideas too. But how could I make a film in America without knowing the country backwards? I wouldn't feel ready to make a film in America unless I knew what colored tie was worn by a lawyer in Boston or how a prostitute talks in Cincinnati. Language, for me, is essential.

How do I know the difference between the speech of a Negro in the South and an emancipated Negro of the North?

How could I start shooting a scene in a New York restaurant at 4:30 in the afternoon if I have to rebuild the atmosphcre in a studio? I can't depend on others.

Michelangelo Antonioni

Reflections on the Film Actor

THE FILM ACTOR need not understand, but simply be. One might reason that in order to be, it is necessary to understand. That's not so. If it were, then the most intelligent actor would also be the best actor. Reality often indicates the opposite.

When an actor is intelligent, his efforts to be a good actor are three times as great, for he wishes to deepen his understanding, to take everything into account, to include subtleties, and in doing so he trespasses on ground which is not his—in fact, he creates obstacles for himself.

His reflections on the character he is playing, which according to popular theory should bring him closer to an exact characterization, end up by thwarting his efforts and depriving him of naturalness. The film actor should arrive for shooting in a state of virginity. The more intuitive his work, the more spontaneous it will be.

The film actor should work not on the psychological level but on the imaginative one. And the imagination reveals itself spontaneously—it has no intermediaries upon which one can lean for support.

It is not possible to have a real collaboration between actor and director. They work on two entirely different levels. The director owes no explanations to the actor except those of a very

From *Film Culture,* nos. 22-23, Summer 1961, pp. 66-67.

general nature about the people in the film. It is dangerous to discuss details. Sometimes the actor and director necessarily become enemies. The director must not compromise himself by revealing his intentions. The actor is a kind of Trojan horse in the citadel of the director.

I prefer to get results by a hidden method; that is, to stimulate in the actor certain of his innate qualities of whose existence he is himself unaware—to excite not his intelligence but his instinct—to give not justifications but illuminations. One can almost trick an actor by demanding one thing and obtaining another. The director must know how to demand, and how to distinguish what is good and bad, useful and superfluous, in everything the actor offers.

The first quality of a director is to see. This quality is also valuable in dealing with actors. The actor is one of the elements of the image. A modification of his pose or gestures modifies the image itself. A line spoken by an actor in profile does not have the same meaning as one given full-face. A phrase addressed to the camera placed above the actor does not have the same meaning it would if the camera were placed below him.

These few simple observations prove that it is the director—that is to say, whoever composes the shot—who should decide the pose, gestures, and movements of the actor.

The same principle holds for the intonation of the dialogue. The voice is a "noise" which emerges with other noises in a rapport which only the director knows. It is therefore up to him to find the balance or imbalance of these sounds.

It is necessary to listen at length to an actor even when he is mistaken. One must let him be mistaken and at the same time try to understand how one can use his mistakes in the film, for these errors are at the moment the most spontaneous thing the actor has to offer.

To explain a scene or piece of dialogue is to treat all the actors alike, for a scene or piece of dialogue does not change. On the contrary, each actor demands special treatment. From this fact stems the necessity to find different methods: to guide the actor little by little to the right path by apparently innocent corrections which will not arouse his suspicions.

This method of working may appear paradoxical, but it is the only one which allows the director to obtain good results with nonprofessional actors found, as they say, "in the street." Neorealism has taught us that, but the method is also useful with professional actors—even the great ones.

I ask myself if there really is a great film actor. The actor who thinks too much is driven by the ambition to be great. It is a terrible obstacle which runs the risk of eliminating much truth from his performance.

I do not need to think I have two legs. I have them. If the actor seeks to understand, he thinks. If he thinks, he will find it hard to be humble, and humility constitutes the best point of departure in achieving truth.

Occasionally an actor is intelligent enough to overcome his natural limitations and to find the proper road by himself—that is, he uses his innate intelligence to apply the method I have just described.

When this happens, the actor has the qualities of a director.

A Talk with Michelangelo Antonioni on His Work

ANTONIONI: Someone once said that words, more than anything else, serve to hide our thoughts. Nevertheless, in answering your questions, I will try to be as direct and honest as possible, as I try to be when I'm working on a film. I didn't come prepared to make a speech, so I've been asking myself what I should say to you and what it is that you want to know about me. I am a film-maker who began making feature films about ten years ago, and who forced himself to follow a certain direction, to maintain

This article is based on the transcript of an open discussion that took place at the *Centro Sperimentale di Cinematografia* in Rome on March 16, 1961, after a retrospective screening of Antonioni's films for students and faculty members, arranged by the Centro's director, Leonardo Fioravanti. It originally appeared in the school's monthly periodical, *Bianco e Nero*. From *Film Culture*, no. 24, Spring 1962, pp. 45-61.

a certain coherence. Now I'm not saying this to pat myself on the back, but I'm saying it because it was the only way I would have been interested in making films. Had I done them in any other way, I probably would have made worse films than the ones I did make.

Now, if you ask me what were the motives and the reasons that led me to make films in this particular manner, I think I can say today that I was motivated by two considerations. (And bear this clearly in mind, these statements are being made *ex post facto* and not *a priori,* that is, I had no conception of them until I actually became involved in making feature-length dramatic films.) The first had to do with those crucial events that were taking place around us immediately after the war, and even later, in 1950, when I first started working in films; the second was simply a technical matter more closely related to cinematography per se. With reference to the first consideration, I will most certainly say that as far as their particular period was concerned, all those so-called Italian neo-realistic films, among which are some genuine masterpieces, were representative of the most authentic and the most valid cinematic expression possible, and they were also the most appropriate. After all, it was a period in which everything happening around us was quite abnormal; reality was a burning issue. The events and situations of the day were extraordinarily unusual, and perhaps the most interesting thing to examine at that time was the relationship between the individual and his environment, between the individual and society. Therefore, a film such as *The Bicycle Thief,* for example, where the main character was a laborer who lost his job because someone had stolen his bicycle, and whose every motivation stemmed from that specific fact, and that fact alone, which in itself was the most important aspect of the film and around which its entire story was centered—this, I say, was the type of film necessary and appropriate for its time. (I know I've said this all before, but I don't mind repeating it because it's something of which I'm profoundly convinced.) It really wasn't necessary to know the protagonist's inner thoughts, his personality, or the intimate relationship between him and his wife; all this could very well be

ignored. The important thing was to establish his relationship
with society. That was the primary concern of the neo-realist films
made at that time. However, when I started making films, things
were somewhat different, and my approach therefore was also
different. I had arrived a little late on the scene, at a time when
that first flowering of films, though still valid, was already beginning to show signs of exhaustion. Consequently, I was forced to
stop and consider what subject matter was worth examining at
that particular moment, what was really happening, what was the
true state of things, what ideas were really being thought. And it
seemed to me that perhaps it was no longer so important, as I said
before, to examine the relationship between the individual and his
environment, as it was to examine the individual himself, to look
inside the individual and see, after all he had been through (the
war, the immediate postwar situation, all the events that were
currently taking place and which were of sufficient gravity to
leave their mark upon society and the individual) out of all this,
to see what remained inside the individual, to see, I won't say the
transformation of our psychological and emotional attitudes, but
at least, the symptoms of that restlessness and behavior which
began to outline the changes and transitions that later came about
in our psychology, our feelings, and perhaps even our morality.

And so I began with *Cronaca di un amore,* in which I analyzed
the condition of spiritual aridity and a certain type of moral coldness in the lives of several individuals belonging to the upper
middle-class strata of Milanese society. I chose this particular
subject because it seemed to me there would be plenty of raw
material worth examining in a situation that involved the morally
empty existence of certain individuals who were only concerned
with themselves, who had no interest whatsoever in anything or
anyone outside of themselves, and who had no human quality
strong enough to counterbalance this self-centeredness, no spark
of conscience left which might still be ignited to revitalize themselves with a sense of the enduring validity of certain basic values.
It was this, unfortunately, which led the French critics quite innocently to define my style of film-making as being a kind of internal
neo-realism. At any rate, this seemed to be the right road for me

to follow at that time. Later, I will also tell you how and why I had adapted a certain technical approach that was directly in line with this choice.

The second consideration that led me along this particular road was an ever-increasing feeling of boredom with the current standardized methods of film-making and the conventional ways of telling a story. I was already instinctively aware of this feeling when I first started working on my early documentaries, especially *N.U.*, which I had filmed in a somewhat different manner than what was then considered the orthodox way of making a film. (You will recall, however, that in 1943 I had already started shooting my very first documentary, which wasn't completed until 1947. Ever since then, in addition to making films about landscapes and places of interest, which were the usual kind of films being done in Italy at that time, I began making films about people, and in a way that was much more intense, much more sympathetic, much more involved.) As far as the documentary form was concerned, and especially with *N.U.*, I felt a need to avoid certain established and proven techniques. Even Paolucci, who was then one of the most noted documentarists, was making his documentaries in accordance with the set standards of the day, that is, in blocks of sequences. Each one of these blocks had its own beginning, its own end, and its own order; when joined together, these blocks constituted a certain parabola that gave the documentary a unity of its own. And they were impeccable documentaries, even from a formal point of view; but I felt somewhat annoyed with all this sense of order, this systematic arrangement of the material. I felt a need to break it up a little. So, having a certain amount of material in my hands, I set out to do a montage that would be absolutely free, poetically free. And I began searching for expressive ways and means, not so much through an orderly arrangement of shots that would give the scene a clear-cut beginning and end, but more through a juxtaposition of separate isolated shots and sequences that had no immediate connection with one another but which definitely gave more meaning to the idea I had wanted to express and which were the very substance of the documentary itself; in the case of *N.U.*, the life of street-cleaners in a particular city.

When I was ready to start work on *Cronaca di un amore,* I found myself with these observations already acquired and with this basic experience already assimilated. So, as I was saying before, when I used that particular technical approach which consisted of extremely long shots, of tracks and pans that followed the actors uninterruptedly (the longest shot in *Cronaca di un amore* was 132 meters and it was the one taken on the bridge), I did it perhaps instinctively, but reflecting upon it now I can understand what led me to move in that particular direction. In effect, I had the feeling that it wasn't quite right for me to abandon the actor at a time when, having just enacted an intensely dramatic scene, he was left alone by himself to face the after-effects of that particular scene and its traumatic moments. Undoubtedly, those moments of emotional violence had had a meaningful effect upon the actor and had probably served to advance him one step further psychologically. So I felt it was essential for me to follow the actors with the camera a few moments after they had completed their performance of the written scene. And though this may have seemed pointless, it actually turned out that these moments were exactly those which offered me the best opportunity to select and utilize on the moviola screen certain spontaneous movements in their gestures and facial expressions that perhaps could not have been gotten in any other way. (Many times, of course, I had the camera follow the actors even without their being aware of it, that is, at a time when they had thought the shot was finished.)

All this experimentation provided the basis for the results achieved in *La Notte.* And I want to say this, that ever since then I believe I have managed to strip myself bare, to liberate myself from the many unnecessary formal techniques that were so common at the time. I am not using the word "formal" in the sense that I had wanted to achieve results that would be strictly figurative. That wasn't the case at all. In fact, this has never been of any interest to me. Instead I have always tried to fill the image with a greater suggestiveness—by composing the shot in a way that would assist me to say precisely what I intend, and at the same time to assist the actors express exactly what they are required to express, and also to assist in establishing a working rapport between the actors and the background, that is, the activity going on behind them as they perform their particular scene.

So, film by film, I gradually began to divest myself of certain precious and professionalized techniques. However, I must say that I don't regret having had them, for without them perhaps I would not have been able to finally arrive at what I feel is a greater simplicity. Now I can actually permit myself to make some minor technical errors. And I do make them. In fact, sometimes I even do it on purpose, in order to obtain a greater degree of effectiveness. For example, certain unorthodox uses of "field" and "counterfield," certain errors regarding position or movement. Thus, I have rid myself of much unnecessary technical baggage, eliminating all the logical narrative transitions, all those connective links between sequences where one sequence served as a springboard for the one that followed. The reason I did this was because it seemed to me—and of this I am firmly convinced—that cinema today should be tied to the truth rather than to logic. And the truth of our daily lives is neither mechanical, conventional nor artificial, as stories generally are, and if films are made that way, they will show it. The rhythm of life is not made up of one steady beat; it is, instead, a rhythm that is sometimes fast, sometimes slow; it remains motionless for a while, then at the next moment it starts spinning around. There are times when it appears almost static, there are other times when it moves with tremendous speed, and I believe all this should go into the making of a film. I'm not saying one should slavishly follow the day-to-day routine of life, but I think that through these pauses, through this attempt to adhere to a definite reality—spiritual, internal, and even moral— there springs forth what today is more and more coming to be known as modern cinema, that is, a cinema which is not so much concerned with externals as it is with those forces that move us to act in a certain way and not in another. Because the important thing is this: that our acts, our gestures, our words are nothing more than the consequences of our own personal situation in relation to the world around us.

And for this reason it seems most important nowadays for us to make these so-called "literary" or "figurative" films. (Obviously, these terms are paradoxical, because I am absolutely sure that no such thing as a literary film or a figurative film exists. There exists only cinema, which incorporates the experience of all the other arts.) I think it is important at this time for cinema to turn towards this internal form of film-making, towards ways of expression that are absolutely free, as free as those of literature, as free as those of painting which has reached abstraction. Perhaps one day cinema will also achieve the heights of abstraction; perhaps cinema will even construct poetry, a cinematic poem in rhyme. Today this may seem absolutely unthinkable, and yet little by little, perhaps even the public will come to accept this kind of cinema. I say this because something of the sort is already taking shape, something which even the public is becoming aware of, and which I think is the reason why certain so-called difficult films today are even achieving commercial success; they no longer remain in the film libraries, they no longer remain in the can. Instead, these films are reaching the great masses of people; in fact, I would say the more widespread they become, the more they are being understood.

ENZO BATTAGLIA (*student of the Centro's directing class*): With reference to that shot in *La Notte* where Jeanne Moreau, at a certain point, moves along that white wall against which she appears almost crushed—was this a planned shot, one that was in the original script, or was it improvised there on the spot? In other words, what I'd like to know is to what extent you plan your shots in advance and to what extent you let yourself be influenced by the locale during the actual shooting.

ANTONIONI: I believe that in every form of artistic endeavor, there is first of all a process of selection. This selection, as Camus once said, represents the artist's revolt against the forces of reality. So whenever I'm ready to start shooting a scene, I arrive on location in a fixed state of "virginity." I do this because I believe the best results are obtained by the "collision" that takes place between the environment in which the scene is to be shot and my own particular state of mind at that specific moment. I don't like to study or even think about a scene the night before, or even a few days before I actually start shooting it. And when I arrive there, I like to be completely alone, by myself, so that I can get to feel the environment without having anybody around me. The most direct way to re-create a scene is to enter into a rapport with the environment itself; it's the simplest way to let the environment suggest something to us. Naturally, we are well acquainted with that area in advance, from the moment we have selected it, and therefore know that it offers the proper setting for the particular scene that's being shot. So it's only a matter of organizing and arranging the sequence, adapting it to the characteristic details of the surrounding environment. For this reason, I always remain alone in the area for about half an hour before I start shooting a scene, whether it's an indoor scene or an outdoor scene. Then I call in the actors and begin testing out the scene, because this too is a way of judging whether the scene works well or not. In fact, it's possible that a well-planned scene that was written while sitting behind the desk, just won't work anymore once it's laid out in a particular locale, so it has to be changed or modified right there and then. Certain lines in the script might take on a different meaning once they're spoken against a wall or against a street background. And a line spoken by an actor in profile doesn't have the same meaning as one given full-face. Likewise, a phrase addressed to the camera placed above the actor doesn't have the same meaning it would if the camera were placed below him. But the director (and, I repeat, this is my own personal way of working) becomes aware of all these things only when he's on the scene and starts moving his actors around according to the first impressions that come to him from being there. So, it is extremely rare that I have the shots already fixed in my mind. Obviously, in the various stages of preparing a film, a director creates images in his mind, but it is always dangerous to fall in love with these formulated images, because you eventually end up by running after images abstracted from the reality of the environment in which the scene is being shot and which are no longer the same as they first appeared while sitting behind the desk. It is really much better to adapt yourself to a new situation, and this is especially so since film scripts today, as you know, are becoming less and less detailed and less and less technical. They are the director's notes, and serve as a model on which one works during the course of the shooting. So, as I was saying a short while ago, improvisation comes directly from the rapport that is established between the environment and ourselves, from the rapport between the director and the people around him, both the usual professional collaborators and the people who just happen to be gathered in that particular area when the scene is being shot. In other words, it is possible that the rapport itself could suggest the outcome of a scene; it could suggest the modification of a line; it could suggest so many things, inasmuch as it too is a method of improvisation. So, I repeat, for this reason I very seldom give much advance thought to the shot but prefer to think about it when I'm there on the scene and when I put my eye behind the camera.

GIULIO CESARE CASTELLO *(film critic and member of the Centro faculty)*: This pertains to a natural setting, but what about the studio where the set is constructed according to a preconceived design?

ANTONIONI: What I said also applies to a studio set.

CASTELLO: Certain reciprocal stimuli inherent in a scene that is shot in a natural environment do not exist in one that is shot in a studio, which, to some extent, always creates a kind of limitation, if for no other reason than there exists a scenography; the set, therefore, is constructed in a specific way and there are certain movements which you simply cannot make, unless you plan and construct the scenography in a different way.

ANTONIONI: Aside from the fact that I've been working less and less in a studio (I've now made two films without once setting foot in a studio), I can say that even there the situation I described holds true. Of course, when preparing a set within a studio, I sketch out an idea for the designer or architect as to what I think the scene should be like, establishing thereby a certain rapport with the surroundings. But not until I actually find myself on the finished set, at that moment and that moment only, do I have the exact feeling of what the scene should really look like. And to some extent even those surroundings, which I myself to a certain extent have set up, can offer me surprises and suggest some changes, some new ideas. And I never reject those suggestions.

Even here, before I start shooting, I remain alone by myself for a period of twenty minutes, a half hour, and sometimes even longer.

ANTONIO PETRUCCI *(member of the Centro faculty)*: If I'm not mistaken, you once wrote somewhere that just before you start shooting a scene, you put yourself in a state somewhat similar to that of a writer in front of a blank page. And yet, undoubtedly, you must have some clue in mind as to what you want to do, just as a writer does; he doesn't sit down in front of a blank page unless he first has a definite idea what he wants to write about.

ANTONIONI: No, but to continue your metaphor, you might say it's more like a writer who has an idea in mind as to what the house in which his character lives should be like, but has not yet begun to describe it. The creation doesn't take place until he describes it. Just as a scene in a film isn't depicted until the actual shooting of that scene takes place. Now there are more than a thousand ways an actor can enter a room and slap someone across the face. But there is only one right way; the other fifty thousand are all wrong. It's a matter of finding the right way. So, when I enter upon a new environment, I feel as though I were in front of a blank page—I have no idea where to begin. And I'm pursued by doubts right up until that moment when I see the material on the moviola screen. Therefore, I would think that even the studio can offer some surprises. Because the moment you place the actors on the scene, then, from the rapport established between the actors and their surroundings—a rapport that is absolutely new and spontaneous—you get an idea as to what should follow, depending on how the situation affects you. If every detail in the sequence were foreseen, well, then there wouldn't be any need at all for the dolly. Today a film is made while in progress; it is written right there on the spot, with the camera.

CASTELLO: This method makes it necessary for you to shoot much more than the usual amount of footage. For example, how many feet of film did you shoot for *L'Avventura* and *La Notte*?

ANTONIONI: Not so much. At least, not an extreme amount. For *L'Avventura,* I shot about 170,000 feet; for *La Notte* about 140,000. So that's not much.

CASTELLO: I would like to ask another question of a more general nature. There being no doubt that everything you did to date was done the way you wanted to do it, inasmuch as you never have to compromise yourself with the producers, is there anything in your films that you yourself reject, anything with which you are dissatisfied, not in the sense that every artist is always more or less dissatisfied with almost everything he has done in the past, but rather something you feel you shouldn't have done or which you should have done differently?

ANTONIONI: Although I'm not completely satisfied with everything I've done—which is something natural and logical—I believe there's no particular film that leaves me more dissatisfied than any other. However, there are certain parts in some films that displease me more than other parts. For example, in *I vinti,* and also some sections in *Signora senza camelie,* which is a film I consider to be a mistake, mainly because I started off on the wrong foot from the very beginning of the film by concentrating on a character who then turned out to be the wrong one. Others may find that this is not so, but for me, knowing what I had in mind, I felt very bitter over the fact that I had to make so many changes from the original idea. However, there are some sequences in the film which I would do exactly the same way today. In *I vinti,* I was particularly dissatisfied with the Italian episode. And even in the French episode, I would now change many things, since I have come to know France a little better since then. Perhaps I'd leave the English episode as it is. But it's very difficult to judge this way, because even in *L'Avventura* it seems to me there are certain things that I don't like anymore; even in *La Notte.* And then, with *La Notte,* I'm still so close to it that I haven't come to like it yet, and I'm not sufficiently detached from the film to really judge it.

FIORAVANTI: In *L'Avventura,* what are the parts that least satisfy you?

ANTONIONI: Well, for example, today I would do the entire party scene at the end in a different way. I don't mean it's not good as it is now: I mean I would just do it differently, perhaps worse, but in any case, differently. Then, certain scenes on the islands, for example, certain things with the father, certain things with the helicopter.

KRYSTYNA STYPULKOWSKA *(student in the Centro's acting*

classes): First of all, I would like to speak about *L'Avventura,* or more precisely, about the significance of its ending, its conception.

I understand one should never put such questions to a director, and for this I apologize, but some of us have spent many hours, actually entire nights, in discussing this very problem because every one of us saw it in a different way. Some said it dealt with an almost Pascalian conception of life, which lays bare the solitude of man, his perpetual failure, his humiliation, his attempt to escape from a world in which there is no way out. Others found in this ending, however disconcerting, a conception of life that is perhaps more optimistic than any of your other films. What are your thoughts on the subject?

My second question, though banal, interests me enormously inasmuch as I'm a student of acting. I would like to know how you work with actors. To be more precise, do you change your methods according to the personality of the actors? For example, let's take three actresses who have worked with you and who are quite different from each other: Lucia Bose, Jeanne Moreau, and Monica Vitti.

ANTONIONI: I think it would be appropriate at this time to read you a statement I made at a press conference given for the opening of *L'Avventura* at Cannes. It pretty well reflects my thoughts regarding the motives and the considerations that moved me to make *L'Avventura* and, in a general way, sort of answers the young lady's question, which I will reply to more directly later on.

"Today the world is endangered by an extremely serious split between a science that is totally and consciously projected into the future, and a rigid and stereotyped morality which all of us recognize as such and yet sustain out of cowardice or sheer laziness. Where is this split most evident? What are its most obvious, its most sensitive, let us even say its most painful, areas? Consider the Renaissance man, his sense of joy, his fullness, his multifarious activities. They were men of great magnitude, technically able and at the same time artistically creative, capable of feeling their own sense of dignity, their own sense of importance as human beings, the Ptolemaic fullness of man. Then man discovered that his world was Copernican, an extremely limited world in an unknown universe. And today a new man is being born, fraught with all the fears and terrors and stammerings that are associated with a period of gestation. And what is even more serious, this new man immediately finds himself burdened with a heavy baggage of emotional traits which cannot exactly be called old and outmoded but rather unsuited and inadequate. They condition us without offering us any help, they create problems without suggesting any possible solutions. And yet it seems that man will not rid himself of this baggage. He reacts, he loves, he hates, he suffers under the sway of moral forces and myths which today, when we are at the threshold of reaching the moon, should not be the same as those that prevailed at the time of Homer, but nevertheless are.

"Man is quick to rid himself of his technological and scientific mistakes and misconceptions. Indeed, science has never been more humble and less dogmatic than it is today. Whereas our moral attitudes are governed by an absolute sense of stultification. In recent years, we have examined these moral attitudes very carefully, we have dissected them and analyzed them to the point of exhaustion. We have been capable of all this but we have not been capable of finding new ones, we have not been capable of making any headway whatsoever towards a solution of this problem, of this ever-increasing split between moral man and scientific man, a split which is becoming more and more serious and more and more accentuated. Naturally, I don't care to nor can I resolve it myself; I am not a moralist and my film is neither a denunciation nor a sermon. It is a story told in images whereby, I hope, it may be possible to perceive not the birth of a mistaken attitude but the manner in which attitudes and feelings are misunderstood today. Because, I repeat, the present moral standards we live by, these myths, these conventions are old and obsolete. And we all know they are, yet we honor them. Why? The conclusion reached by the protagonists in my film is not one of sentimentality. If anything, what they finally arrive at is a sense of pity for each other. You might say that this too is nothing new. But what else is left if we do not at least succeed in achieving this? Why do you think eroticism is so prevalent today in our literature, our theatrical shows, and elsewhere? It is a symptom of the emotional sickness of our time. But this preoccupation with the erotic would not become obsessive if Eros were healthy, that is, if it were kept within human proportions. But Eros is sick; man is uneasy, something is bothering him. And whenever something bothers him, man reacts, but he reacts badly, only on erotic impulse, and he is unhappy. The tragedy in *L'Avventura* stems directly from an erotic impulse of this type—unhappy, miserable, futile. To be critically aware of the vulgarity and the futility of such an overwhelming erotic impulse, as is the case with the protagonist in *L'Avventura,* is not enough or serves no purpose. And here we witness the crumbling of a myth, which proclaims it is enough for us to know, to be critically conscious of ourselves, to analyze ourselves in all our complexities and in every facet of our personality. The fact of the matter is that such an examination is not enough. It is only a preliminary step. Every day, every emotional encunter gives rise to a new adventure. For even though we know that the ancient codes of morality are decrepit and no longer tenable, we persist, with a sense of perversity that I would only ironically define as pathetic, in remaining loyal to them. Thus moral man who has no fear of the scientific unknown is today afraid of the moral unknown. Starting out from this point of fear and frustration, his adventure can only end in a stalemate."

That was the statement I read in France. I believe one can deduce from its premise the significance of the film's ending, which, depending on how you look at it, might be considered either optimistic or pessimistic. Georges Sadoul has made a little discovery which I later found to be in agreement with what I had intended when I shot the final scene. I don't know if you still remember it. On one side of the frame is Mount Etna in all its snowy whiteness, and on the other is a concrete wall. The wall corresponds to the man and Mount Etna corresponds somewhat to the situation of the woman. Thus the frame is divided exactly in half; one half containing the concrete wall which represents the pessimistic side, while the other half showing Mount Etna represents the optimistic. But I really don't know if the relationship between these two halves will endure or not, though it is quite evident the two protagonists will remain together and not separate. The girl will definitely not leave the man; she will stay with him and forgive him. For she realizes that she too, in a certain sense, is somewhat like him. Because—if for no other reason—from the moment she suspects Anna may have returned, she becomes so apprehensive, so afraid she may be back and still alive, that she begins to lose the feeling of friendship that she once had for Anna, just as he had lost his affection for Anna and perhaps is also beginning to lose it for her. But what else can she do but stay with him? As I was saying before, what would be left if there weren't this mutual sense of pity, which is also a source of strength. In *La Notte* the protagonists go somewhat further. In *L'Avventura* they communicate only through this mutual sense of pity; they do not speak to one another. In *La Notte,* however, they do converse with each other, they communicate freely, they are fully aware of what is happening to their relationship. But the result is the same, it doesn't differ. The man becomes hypocritical, he refuses to go on with the conversation because he knows quite well that if he openly expresses his feelings at that moment, everything would be finished. But even this attitude indicates a desire on his part to maintain the relationship, so then the more optimistic side of the situation is brought out.

CASTELLO: I find it a bit ridiculous, this wanting to establish whether an ending is optimistic or pessimistic. However, I have noticed there is a certain divergence of opinion. I find the ending of *L'Avventura* far more optimistic than that of *La Notte*. And yet there are some who find *La Notte* more optimistic.

ANTONIONI: Once, in a situation similar to this, Pirandello was asked some questions about his characters, his scenes, his comedies. And he replied: "How should I know? I'm the author." Now for the young lady's second question about acting. With actors, I use certain ideas and methods which are strictly personal, and I don't know if they are right or wrong. Looking back at what has been my experience with actors, I can say that I directed them in a certain way only because I didn't care to work in any other way since my way seemed to give me the best results. And then, I am not like those directors, such as De Sica and Visconti, who can "show" the actor exactly how the scene is to be acted. This is something I wouldn't know how to do inasmuch as I myself do not know how to act. I believe, however, that I know what I want from my actors. As I see it, an actor need not necessarily understand everything he is doing. In this respect, I always have a great deal of trouble when I first begin working with my actors, especially with some foreign actors. There is a general belief that actors must understand everything they do when enacting a scene. If this were so, then the best actor would be the one who is the most intellectual, which is simply not the case; the facts show us that often the reverse is true. The more an actor forces himself to comprehend the meaning of a scene, the more he tries to achieve a deeper understanding of a given line, a sequence, or the film itself, the more obstacles he sets up between the really natural spontaneity of that scene and its ultimate realization. Aside from the fact that by doing such, he tends to become, in a certain sense, his own director; and this is more harmful than beneficial. Now, I find it's not necessary for a director to have his actors rack their brains; it's better, in every respect, for them to use their instinct. As a director, I shouldn't have to consult with them regarding my conception of the way I feel a scene should be done. Otherwise, by revealing to them what is after all my own personal plan of action, they automatically become a kind of Trojan horse in what is supposed to be my citadel, which is mine by virtue of the fact that I am the one who knows what I want from them and I am the one who knows whether their response to what I ask for is good or bad. Inasmuch as I consider an actor as being only one element in a given scene, I regard him as I regard a tree, a wall, or a cloud, that is, as just one element in the overall scene; the attitude or pose of the actor, as determined under my direction, cannot but help to effect the framing of that scene, and I, not the actor, am the one who can know whether that effect is appropriate or not. Furthermore, as I said previously, a line spoken by an actor where the camera is facing him from above has one meaning, while it has another meaning if the camera is facing him from below, etc., etc. Only the director can judge these things, not the actor. And the same applies to intonation, which is primarily a sound and only secondarily a line in a piece of dialogue. It is a sound that should be made to integrate with the other sounds accompanying a given image, and at that moment, when the actor speaks his line, all the sounds, including his delivery of that line, that combine to make up the total sound pattern appropriate to that image or sequence, are not there yet. The actor pays no attention to all these details, but the director does. And that's not all. Even improvisation is a factor in connection with this particular subject. For instance, when an actor makes a mistake in delivering a line, I let him make that mistake. That is, I let him go ahead with his mistake because I want to see how it sounds, how it works, before he goes ahead and corrects that mistake. I want to see whether I can somehow utilize that mistake. Because at that moment his mistakes are the most spontaneous things he can give me, and it is that spontancity of his which I have need of, even though he gives it to me against his will. When going through a scene before shooting it, I often try out certain pieces of dialogue or certain actions which may not have anything to do with the actual scene itself, and I am forcefully embarrassed when the actors ask me for explanations. Because beyond a certain point, I don't want to tell them anything. When I was doing *Il Grido,* that excellent actress Betsy Blair wanted to go over the script with me, and she would ask me for an explanation of every line. Those two hours I spent with her going over that script were the most hellish hours of my life, since I was forced to invent meanings that weren't there at all. However, they were the meanings she had wanted me to give her, so she was satisfied. And this should also be taken under consideration.

There is another reason why I feel it really isn't necessary to explain every scene to your actors, for if you did so that would mean you'd have to give the same explanation to each actor. And this would not do, at least not for me. In order to get the best results, I know that I have to say one thing to one actor and something else to another actor. Because I am supposed to understand his temperament, I am supposed to know how he reacts, that when affected a certain way, he reacts a certain way, and when affected another way, he reacts differently. So it's not possible to use the same approach with every actor. To the director, the scene itself remains always the same, but when I approach the actors, in order for me to obtain the desired results, by explanations to them have to vary in accordance with the nature and temperament of each actor.

STEFANO SATTA *(student of the Centro's acting classes)*: Although *L'Avventura* and *La Notte* both end with a new awareness on the part of the protagonists (you mentioned a mutual feeling of pity) while *Il Grido* ends with a suicide, it seems to me that *L'Avventura* and *La Notte* are more imbued with agony and despair than *Il Grido*. Is this merely coincidental or is it actually because of the different social climate involved?

ANTONIONI: This is a question the critics can answer more efficiently than I can. You are not really asking me a question, you are making an observation. In other words, what you're telling me is that *L'Avventura* and *La Notte* succeeded in achieving their aims while *Il Grido* did not. When the critics said—with regards to *Il Grido*—that I was cold, cynical, and completely inhuman, they evidently weren't aware of what I was trying to say. Perhaps I was not precisely aware of it myself at the time, and it only became clear to me after having done the other two films. Perhaps *L'Avventura* and *La Notte* help somewhat to explain *Il Grido,* which, if shown in Italy today might receive a greater success than when it first came out. I would say that *Il Grido* is a more pessimistic film, more full of despair, which may be due to the fact that I myself, at that particular moment in my life, was in a certain state of depression. So if the film didn't reflect this, I'd really be surprised.

SATTA: I would like to express myself more precisely. In *Il Grido* I found a greater feeling of human warmth that I did in *L'Avventura* and *La Notte*.

FIORAVANTI: I think he means that *Il Grido* ends in a more dramatic and tragic manner, that is, with a suicide; but, in certain aspects, he finds this film is actually more optimistic than either *L'Avventura* or *La Notte,* which seem colder to him in spite of the fact that they contain certain glimmers of hope.

ANTONIONI: But insofar as this human warmth is no longer of any value to the protagonist, insofar as it doesn't help to prevent him from destroying himself, the ending of this film is more pessimistic than the others. I don't know. In spite of everything, this quality of human warmth as expressed by the main character in *Il Grido* doesn't serve him at all as any link to the rest of humanity. He is a person who is no longer attached to life.

SATTA: I would like to ask you another question. Regarding the final scene in *La Notte,* I feel that you have departed from your usual style; in the sense that whereas you have been accused at times of making your characters say so very little to each other, in the final scene of *La Notte* almost the opposite is true. With that final conversation between the husband and wife it almost seems that you want to give an explanation for the benefit and comfort of the spectators.

ANTONIONI: I don't know if it gives that impression or not. Actually, that conversation, which is really a soliloquy, a monologue by the wife, is a kind of summing-up of the film to clarify the real meaning of what took place. The woman is still willing to discuss, to analyze, to examine the reasons for the failure of their marriage. But she is prevented from doing so by her husband's refusal to admit its failure, his denial, his inability to remember or unwillingness to remember, his refusal to reason things out, his incapacity to find any basis for a new start through a lucid analysis of the situation as it is. Instead, he tries to take refuge in an irrational and desperate attempt to make physical contact. It is because of his stalemate that we do not know what possible solution they could come to.

CHRISTA WINDISCH-GRATZ *(student of the Centro's acting classes)*: Between *L'Avventura, La Notte* and *Il Grido,* I particularly liked *Il Grido.* I liked the ending of *Il Grido* because it clarifies something, it arrives at a definite conclusion, one that is perhaps too cruel, that needn't be so, but nevertheless that's the way it is. Whereas *L'Avventura* and *La Notte* leave me cold because they don't come to any definite conclusion.

ANTONIONI: Lucretius, who was certainly one of the greatest poets who ever lived, once said, "Nothing appears as it should in a world where nothing is certain. The only thing certain is the existence of a secret violence that makes everything uncertain." Think about this for a moment. What Lucretius said of his time is still a disturbing reality, for it seems to me this uncertainty is very much part of our own time. But this is unquestionably a philosophical matter. Now you really don't expect me to resolve such problems or to propose any solutions? Inasmuch as I am the product of a middle-class society, and am preoccupied with making middle-class dramas, I am not equipped to do so. The middle class doesn't give me the means with which to resolve any middle-class problems. That's why I confine myself to pointing out existing problems without proposing any solutions. I think it is equally important to point them out as it is to propose solutions.

BANG-HANSEN *(student of the Centro's directing class)*: I would like to know to what extent you believe lucidity could be a form of salvation or a way out.

ANTONIONI: Now, look, lucidity is not a solution. In fact, I would say it puts you at a greater disadvantage, because where you have lucidity there is no longer any reason for the existence of a scale of values, and therefore one finds one's self even more at a loss. Certainly, I am for lucidity in all things, because this is my position as a secular man. But in a certain sense I still envy those who can draw upon their faith and somehow manage to resolve all their problems. But this is not so with everyone. You ask me questions of such magnitude that I feel I'm much too small to answer them.

PAOLO TODISCO *(student of the Centro's acting classes)*: To go back to your experiences with actors, you said that you try to create a characterization, giving the actor a minimum amount of directions, and then wait to see how he himself develops a certain theme.

ANTONIONI: No, that's not quite right. I never let the actor do anything on his own. I give him precise instructions as to what he is supposed to do.

TODISCO: Okay, then here is my question: In your films, you have worked with the following three actors: Lucia Bose, Steve Cochran, and Monica Vitti. Three kinds of experiences, three different types of actors: Lucia Bose, who has done very little before she started working with you; Steve Cochran, whose experience is that of a school much different than ours; and Monica Vitti, who comes to films from the stage. Which of the three gave you the most difficulty?

ANTONIONI: Steve Cochran. Because he is the least intelligent of the three.

CASTELLO: Just a moment. Only a short while ago you said you didn't want intelligent actors; you wanted it this way yourself, so why do you regret it now?

ANTONIONI: Let me explain. He was less intelligent in the sense that when I specifically asked him to do something, he simply refused to do it. If I gave him certain directions and told him to follow those directions to the letter, he would abruptly tell me, "No." "Why not?" I would ask him. And he would reply, "Because I'm not a puppet." Now that was too much to tolerate . . . After all, there's a limit to everything. As a result, I had to direct him by using tricks, without ever telling him what it was I wanted.

GUIDO CINCOTTI: But it was resolved one way or the other. Either Cochran finally resigned himself to following your directions or else this underhand method you used went well. Because the end results were excellent.

ANTONIONI: No, because he just went ahead and did everything he wanted—only he never became aware of the tricks I had to use in order to get what I wanted from him. With regards to Lucia Bose, I had to direct her almost with a sense of violence. Before every scene, I had to put her in a state of mind appropriate to that particular scene. If it was a sad scene, I had to make her cry; if it was a happy scene, I had to make her laugh. As for Monica Vitti, I can say she's an extremely serious actress. She comes from the Academy, and therefore possesses an extraordinary sense of craft. Even so, there were many times when we were not in agreement on certain solutions, and I was forced to beg her not to interfere in my domain.

TODISCO: It is said that a stage actor generally creates some difficulties for the director of a film. Now have you had such difficulties with, for example, Monica Vitti, who was originally a stage actress?

ANTONIONI: No, I wouldn't say so. Because Monica Vitti is a very modern actress, so even in her theatrical career she never had those attitudes which can be defined as "theatrical." Therefore, I didn't have any great difficulty with her. And then Monica Vitti is extraordinarily expressive. This is a great quality for a film actor. Perhaps on stage this expressiveness was of less value to her; that is, if an actor does have such a quality, it is all the better, but if he does not, it doesn't really matter much; what is more important for the stage is the actor's attitude. At a distance of one hundred feet, the actor's facial expression is lost, but in a film what counts the most is the actor's expressions. And Monica Vitti has an extremely expressive face.

MARIO VERDONE *(film critic and member of Centro's faculty)*: Actually, what is your opinion about the contribution music can make to a film? I say actually because it has seemed to me this contribution has diminished in your last two films.

ANTONIONI: I think music has had and can continue to have a great function in films, because there is no art form which the film medium cannot draw upon. In the case of music, it draws directly, and therefore the relationship is even closer. It seems to me, however, that this relationship is beginning to change. In fact, the way music is being used today is quite different than it was used ten years ago. At that time music was used to create a certain atmosphere in order to help get the image across to the spectator. Earlier, of course, in the period of the silent film, there was the old pianola, which was originally used to hide the noise of the projecting machine and then, later, as a means to emphasize the images that passed over the screen in absolute silence. Since then, the use of music in films has changed a great deal, but in certain films today it is still being used that way, that is, as a kind of external commentary. Its function is to establish a rapport between the music and the spectator, not between the music and the film, which is its proper function. Even to this day, especially in certain films from Hollywood, a battle scene is accompanied with violent symphonic crescendoes from a full orchestra; a sad scene is always accompanied with violin music because it is felt that violins create an atmosphere of sadness. But this seems to me to be a completely wrong way to use music, and has nothing whatever to do with cinematography.

There are, of course, certain films where music is used in a more meaningful way, as a means to complement the images, to heighten and intensify the meaning of the image. And this has been done with certain scenes in *L'Avventura* and in Resnais' *Hiroshima Mon Amour*. And I must say that the music really worked well in these cases, that is, it expressed what the images themselves intended to express, it was used as an integral part of the image. Having said this, however, I must also say that I am personally very reluctant to use music in my films, for the simple reason that I prefer to work in a dry manner, to say things with the least means possible. And music is an additional means. I have too much faith in the efficacy, the value, the force, the suggestiveness of the image to believe that the image cannot do without music. It is true, however, that I have a need to draw upon sound, which serves an essential "musical" function. I would therefore say that true film "music" has not yet been invented. Perhaps it might be in the future. Until that time comes, however, I feel that music should be spliced out of the film and spliced into a disc, where it has an autonomy of its own.

PETRUCCI: In connection with this, I want to bring up the entire sequence in *La Notte* that takes place in the streets of Milan. It is clear that when those street sounds, those automobile horns, etc., are isolated from their corresponding images, they have no meaning in themselves. At the same time, however, when heard in relation to those images, their function is exclusively a musical one.

ANTONIONI: Of course. But there must be a mutual rapport. That is, the images cannot stand alone, without those sounds—just as those sounds would have no meaning at all if they were detached from the images.

VERDONE: I seem to find a certain predilection in your films for contemporary art. Not so much with regards to the paintings of Morandi which are seen in *La Notte* or of the abstract paintings seen in *Le Amiche,* but more so in your framing of the image itself, in your manner of seeing things, for example, a white wall or a gravel path or some wooden boards nailed to a window. That is, you seem to have a predilection for a kind of painting which might be called non-painting, like that of Burri, or a sculpture by Consagra, or similar artists—I could cite Vedova, Fontana, etc., etc. I would like to know if this is accidental (and I'm sure it's not since it seems to me nothing is accidental in your films), or is there a definite rapport between contemporary art and your latest films?

ANTONIONI: I have a great love for painting. For me, it is the one art, along with architecture, that comes immediately after film-making. I'm very fond of reading books on art and architecture, of leafing through pages and pages of art volumes, and I like to go to art shows and keep in touch with the latest work being done in art—not just to be *au courant* but because painting is something that moves me passionately. Therefore I believe all these perceptions and this interest have been somewhat assimilated. And, naturally, having followed modern art, my taste and my predilection for a certain style would be reflected in my work. But in framing a shot, I certainly don't have any particular painter or painting in mind; that's something I avoid.

PETRUCCI: I'd like to ask you a question about something you mentioned before, concerning your earlier work and its particular tendency, from a a technical point of view, towards using long shots, long tracks, long pans, etc. We have not seen any widespread indication of this in your latest films. Can we therefore assume that a change has taken place in your method of expression, that you are now using your technical means of expression in a different way?

ANTONIONI: When I began *Cronaca di un amore,* as I said a short while ago, I did not consciously intend to make a film in that particular way, that is, it was not a preconceived style that was evolved while sitting behind the desk. But when I started climbing on the dolly to follow the actors around in the first scene, I saw that it wasn't essential to cut right at the specified end of that scene, so I continued shooting on for a while longer. As I already said before, I felt an urge to keep the camera on the actors even after the prescribed action was completed. Evidently, I did this because I felt the best way to capture their thoughts, their states of mind, was to follow them around physically with the camera. Thus the long shots, the continuous panning, etc. Later, however, as I went along (and here I should say that even in making this film I worked quite instinctively) I became aware that perhaps this was not the best method after all, that perhaps I was concentrating too much on the external aspects of the actors' states of mind and not enough on the states of mind themselves. Perhaps it would be better, I thought, to construct the scene and try different camera movements and montage so that by setting up the camera at one level, then using a certain pan in a preceding or following shot, I could obtain the results I wanted. In short, I realized that just one specific technical approach was not enough to obtain the particular type of shots I would need to go beyond the literal aspects of the story, but that it was necessary to work more closely with the material itself, selecting those particular objects in the scene by various methods.

FRANCO BRONZI *(student of scenography)*: When speaking with some of the student directors here at the Centro, there are certain times when we students of scenography meet up with some rather strange notions. We find that student directors or young directors have the feeling that scenography is not very important. It seems that as far as they are concerned, to shoot a scene against a natural wall of a building is more or less the same thing as shooting a scene against a wall constructed in a studio. According to your way of thinking, is scenography an important contributing factor in the successful realization of a film?

ANTONIONI: I wouldn't say it isn't. It could be. It depends on the type of film you make. For example, in the next few months I'll be doing a film where I don't think I'll have any need of a studio, but immediately after that, at least if I don't change my mind and start something else, I'll be doing another film entirely inside a studio. For it will be done in color and I want to inject my own color scheme, that is, I want to paint the film as one paints a canvas; I want to invent the color relationships, I don't want to limit myself by one photographing natural colors. In this case, scenography becomes an extremely important element. There is also something to be said for scenography when one shoots a film outdoors and wants to obtain a specific kind of background—then scenography is as important as it is in a studio. Today there are several film-makers who are working in somewhat the same way I have and will be working. Resnais, for example, is one of these, as well as several young film-makers like Godard and others. They actually intervene and change the natural setting of the environment, and even go so far as to paint walls and add trees. It's not a matter of merely selecting a place and accepting it exactly as it is. A natural setting provides you with enough of an idea of the background required for the realization of a scene, but even outdoors one should intervene and make what changes are necessary. So therefore scenography *is* important.

GIAN LUIGI CRESCENZI *(student of the Centro's acting school):* In the film *Le Amiche* we have the portrayal of a painter who is going through a certain crisis. In *L'Avventura* was have the portrayal of an architect who neither plans nor designs but merely calculates figures and draws up estimates for construction materials. In *La Notte,* Mastroianni is a writer in crisis. I would like to know if these three characterizations, which are analogous to one another, not only in terms of their professional crises but also with regard to their personal affairs, were conceived by you for the purpose of examining a certain type of individual in order to draw some conclusions about his particular situation, or was this similarity in your choice of character type simply coincidental?

ANTONIONI: It seems rather odd that you would think it could be a coincidence. Obviously, when I select the profession of a character for one of my films, I know very well what I'm doing. I choose intellectual types mainly because they have a greater awareness of what is happening to them, and also because they have a more refined sensibility, a more subtle sense of intuition through which I can filter the kind of reality I am interested in expressing, whether it be an internal reality or an external one. Furthermore, the intellectual, more than others, is the type of person in which I can find the symptoms of that particular kind of crisis which I am interested in describing. If I take an insensitive type, a rough and rugged type, he wouldn't have any of the particular problems I'm concerned with and the story would end right there. So I don't quite know what you mean. Do you want to know if I'm searching for a single character type that would be representative of everyman? I don't understand.

CASTELLO: Perhaps he means to ask if there exists a certain development from one character to another; whether your ultimate objective is to create a general character who would be representative of the intellectual in crisis, or if each character is independent of the other.

ANTONIONI: No, I don't believe the individual characters in the various films are meant to be representative of a certain type of man. Naturally, I shall make a film that will bring an end to this cycle of films which are dedicated, so to speak, to the emotions. As a matter of fact, at a certain point in the film I'm now working on—although it too is mainly concerned with the relationships of human sentiments—due to the very nature of the story itself, this particular theme is given less prominence than it had in the other films and paves the way for the introduction of other themes.

Fritz Lang

*

H A P P I L Y
E V E R
A F T E R

I HAVE BEEN involved in the creation of motion pictures for more than thirty years, as a writer or as a director, and mine has been a varied life full of surprises, both pleasant and unpleasant. But from the beginning one experience has been commonplace—that of being asked to state succinctly, in words of one syllable, a "formula" for making motion pictures.

The question is not always phrased in just that way. I may be asked to state my rules for creating suspense, to list *precisely* the qualities necessary for a film story or to analyze with fine exactitude those places in a motion picture where dialogue can or cannot be used, etc., etc., but all of the questioners want the same thing (I want it too)—a sure-fire formula for success.

No matter how the demand for a magic "formula" is put to me, my answer does boil down to three one-syllable words—*I don't know.* I don't know any *rules* for creating suspense. I wouldn't attempt to list the qualities necessary for a film story. If I did, tomorrow someone would be sure to film successfully a story having none of the qualities I listed. As for rules about the use of dialogue —again, I don't know. I only know that out of a multitude of experiences, out of successes and failures (I've had my share of both), I've developed a kind of automatic reflex device which

Originally published in *Penguin Film Review,* no. 5, January 1948, pp. 22-29.

guides my work, which has usually served me fairly well and which I hope will continue to do so.

I am disclaiming the possession of rules and theories because I want it understood that whatever thoughts I express here I know to be inconclusive and subject to change. I prefer that such ideas remain fluid, believing set formulations, rules and rigid procedures to be for me the deadly enemy of creativeness. Even should I appear to formulate a rule, I believe that *if* the rule exists it exists to be broken. I am merely setting down here a few random thoughts about one aspect of picture-making—the question of happy versus unhappy endings.

A friend of mine who is a fairly worldly member of the motion-picture audience started it all when he confessed to me that he will not go to see a movie which he knows to have an unhappy ending, and he assured me that a majority of the people he knows feel the same. His confession disturbed me a little. I thought I had long since resolved for myself this question of how a picture should end through the simple truism that each picture should have the ending which belongs to it, and if it rings true it will be accepted. But I found this truism to be insufficient and meaningless in the face of what I assume is a general audience demand for, willy nilly, a particular kind of ending. As a picture creator as well as a businessman, I respect the audience, which I believe to be moving towards better standards and higher truths on the screen, as well as in life. Yet in this apparently arbitrary demand for "Pollyanna" there seemed to be, on the surface, a contradiction of my evaluation of my audience.

I am always suspicious of assumptions which discredit the audience, because they are so often used as excuses for lazy, untalented or inept production. I realize it has always been stated authoritatively by "authorities" that the motion-picture audience's preference is for happy endings, and it seems to be *generally* true that pictures with "unhappy" endings are not as well received at the box-office as are those which proclaim "all's right with the world." Still, I question the easy conclusion that an immature, Pollyanna audience in its demand for Pollyanna pictures makes the production of good (mature) pictures impossible. I suspect that such a judgment is a handy rationalization for people who are themselves too immature to look for audience needs behind audience demands, in order to give the audience the substance as well as the form it craves.

The happy ending is a relatively late development in serious drama and is peculiar to the western world. Apparently it was only in a society where the individual could achieve dignity and could at least hope for a happy ending for his own life, that he enjoyed seeing such possibilities dramatized. Even today the peoples of Asia, of India prefer tragedy, finding in it a catharsis, a release from the universal sorrow of their lives.

Life in the western world, particularly in the United States, where there is usually the assurance of food for weeks or even months to come, where millions of common people exercise some choice over how and where they live, where at least a fair proportion of the population enjoys such glittering marvels as bathtubs, automobiles, refrigerators, would constitute to a Chinese peasant or to an Untouchable of India an unbelievable fantasy. To the average American of the last century, whether native born or immigrant, these same possibilities were marvelous but by no means fantastic. For a majority, a good and happy life was realizable. Even western Europe, until the last year, offered its peoples great individual hope, a promise of fairy-tale endings for many, many lives. In such a world of greater material comforts, broadened human freedoms with greater emphasis on the worth of the individual, it is no wonder that people took delight in seeing and hearing over and over again the old fairy-tale assurance, "and they lived happily ever after."

The First World War brought changes to the western world. In Europe, an entire generation of intellectuals embraced despair. In America, too, intellectuals and artists turned to a rocky wasteland, trying to outdo each other in pessimistic outcry. All over the world, young people engaged in the cultural fields, myself among them, made a fetish of tragedy, expressing open rebellion against the old answers and outworn forms, swinging from naïve nineteenth-century sweetness and light to the opposite extreme of pessimism for its own sake. In the end, our audience, even in

Europe where a new life was being built out of the wreckage of the old, rejected our despair (at the box-office!) and we, with many groans, gave in to the "bad taste" of the audience while casting wistful glances back into the purple gloom in which our "artistic" spirits had thrived. Yes, it was a fight I shared, the fight for the "unhappy ending," but today I believe I was tilting with windmills.

Today, at the end of the Second, and even worse, World War, another generation of young intellectuals is raising the slogan of "artistic" despair. And today's audience in both Europe and America is again rejecting them. You *may* say that because the war left the American people comparatively untouched, in their innocence and immaturity the future looks richer and more promising than ever before, so it is senseless *optimism* which makes them seek light and frivolous film fare. Granting that America's war experience was in no way comparable to that of Europe and that many realities of the struggle against Fascism were not realized by a majority of Americans, I doubt if Americans look ahead to an easy life. These are a people who too recently saw bread lines and mass unemployment and who today again see their savings melting away in inflation and in a period labeled "prosperity" know that again millions may be unemployed. I do not think the American people are naïvely optimistic, but if they are, what of the people of Europe who also reject pessimism and despair? Are people looking for an escape from reality because of the misery of their lives, seeking soothing assurances as children turn from hunger and pain to the assurances of a mother?

We must look farther for our answer to what the audience wants and what it needs. We must look farther if we claim any responsibility beyond that of making invested dollars multiply in profits. And we must look farther even to assure continued profits.

I believe in artistic rebellion. I think new approaches, new forms are needed to reflect the changed world we live in. But I don't think the only alternative to sugar is poison. If we keep our ears and eyes open, I think we shall discover that our audience is somewhat sickened by sugar but knows it is more nourishing and far safer than arsenic.

These last months, there have been dozens of articles on Hollywood's concern over European, especially British, competition. Part of our answer *can* be found in the undoubtedly increasing popularity of English and European films in the U.S. and abroad. Is it an even *happier* dream-world that people find in these films? The answer obviously is no. But it is no more true that they find a general negativism. Most of the films from abroad which I have seen tell another story of the individual hero who solves his problems and lives happily. There are exceptions, notably *Open City,* but of this I will speak later.

The problem for me boils down to a question of *concept,* of positive or negative concept—of how we look at the world. Classic tragedy was negative, in that it showed man trapped by Fate, as personified by the gods, drawn helplessly to his doom. In an age when man was puny in the face of nature, there was a magnificence in this concept which gave man, even in his almost inevitable failures, a sense of dignity. Too often, modern tragedy, unable to draw on a mystic belief in prearranged Fate, is *merely* negative, showing a triumph of evil and a waster of human life *for* nothing and *because* of nothing. It is this negativism which our audience rejects. Yet classic tragedy is certainly as unacceptable to a modern audience, to people who in one generation have conquered more and more diseases, doubling and trebling life expectancy, who have made time a servant and space a toy, who have harnessed the energy of the universe. No matter what unsolved problems we have of keeping our world at peace and of distributing equitably the abundant riches of the earth, we believe problems *can* be solved because we have seen so many solved. We believe in a limitless future, one world, trips to the moon and then to the galaxies beyond our solar system. How can we say that man is trapped by fate, believing man is mighty?

It is not the intellectuals and dilettantes who believe in this power of mankind. Nameless millions, engaged in bitter day-to-day struggle, believe somehow in a brilliant living future—insist it is impossible that men live and die for nothing. When Norman Corwin, in his recent One World tour, asked people of all races and nations about their hopes and fears for the future, he received most often optimistic answers. And one man seemed most eloquently to sum it up when he told Corwin that atomic power is not the strongest thing in the world, since "man is stronger."

So what are our alternatives, as film creators responsible to our own time? The traditional happy-ending story is a story of problems solved by an invincible hero, who achieved with miraculous ease all that his heart desired. It is the story of good against evil, with no possible doubt as to the outcome. Boy will get girl, the villain will get his just deserts, dreams will come true as though at the touch of a wand. Our audience prefers such a story to tragedy, and I think the audience is right in its preference. But I am sure there is something further which will answer the real cultural needs which lie behind the audience's demands. And it is the immemorial function of artists to *lead* the way along the paths of cultural development.

I spoke earlier of *Open City,* which has enjoyed great success abroad and which even in America, with limited distribution, has run for more than a year in several large cities. No one would advocate a traditional happy ending for *Open City.* A European audience would not accept a picture which shows a superman hero triumphing easily over the forces of Fascism. Europe knows better. Even an American audience would not accept such a solution to such a problem. (As an example, I cite one of my own pictures, not because it is the best or only example, but because I am naturally most familiar with the problems and choices in my own work.) In 1943, when I made *Hangmen Also Die,* which I made primarily for Americans, who then knew next to nothing of the nature of Fascism, I ended the picture with the anti-Fascist professor going to his death along with the other Czechoslovakian hostages. I did not want to tell Americans that Fascism would crumble at the first breath of resistance, and I did not think they would believe it if I had told them. But I don't consider either *Open City* or *Hangmen Also Die* tragedies in the sense of negativism or despair. Both of them show man triumphant in himself, in his own sense of dignity. Both of them pose tremendous problems, but proclaim the solution through man's courage and sacrifice for those who live after him. This is not man as the victim of Fate or man dying for nothing.

It is interesting to note here that what constitutes a happy ending must be qualitatively different to people conditioned by modern democratic life than, for instance, to the people of Nazi Germany. A happy or affirmative resolution of a story must be based upon the ideals and ethical concepts of the audience. It is also significant that in the Fascist states there was a marked return to the mystical concept of Fate, as it existed in classical tragedy.

I think we can all agree that when we deal with the largest life-and-death questions—war, Fascism, depressions—as they affect millions, the audience does not want the traditional happy ending. *The Best Years of Our Lives,* a motion picture which achieved last year's greatest success, has nevertheless been criticized by people on all levels of life for the kind of ending which they sensed was forced upon it. It seems to me that this very strong motion picture would have been immeasurably strengthened if it had resolved the stories of the three returning veterans in terms of a recognition by them of their obligation to struggle for a good life, instead of having a good life fall into their laps—a happy ending achieved through thought and feeling rather than through miraculous events.

When I made *Woman in the Window,* I was chided by critics for ending it as a dream. I am not always objective about my own work, but in this case my choice was conscious. If I had continued the story to its logical conclusion, a man would have been caught and executed for committing a murder because he was one moment off guard. Even were he not convicted of the crime, his life would have been ruined. I rejected this logical ending because it seemed to me a defeatist ending, a tragedy for nothing brought about by an implacable Fate—a negative ending to a problem which is not universal, a futile dreariness which an audience would reject. *Woman in the Window* enjoyed a considerable success, and while it may be hindsight on my part, I think that with another ending its success would have been less.

To state my general thesis— I think the audience's apparent preference for happy resolutions is more accurately described as a preference for *affirmative* resolutions, as a desire to see dramatized the rightness of its ideals and the *eventual* achievement of its hopes. The death of a hero, if he dies for an acceptable ideal, is not a tragedy. The death of a protagonist, if he dies because he lives counter to an ideal, is affirmative. While my picture *Scarlet Street* may not seem to fall in easily with my thesis, I feel the audience in general was satisfied with its unstated affirmation that evil in its many forms—the evil of crime, of weakness, of deceit—must reap some sort of physical or mental punishment, and not punishment by Fate, but created by the characters themselves, each one of whom—the boy, the girl and the old man—chooses an easy road to happiness without regard for moral and ethical standards.

To sum up: Classic tragedy served as a catharsis in a society where the individual man could hope for little beyond a sense of his own dignity as he faced the overwhelming forces of nature. The happy ending, known previously in legends and fairy-tales, was accepted in so-called realistic drama in the western world when man, emerging from centuries of bitter struggle, realized his struggle against nature could be won. Prior to the First World War, the happy ending was usually a naïve presentation of the inevitable triumph of virtue. Following World War I, rejecting the intellectual swing to despair, people tended more and more to the *affirmative* ending, in which virtue triumphs through struggle. Today, following World War II, this tendency in the taste of the American and European audience is even more marked.

Today, the peoples of America and Europe cling stubbornly to their belief that problems *can* be solved. The difference (and all to the good) is the quality of their belief. It is this difference in quality which our pictures must capture, the greater maturity expressed in the people's belief that the future does not come of itself—it must be achieved. The highest responsibility of the film creator is to reflect his times. If the people believe in the future, the film creator must also believe in it. And if they search for ways to achieve the future, he must chart the ways.

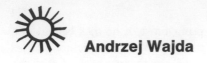

Andrzej Wajda

*

DESTROYING
THE
COMMONPLACE

MY LIKING for contrast is primarily due to the obvious fact that the Cinema is a visual art. Films, which used to be "the great mute art," have become "great talkies"; everything began to be dull, when it was expressed in banal forms. The most important place was given to speaking actors. Almost the whole of world cinematography forgot the delightful possibility given to films—the ability to observe events, to be a witness. Now we are looking for a way out. And just as the lapidary quality of poetry is the opposite of the wordiness of prose, so the way out of the boredom of commonplace dialogue films is intensity in the use of detail, and its mutual contrast.

This passion for contrast is the reason my name has been linked with that of Buñuel. I was already linked up with Buñuel before I knew his films. I saw them in Paris for the first time, and indeed I recognized my teacher in them. Especially in *Los Olvidados* and *The Golden Age*.* But what I find attractive in Buñuel is not his "cruelty" but his courage in showing everything human without bowing before morality or esthetics. Buñuel believes that the human mind can be shown in the language of pictures a much more true language than that of dialogue, and that the most deeply

From *Films and Filming,* June 1961, pp. 7, 41; adapted from an article in the Polish paper *Ekran.*

* Generally known by its French title, *L'Age d'Or.*

hidden layers of intimate human thought are dependent upon situation.

I am still profoundly impressed by *The Golden Age*. There is one scene there to which I like to return; it is a true indication of this great artist's tendency. It takes place in a great salon where the guests are grouped round a buffet, eating and drinking. Suddenly the door is thrown open and a carriage and pair drives across the salon and disappears through another door. Nobody notices the carriage because they are all preoccupied with themselves.

It is impossible to describe this scene, because the significance lies in the visual contrast between the contented guests and the carriage driving across the room. Buñuel wants to get out of the rut of banal situations and does not try to present a realistic interpretation of phenomena.

Symbolism uses ready-made, accepted images. If we are agreed that a bunch of roses means love, a director will use it in a film to mean just that. But what Buñuel does, and what I try to do, is to create new images, new series of images which could play the role of symbols. You surely know the saying: "The first man to compare a woman to a flower was a genius; the second was a fool."

But in *Ashes and Diamonds* and *Lotna* I nevertheless willingly use the existing wealth of images, of national metaphors. I do not make films for Japanese or for Parisian audiences; I myself am a part of the public for whom I work, and so I must use images which are accepted and generally understood. That is the only hope I have of saying something new. This has no bearing on the fact that I reject symbolism as a method.

Misunderstanding is met with when the word "naturalism" is used in a pejorative sense. When a pair of lovers catch sight of a corpse, or when the camera "bores" into bleeding flesh, that calls forth the word "naturalism." But it is more of a "revolt" against accepted esthetic standards. I understand the word in a historical sense, as a trend in nineteenth-century art. In any other sense it can only mean extreme fidelity, a literal approach about which there can be no doubt. And these definitions cannot be given a pejorative sense. "Naturalism" is the opposite of my intentions, because what I aim at is the creation of spasmodic situations with no attempt at observing the principle of probability—situations which give me the opportunity of expressing myself much more convincingly than I can by mere fidelity.

Buñuel does in fact open new perspectives for World Cinema, but he is practically alone. At the present time there is no *avant-garde* film movement in Poland or anywhere else. We could not really call the Polish "experimental" films *avant-garde,* nor McLaren's studies,* nor the English Free Cinema.** Here it is rather a case of broadening normal means of expression, and no more profound art trend could rise from these tendencies. There are only individual personalities.

And what about *la nouvelle vague?* For me it simply doesn't exist. I talked on this subject in Venice. This is rather a new organization in film production, getting away from the principle of the "film that costs tens of millions," financed by the producer who dictates a certain standard of taste. The "new wave" directors make good films for a fraction of this sum.

I do not deny that they have achieved progress, because they have started to overcome the idea that the Cinema is such an expensive business that it must be guided by the criterion of profit. Of course, if photography and the films had not robbed painting of its monopoly in portraiture of the world, the world would be two hundred years behind now. It is possible that the experiment in organization and production introduced by the "new wave" will cause a revolution in this field. But the results for art? Scattered and transient.

Hiroshima is a fascinating film; the use of means of expression, the combination of documentary and film technique entrances me. But the linking-up of those two places, Hiroshima and Nevers,

---

* The animated films of Norman McLaren, who specializes in drawing sound and picture directly onto the celluloid base. Most of McLaren's films have been made for the National Board of Canada.

** A British documentary movement of the 1950's, the aims of which, as expressed in their manifesto, were to make films "which share an attitude: a belief in freedom, in the importance of the individual, and in the significance of the everyday." The leading film-makers in the movement were Lindsay Anderson, Karel Resiz, and Tony Richardson.

does not seem suitable to me. And the Camus film, *Black Orpheus,* was nothing but a colored and badly acted tourist agency advertisement. In my view the *avant-garde* must be something quite different—people with something to say, who know that they cannot say it in the old way.

Of all the national film styles American and Japanese are most to my liking. The latter seems most significant to me, especially Kurosawa's films. I have seen the latest version of *Macbeth* under the title of *Throne of Blood,* with Mifune in the chief part. It is a great experience. I feel Kurosawa is the only director who has succeeded in putting the *whole* of Shakespeare on the screen. You are struck by the incredible force and tension of the acting, essential for interpreting the passionate heroes of Shakespeare.

As for American Cinema, you can really only speak of individual directors who have got above the dictatorship of banality, like John Ford, Elia Kazan, Fred Zinneman, and Laslo Benedek. Altogether the Cinema of the world today is marked by personalities: Clair, Renoir, Bergman and so on.

Bergman, for me, is a dreadfully literary director. He starts not only from an idea, but from literary situations as well. Not long ago I read Berent's *Living Stones*—I had not then seen the scenario to Bergman's film. There's a sort of "Young Polish" stream of his films. Obviously a Swedish equivalent which goes back to the painting of the Swedish Malczewskys and Wojtkiewiczes. But Bergman knows what to take from his sources. As a phenomenon he is alone, too, with no followers. His best films seem to be *The Magician* and *Summer With Monica.*

But let me get back to Polish matters. I was against coining the phrase "Polish Film School" because I felt there were still too few unifying moments for us to be able to speak of a "school." But now I see the opposite is happening.

The people who were so full of enthusiasm are rapidly retreating and letting the "school" fall into disfavor. And I am just beginning to admit its points. There is no doubt that a number of films have been made in our country dealing with moral problems of today, and based on the conviction that the film is not a means of entertainment but an instrument, a means of expressing important problems. We should also remember that these films were not made in a vacuum, but were meant for observant and sensitive audiences. For film workers this realization that their work will come before such an audience is a great creative incentive.

But it was not only the existence of such an audience that helped in the making of these films. There was also the standpoint of the film industry itself. I do not think that much could be achieved by jumping suddenly from one type of organization to another, in an atmosphere of unclarified criteria. We must remember that what is done one year does not bear fruit until the next.

And style becomes increasingly important. I think that color on the screen must be applied in physiological doses, not mechanically. That is why we do not "observe" color, it means little to us and we are not conscious of it. After some time the viewer does not look at a color film any differently than at a black-and-white film. Color is a factor in art, and must be used where it has a function to fulfill, where it should be noticed. That was Eisenstein's approach to the question. Thus in his *Ivan the Terrible,* the second part, we see colored faces contrasting with a neutral gray background. But this way of "bringing out" color on the screen is very difficult.

Every scene in a film is determined by its place, by what goes before and what follows. That is the basis of film drama. I realized this long ago, when I was still a student. I once saw a showing of Rossellini's *Rome, Open City,* arriving in the cinema at the moment when the Gestapo woman agent is retreating before the sight of the tortured Communist. Carla Revere acted this scene in a very schoolgirl, primitive way, but taken together with the previous scene with Manfredi lying on the ground, it was most effective and nobody would have been able to see in it the "primitive" acting I remembered when the film is seen as a whole.

I think the real place for judging an actor's ability is on the stage. In the cinema there are many factors which affect the acting, the dramatic direction, the montage, the atmosphere created. In addition the attention of the audience is not concentrated. That is why amateurs can play successfully in film while on the stage it is out of the question. Here the actor has the audience's attention fixed on him and he must know his job.

It is in the theatre that I find the greatest achievements in acting today. In *Titus Andronicus* Olivier created a greater work of art than in his films. There is no film equivalent of the genius displayed in the Piccolo Teatro di Milano, which is a theatre based on pure acting, independent of a text. Where the support of words has been taken away the actor must turn to the most secure element in his art—his own "liveliness"; he must express the content of his role in gesture, expression and pantomime.

The Piccolo Teatro is my ideal of acting in the sense of stage-craft. But not as a definition of the actor's art. I think the greatness of acting lies precisely in its quality of being undefinable, in its passing the limits of the describable, in its existence beyond the actor's silhouette, his visual likeness. We might say a shadow moving in front of a man.

But this is not true of acting alone. This is the basis of art in general. We meet a mystery we cannot define exactly. Especially in contemporary art—painting, music, poetry seek out the finest details and search in them for the mystery of the universality of things. That is why contemporary art does not start from general analysis. It goes in the reverse direction—from the detail to the universal.

The point is not that the world is "varied" but that everything in it has become a separate artistic and philosophical problem. That is what distinguishes the artist from the "ordinary" man; he is always questioning and everything is a problem. The artist can enter the world of things, reveal the relationship between people and things, between two silent people. The more ordinary and banal the situation, the more hidden truth there is in it waiting for us to explore. Today the Cinema uses tricks and banalities blindly, and yet it is the development and unraveling of these that is the purpose of art.

It is the task of the Cinema to overcome the barriers of the commonplace. We have gone through the phase of surrealism—and nothing can deter the influence of this trend which forces us to go on revealing new significance in the things around us.

Josef von Sternberg

*

ACTING

IN

FILM

AND

THEATRE

"THE MANAGER: Not at all. Your soul, or whatever you
like to call it, takes shape here. The actors give body and
form to it, voice and gesture. And my actors—let me tell
you—have given expression to much better material than
this little drama of yours, which may or may not hold up
on the stage. But if it does, its merit, believe me, will be due
to my actors.
THE FATHER: I don't dare contradict you, sir; but it is tor-
ture for us who are as we are, with these bodies of ours, to
see those faces. . .
THE MANAGER: (Cutting him short and out of patience)
Good heavens! The make-up will remedy all that, the
make-up. . ." —PIRANDELLO

THE RICE FIELDS of Java remain in my eyes as if I had been there
yesterday. Standing in the center of these lovely green stretches
furrowed with quiet water are the most interesting scarecrows that
can be found on earth. High over the rice on bamboo stilts is a
palmleaf-covered hut and long strings with hundreds of tiny bells
reach from it to the far corners of these plantations. When the
birds come for the rice, a graceful Javanese woman lazily stretches
out a shining copper hued arm and frightens the birds away with
an eerie tinkle.

From *Film Culture*, I, nos. 5-6, Winter 1955, pp. 1-4, 27-29.

The actor is the opposite of a scarecrow—it is his function to attract. The easiest way to attract is to be beautiful. Arnold Schoenberg's wife once said to me with a good measure of unnecessary passion: "How can a person think and not engrave the face with ugly wrinkles?" Though this is far-fetched, it may not be entirely without foundation. It is not particularly necessary to think deeply, but it is, perhaps, superfluous for a handsome person to think deeply. Fortunately, the ability of an actor to think is not subjected to the same strain as his appearance.

The sing-song girl, wheeled in a festively lighted jinricksha through the streets of China, has a simple task. The girls who live on flower boats have a simpler task. They are not required to sing or to move. Not always is entertainment expressed in this primitive form. The rice-powdered geisha in Japan is many steps higher and often has achieved enough grace and intelligence to make her charm and wit the prime essentials. The theatre tries to make use of all these values. Generally speaking, the original attraction of the theatre was carnal rather than intellectual, and is still so today.

But no matter how beautiful men or women may be, they rarely are content to live by looks alone, and the theatre has witnessed interesting combinations of beauty and intelligence. Beauty alone has little lasting effect and so, because of the necessity to interpret elements other than empty beauty, the stage accumulated many who were forced to combine a portion of brain with a portion of beauty.

Though the balance to date is strongly in favor of good looks only, we can observe side by side with it old age and ugliness. This would not be tolerated on the stage without compensating qualities. And we often find those who have grown old with countenances so noble that we know their possessors have worked hard to remove every trace of cheap sentiment. Even when an actor has an apparently repulsive face, his features, on closer inspection, have a baseness of classic quality; and in the ugliest faces are found twinkling eyes determined to present their masks relentlessly to portray the basest instincts for critical inspection.

Trained memories that know the classics, ability to simulate

age or youth at a moment's notice, joy and grief projected by
precise control of feeling, personal suffering forgotten to portray
impersonal happiness; a vast army of actors and actresses lurk in
every cultural center to carry out the innermost thoughts of
dramatists, to whom few, if any, human impulses have remained
secret. What sort of human being is this actor and how does he
differ from those who form his audience?

The most essential qualification in an actor must be not to
conceal himself but to show himself freely. All those things which
move the engine of our life and which we do our best to conceal
are those the actor must do his best to show. What we are most
ashamed to acknowledge he does his utmost to accent. No corner
is dark enough for us to hide our love, no stage is bright enough
for him to display it. The idea of killing inspires us with horror—it
fills the actor with celestial delight to hold a dagger or pistol in his
hand. Death to us is not pleasant, but no actor I have ever known
fails to relish the idea of showing the agonies of abandoning life,
gasp by gasp. His life begins when the eyes of others are leveled at
him, it ends when he exits from the stage. He is helpless in the
face of flattery and dreams of applause when he shuts his eyes at
night. He prefers being hissed to being ignored, and his private
life can be an unpleasant break in his design for living.

These traits have been registered for many centuries, and
often with little affection. Lucian writes in the year 122: "Take
away their mask and tinseled dress, and what is left over is ridiculous!" Hazlitt in 1817: "It is only when they are themselves that
they are nothing. Made up of mimic laughter and tears, passing
from the extremes of joy or woe at the prompter's call, they wear
the livery of other men's fortunes; their very thoughts are not
their own."

A doctor I knew had many contacts with actors and told me
that when he was much younger he had been constantly puzzled
by finding symptoms of claustrophobia every time he was called
in to treat an actor.

Claustrophobia is the fear of being confined in a closed room.
He mentioned this to Sigmund Freud. Freud took the doctor by
the shoulders and shook him like a puppy when he was asked

why every actor had this phobia, and roared that everyone with claustrophobia becomes an actor.

It is related that when Sir Henry Irving heard that another actor was going to play Hamlet he exclaimed: "Good God! How does he know he won't do himself a grievous physical injury!" I should like to add that the audience, too, can be badly hurt.

Acting is not the memorizing of lines while wearing a disguise, but the clear reconstruction of the thoughts that cause the actions and the lines. This is not easy. In the finest sense of the word, the actor is not only an interpreter, and not only a carrier of ideas that originate in others, but himself can be (though not without difficulty) a good creative artist. He is the mechanic who can take the word of the playwright and the instructions of the director and fuse the two with all the complicated elements of which he himself is composed to give fluent voice to inspiring ideas, with an effect so strong that one is impressed with the meaning of even the simplest word. It is his function at his best to tear emotion and mind apart and put them together again in orderly condition.

The actor also can take the loftiest sentiment and make it ridiculous, and he can take what apparently is an absurd idea and with it illuminate the most obscure problem. He can give us clear sight instead of darkness as readily as a flash of lightning can show what the deepest night contains. He can portray sin for us in its ugliest form and can purge any evil desire by depicting the brutality of the criminal and his tormented history. He offers us breathless excitement and thrill, no less strong because it is vicarious. He can take our thoughts into his body, and return them safe and sound when the curtain falls.

He makes us laugh at human stupidity, and though we prefer not to recognize ourselves, we always notice the resemblance to a neighbor. He can make us howl at the most powerful king, and make us respect a fool.

He can make the ugliest qualities attractive by investing them with charm and grace, and he can take a fine sentiment and deliver it to be absurd.

Those who sometimes stand in the snow and rain to see a tired actor, divested of his trappings and paint, come hurrying out of the stage door, may or may not know that this exhausted animal has just pulled out of himself energy enough to swim the English Channel. But there are some enthusiasts who have sensed that it can be as heroic to struggle with brain and nerves as it is to conquer the elements and have been so responsive that they have carried the actor for miles on their shoulders to his home. They still do that to bull-fighters when the bull-fighter succeeds in making vivid the qualities of skill and courage. But a maddened bull is easy to see. Not so easy to perceive is the problem of the actor.

Life itself may often teach us little except discouragement, pettiness, and care, and we are grateful to those who recall our ideals and inspire courage and give us new and unsuspected strength. The actor can make us walk out of a theatre with determination to conquer our fears, and he can empty our bag of troubles as if we were newly born. The actor can make us aware of the beauty of something we have seen every day and until now thought ugly—he can make us feel as if we have never before really seen a human being, but he can also make us feel as if we never want to see another.

Some of us are partial to the idea that all the world's a stage with exits and entrances, but for the moment, I confine myself to the man or woman who is professionally known as an actor or actress, and who is paid for it, sometimes with bags of gold, though more often with copper pennies. The pay that an actor receives is not a measure of his worth and many a strutter, making as much noise as a sack full of tin cans, has become rich. The acquisition of wealth is a study in itself. Were quality valued according to income, the armament profiteer would be the greatest actor. One of the startling tragedies in our profession was caused by paying an actor ten thousand dollars a week and not permitting him to act at all.

I have known many actors and actresses. Some of them were good and some of them were bad, but among the good ones I often found many despicable traits and, among the worst, fine qualities. I don't believe that actors are essentially different from others, nor that they all get on a stage, nor that they all remain actors. I do believe that they seek exposure more than others, and that a lack of self-esteem drives them to solicit praise and applause. The key to this behavior is the same as the key to the behavior of others—it is to be found in the first few helpless years of life.

Since I cannot discuss the great actors who were before my time, my observations must be based on those whom I have myself witnessed. I did see Sarah Bernhardt both on the stage and in films, but only when she was old and crippled, and I have seen all those reputed to be great since. Not always was I impressed. I have been moved and inspired by many lesser-known actors and actresses on hundreds of different stages in many corners of the world. But rarely, if ever, have I been inspired or moved by a performer in the films, though I may have been impressed by the film itself.

There is a very important technical reason for this. On the stage an actor is sent out before an audience on his own, though he may be instructed to the hilt. But, once in front of the footlights, he must establish his own contact with the audience and build a continuity of action and thought. The destiny of his performance is in his own hands.

He can gauge the response of the audience clearly—or at least not disregard its testimony easily. He would be a fool to ignore the fact that an intended joke fails to gain response or that an exaggerated gesture is greeted with tittering. (I do not rule out the possibility that fools fail to achieve success.) He is the boss of his own body and of his own mind, knows without any doubt the direction from which he is being watched and himself relays directly everything he thinks and feels to the audience.

All this is not the case in motion pictures. Though the photographed actor is popularized and reproduced so that he can be adored in Bombay, as well as in Milwaukee, and, unlike the actor in the flesh, can appear in both places at the same time, this is accomplished by a mechanism which does not confine itself to multiplication alone. This mechanism not only distributes the actor like popular dolls turned out wholesale, but it actually makes those dolls look as if they could move and speak by themselves. A child, a shark or a horse is made to act the same way as a great actor—easier, as a matter of fact, since they do not resist so much. But whether children, animals, or actors, they are invested with an intelligence that apparently stems from them. In film cartoons, when a tail-wagging duck goes into action, the audience knows at once that behind it there is someone that causes it to move and squawk. When the ventriloquist takes a puppet out of a box, it also is accepted as a unit of intelligence, but the audience is not for a moment deceived about its being a dummy, though it may not care whether it is or not. But when a film actor, who undergoes much more manipulation than a duck or dummy, begins to function, he is judged, praised and condemned, even by our best critics, on the basis of being a self-determining and self-contained human being. This is not so. Actors are usually tricked into a performance not too dissimilar from the process employed by Walt Disney or Edgar Bergen.

In films we have a large assortment of actors with a variety of looks and talent, but they are as powerless to function alone as is the mechanical dummy before he is put on his master's lap and has the strings pulled that move head and jaw. I doubt if many are intensely interested in the mechanism that moves an actual dummy, and it is possible that no one is interested in the strings which move the stars of our day, but I am going to discuss the strings anyway, though they are tangled up badly, pulled by many, and laboriously concealed, after the movements have been made.

Though not wishing to imply that the result may be favorable, it is possible for the actor on the stage to select his material and to appear directly to the audience without any distortion of purpose. But this is impossible in films. Here a complicated machine extracts an essence from the actor, over which the actor has no control. He can be superior to another in proportion to his personal superiority, but his ultimate importance is regulated by manipulators who demand and receive a pliability which, given graciously, results in his advancement, and given reluctantly, causes him to be discarded.

In Paris, the artists lovingly employ a phrase of Cezanne's

"Le bon Dieu est dans le détail." May that be my justification for going into detail, even where detail may be unpopular. The more I ponder on the problems of the artist, the less they resemble the problems of the actor.

Though the actor in the theatre and in films is interchangeable, and can even be active in both media at the same time, there are some generally observable distinctions. On the film stage, in contrast to the theatre, the actor rarely knows where the audience is going to be nor usually cares. Often three cameras are aimed at him from three different directions. He can note (to his surprise) a camera leveled at him from ten feet above and a camera looking at him from the ground, both from opposite directions and both recording his movements simultaneously. If he communicates with the camera attendant, he can persuade him to define what parts of his person will be included. He, himself, can never judge whether he is close or if his whole body is seen, since the determining factor is not his distance from the camera, but the focal length of the lens used.

His face is so enlarged that its features may no longer be viewed without discomfort. An inadvertent light can make his nose look like a twisted radish, or it can completely obliterate the expression of his eyes, which usually is a mercy. Though the actor normally is made to look better than he is, the bad use of a lens or the camera placed at a bad angle can produce an effect over which he has no control.

His voice can be garbled beyond recognition by the sound apparatus (unfortunately, it usually is only reproduced), and he can be made voiceless by the dangling microphone swinging in a direction in which he cannot aim his words.

No accumulation of emotion or continuity of thought is easy, if at all possible, to the film actor, as the technique of making a film is such that it sometimes requires the player to enter his house from the street three months after he made the street scene, though afterwards the action on the screen takes place in sequence. The exigency of film production may require the street scene to be taken on the sixth day of October and the scene of the house which we see him enter a second later on the fifth of

January the following year. (That shrewd arrangement is called a schedule.) The actor has the most extraordinary difficulty in remembering what sort of necktie he wore three months ago, without adding to his concern exactly what he thought or felt. Notes and drawings on the pattern and color of his necktie help a little.

If he is a genius and gifted with great memory, even then he is at the mercy of the instructions given him by whoever happens to be the most convincing person around. The most convincing person is usually the property-man, the script-girl, his servant, or the boy who measures the distance of his nose from the camera.

I have been asked often why it is necessary to be disconnected in the making of a film. Why cannot a film be taken in continuity so that the distressed actor will know precisely what he is doing? Aside from the fact that there is rarely room enough to put up all the sets at once, or to construct, let us say, a replica of a street to connect with the house which the actor must enter, a film takes from four weeks to an occasional six months to complete. It usually takes an hour and a half to show the finished work. Somewhere in this loss of time you will find the reason for not making a film in continuity. It takes time to build sets, to place the camera and the lights, and to instruct the actors, though this last function is considered wasteful by all but a few directors.

No longer a new medium, the film has absorbed countless men who have attempted to find better ways to good results, and uninterrupted continuity of action has been found too difficult. The actor in motion pictures, as on the stage, is told what to do, but there is no dress rehearsal before an audience, nor a collective tableau to give him any indication that he has been told the right thing. Only the finished product reveals that—and then clearly.

But the finished product is not finished with the actor, but with a pair of scissors. These are flourished afterwards by someone who has little idea (usually none) of what was originally intended and he can remove the most precious word from the mouth of the actor or eliminate his most effective expression. This posthumous operator, known as a cutter, literally cuts the actor's words and face. He can make a stutterer speak rapidly and a person of slow thought think quickly. He can also reverse that process and does not hesitate to do this often. He can change the tempo and the rhythm of the actor's walk and his purpose. He can retain pieces of the performance which the actor fails to consider essential because at that moment he was no longer acting, but thinking of lunch; and with an easy snip of the shears, he can destroy the one expression the actor valued most—or the phrase he thought would make him immortal.

He can retain pieces which make hands and legs look like slabs of blubber (physical distortions are less ridiculous than mental ones), and he can cause the most thoughtless women in the world to think by retaining parts of her anatomy that she planned to conceal.

Not only does the cutter cut, but everyone who can possibly contact the film, even including the exhibitor who is to show it, has plans and often the power to alter the film. Actually were each one permitted to exercise his genius for improving a film, nothing would be left but the title, and that is usually debated, too, until the night before the film is shown.

Far from being responsible for his own performance, the actor cannot even be quite certain that the final result will not disclose the use of a double or even a voice which is not his. In any form of physical danger, usually featured in the motion picture, the actor is replaced by someone who is supposed to look like him, and though the actor often is willing to take the physical risks himself (rather than the mental ones), the producer is not so willing since a bodily injury means delay. As for the voice, he may for some reason be unable to sing, or what is more common, be unable to talk.

I have myself replaced the voices of many actors with their own voices from other scenes and in many cases have replaced their voices with the voices of other actors, thereby using the voice of one man and the face of another. Though this is not usual, it can always be done and is to be recommended. (The ideal film will be a synthetic one.)

In *An American Tragedy,* I replaced the voice of the man

who played the important part of the judge in the famous trial. This man was not a bad actor, but only too late did I discover that his diction betrayed an accent which was inconsistent with the intended portrayal. I was asked afterwards how I had failed to notice this accent. I confessed my fault but pleaded that the actor had impressed me by not speaking when I met him. Rather than replace the actor himself and hurt his feelings, I replaced his voice, without anyone being the wiser for it, except the actor who must have experienced no mean surprise to see his mouth open and speak with a voice not his. This process is called "dubbing" and is extensively used.

I have corrected faulty diction and exaggerated sibilants by using pen and ink on the sound track that runs with the film; and it has been announced that someone had succeeded in writing on the sound track markings so skillfully resembling the photostatic image of words that, when projected, the human language was heard. Imagine writing the sound of a human language with pen and ink—or changing the human language not only with pen and ink but with the slightest twist of a dial or alteration of speed raising or lowering the pitch of a voice.

Since few are dissatisfied with the voices of our popular actors, little such manipulation is normally indulged in, but ample sections of speech are always eliminated without the actor's participation, and every actor has been asked to make what is known as "wild track," sometimes by telephone. This "wild track" is made to be placed in some section of the actor's performance when his back is turned or when he accidentally waves a hand so that it looks as if he were talking. This "wild" part is usually some tender sentiment that has been omitted by the author or director and which is now recorded separately and then injected into the image of the actor. But normally the voice and body of the same actor is used, though long after he has finished he may be recalled twenty times by twenty different men to patch up something which afterwards passes for a memorable characterization.

Personally, I have frequently been forced to cheat sentiment into the "finished" performance by concealing flaws and revealing meanings with sound and music (all this is done afterwards without knowledge or authority of the actor), and I have had no end of trouble disguising what is technically known as a dry mouth, which means the clicking of the actor's tongue against the roof of his mouth is recorded so that it sounds like the clatter of hail. Such an actor has to be continually lubricated by having large quantities of water funneled into his mouth, which process does not improve a performance.

Intelligent performances have been coaxed out of idiots who have not been able to walk across a room without stumbling, and I have seen intelligent men and women made to appear like half-wits without their being aware of it until they sat in the theatre and beheld the transformation.

Though one can hold the film actor responsible for his person, one cannot hold him responsible for his performance. The more the actor knows about the films, the more he will realize his helplessness and seek to determine the selection of director, cameraman and story, and that process of ultimate demolition known as editing or cutting. But worse than that, until quite recently, not even the most prominent director, except in rare cases (where it could not be prevented) was permitted to cut the film, since the usually anonymous producer had only this opportunity to actively participate as a creative craftsman.

Not many actors have even achieved the position where they can control the factors which influence their career, and when they have, they rarely, if ever, have been able to avoid failure. The history of motion pictures is littered with the wrecks of players who achieved control of their own productions, though there have been two or three unimportant exceptions.

The average film actor, capable or not, prefers to be called upon to turn on his emotions like water from a tap at nine in the morning—emotions that normally take time to develop—and at the request of even the most incompetent director, the trained star or supporting player will, without too much questioning, laugh hysterically or weep, with or without the aid of tickling or glycerine—and be content in the belief that he is considered to be performing the work of an artist.

It is naturally easier for the actor of little ability to adapt him-

self than for one with great intelligence, as the system of producing films is more often than not a severe shock to anyone whose
mind has made some progress since childhood. But an actor is
not easily shocked, and so he goes about the task of learning,
as swiftly as he knows, just where he fits into the crossword puzzle
of films; how he can function best and how he can sneak past the
controls. When he finally is so experienced that he manages to do
what he thinks is best without authoritative restraint and guidance, the result is not good.

Not the system alone, but the intricate mechanism and unavoidable complications are against the actor. Usually organized
by men who have no sympathy with problems that require thinking, the confusion of the normal studio is ghastly. Everything is
ordered except the work of those who actually make a film.

When the film actor enters a set in the morning, the chances
are that he has never before seen it (he may even not have heard
of the director), but five minutes later he is required to behave
in it as though it were a home of twenty years standing and to
be familiar with every object. That is not very difficult. He is required to act as though he were alone, but from every possible
lurking place electricians and other workers inspect each movement. They are indifferent to his problems and yawn at the
slightest provocation, and he must purchase their tolerance with
forced good fellowship. He soon is used to that, too.

He may be required to throw his arms around another actor
and call him his best friend—without having seen this individual
two seconds before playing such a scene. He is induced, and sometimes prefers, to play ardent love scenes to a space near the lens
which, in the absence of the leading lady, who is reclining in her
dressing room or still emoting in another film, represents her until she can appear. This doesn't bother him at all, for if the woman
is present, who for the moment represents the love of his life, she
is asked to look beyond him or at his ears, as otherwise the
camera, due to the fact that film lovers are not separated by normal distance, makes them both appear to be cross-eyed.

The actor is often not given a manuscript until half an hour
before having to act a part (I am told there exist actors who

read an entire script and not only their dialogue excerpts) and must take instructions like a soldier to turn and walk to the left or to the right, and be content with the assurance that he is doing nothing wrong and will learn more by and by. If he rehearses too long he is put down as difficult and his reputation suffers. But he never feels that he needs much rehearsal, though he does feel that the other actors need it badly.

With the exception of a very few, whose abnormality should be discussed in detail, I have never known an actor to spend so much time on the inside of his head as on its outside. Apparently, the make-up is really worth taking trouble with, and this phase of his interpretive ability is never neglected. I am considered a martinet because of my insistence that an actor listen to my instructions without dividing his attention with a close study of his curling irons, whiskbrooms, powder-puffs and "fan" magazines. But normally, the director will not insist on being listened to very closely (he may then appear to be delaying the schedule), and his performer lends an ear while the other is belabored by a group whose sole purpose it is to make his appearance ready for the ordeal of acting. Generally speaking, an electrifying statement like: "Come on, Charles, put this over and we'll knock off for lunch" suffices. Melting make-up is then patched with hasty hands, he is brushed off, hustled and thrust into lights which generate enough heat for a Turkish Bath, and given those aids, he coolly portrays a man of the world while the perspiration runs down his back and puddles at his feet.

If the words he then has to speak in a superior manner prove too much for his memory, he reads them from a blackboard, which is placed out of sight of the camera. These words are usually chalked up by someone whose spelling is on the archaic side. Some of the greatest speeches in film history have been put together from thirty different attempts to read them. Sometimes these speeches have been pieced together from efforts to get the actor to speak them that ran over a period of a month. In showing such a speech afterwards to the thrilled mob, it can be noticed that instead of seeing the actor deliver this speech, say the Gettysburg speech, one hears the words while other actors are shown listening with open mouths. Their mouths are not opened because of admiration for the orator's memory.

No, in the film world the actor loves to be known as a man who walks on the stage, views the situation with an eagle eye, establishes quick contact with all the sundry, and then if his name is, let us say, Spencer, to be known as "One Take Spencer." He will value such a nickname more than a gangster who establishes his menace by being lovingly called "Machine Gun Kelly." I once had an actor who said to me while we were rehearsing: "They call me One Take Warner." It took all day to get him to say "Good morning." But to take a scene more than once, though the acting may be execrable, is to waste film, unless the actor fumbles his lines. Believing that every time he opens his mouth the audience will be staggered with delight, the actor is offended if it is intimated that placing words in proper rotation and breathing with relief after every comma is not sufficient to embody them with meaning.

But let me continue to describe this intellectual atmosphere. Peter Arno succeeded in epitomizing the whole absurdity of the usual film stage in a cartoon which shows an actor energetically climbing into the bed where his leading lady languidly reposes and being introduced to her by the director as he prepares to lie down at her side. Of course, Arno exaggerates, as the chances are that the actor will have to introduce himself. With some exceptions, actors do not mind that. What they do mind is being ignored. There are but few actors who like to hide. Recently I passed one who was recognized in a theatre lobby by a tourist who approached him and said: "Aren't you in the movies? Your face is familiar." The actor turned pale, mumbled: "My God!" and vanished.

But as a rule, the actor does not vanish quickly enough. Particularly on the screen, where a second often seems to be endless. The one who insists on staying before the camera the longest is the star-actor, and one would think that he ought to remember that he did not become a star that way. But being a star gives him prerogatives. When he portrays, let us say, an explorer, he will do no more than don the smeared uniform selected by the wardrobe, and then enter the stage not as if after an exhausting and dangerous journey, but as if he had just left his dressing room. The director who points out the difference in distance will not remain his friend, I presume. (Directors are usually chosen by their ability to get along with actors, and with other less essential functionaries.) As for a minor player, who, for example, is to portray a monarch, nobody bothers much with him. He is practically booted onto the set by an assistant who, in addition to this doubtful method of inducing the proper kingly mood, has just shouted, "Hey, Emperor, what the hell is the matter with you? Didn't I tell you to be here on time?" The same actor will immediately assume the part of a noble ruler distinguished for his wisdom, and issue commands to a benign minister who, yesterday, played an apoplectic sheriff in a film in which the king was a horse-thief.

It is also easy to understand that striking story about the man with a real beard, who was called in hurriedly from the street because the director suddenly had the idea that he wanted a man with a beard to walk across a scene. The beard demanded to read the manuscript. The crew on the stage, the actors who were waiting for this man, the director and his staff, could not credit their ears. Why should a man who merely had to walk across a stage demand a manuscript? The extra, who needed ten dollars very badly, nevertheless insisted, and said that unless he read the manuscript he would not know how to walk or what its purpose was in relation to the story and therefore could no more walk than he was able to fly. It is a tolerably apt commentary on motion pictures that this inquisitive actor was instantly displaced by another beard which did not care how it walked or what for. I later heard that the first man shaved.

But it is not easy to understand why the motion picture actor insists on being rated as a creative artist. He may be a hero or an exceptionally charming individual with fantastic energy. He may be worth everything he gets, which in the long run is usually taken from him. He may be one who chooses this rash way of earning a livelihood rather than another, but creative art has other servants and other standards and is based on no such nonsense.

I was the first to deal with the film machine in *The Last Com-*

mand, in which the late Emil Jannings played the part of an extra. If anyone remembers this film of long ago, he might recall
that Jannings, who had been Commanding General of the Russian
Army, is propelled by fate to Hollywood and there chosen from
the ranks of the extras to depict his own history. The picture ended
with Jannings driven mad and dying in the belief that he was once
more in real command. But this ending was poetic, like all my
endings. The film actor is not driven crazy—he is driven to become the idol of millions.

And the length of time in which he retains his popularity does
not depend upon him, but upon his stories, current fads—and his
directors. The supporting players usually last the longest in their
screen life because they do not carry the burden of the failures.
They are selected according to types catalogued as fat, thin,
monks, doctors, baldheads, beards, soldiers, detectives, diplo-
mats, leg girls, emperors, etc., and heaven help the man who
has once played a monk and thinks that on a better day he may
be a doctor.

The star is typed as much as the supporting player and strongly
identified with the part he plays, not only by public and critic,
but by himself (though one hears once in a while that some actor
or actress aspires to play something that sounds better than the
piffle that made them stars) so that he usually assumes the good
or bad qualities for which he has been noted and is only with
difficulty weaned away from them when another part requires
other qualifications. The difference in Jannings' household when
he entered it as a general and when he came home as a film extra
was appalling. He would on one day flick the maids with his whip
when asking for a cigarette and on the next plead with them in a
broken voice for permission to enter.

The nature of his work in film does not allow the actor much
energy for the contemplation of abstract virtue and he therefore
seeks his praise where he finds it in abundance, and he will avoid
any extraneous issues by talking only about himself or about his
part and will not listen to others unless he knows his turn will
come.

But there is a reason for this lack of balance in the flustered
life of the film actor. It is induced by the abnormal demands made

on him. He is asked to play a climax first and the scenes leading to it afterwards. He may play an ardent love scene on the first day of the production, and show how he casually met the girl, originally, after he played the father of her child. These acrobatics are strenuous and exhausting and drain nerves which are needed to restore normality.

Remarkable is the stretching of emotions which must be interrupted in flow by hours of preparation for each scene, and sometimes by the finish of the day's work which, likely as not, breaks off in the midst of complications that scream for completion, say: when an actor is told that someone followed his wife and saw her enter a hotel with a stranger and register under an assumed name. The suspense will not be broken until nine the next morning.

Failing to be guided by the director, the sole guide to which he will trust is whether he feels a scene or not. And no worse guide can be imagined. Acting is not quite so simple. Nor do many directors care to guide the actor, since they thereby assume a responsibility they may not wish to carry—nor do I presume that all directors are capable of guiding the actor.

But then the vital interests of the normal film are above acting. Though he will battle to have as many words or close-ups as the other, he will not inspect the content of the words or the meaning of the enlargement. He will insist that his dressing room is as good as the other fellow's and that his lunch when he motors to location is at least as palatable as the director's, and that when he returns from location that only those ride with him who think him irresistible.

Acting is not made-up nor is it memorizing words. Nor is it feeling a scene. An actor must not only feel but be able to guide his feelings, and his delivery must contain criticism and comment on what he is expressing. He must know when to restrain and when to let go and his intellect must always be in advance of his impulse. He must know why the words that he speaks were written and whether they were given to reveal or to conceal his thoughts. He must be able to listen to the other actor and to consider what he hears, and not merely think of his cue and then act in his turn uncolored by what the other had conveyed. His person may be less visible than the ideals he is expressing, and he must know when his image interferes with or represents these ideas. Most of all he must be in control of the effect he wishes to cause. His humility as a human being must be genuine and not coupled with false modesty because he feels himself to be important. There is no such thing as an important actor or an unimportant one, there is only the actor who gives full expression to the purpose to which he owes his presence. Wherever such a purpose is unclear or shallow, no actor can do anything but be likewise.

We observe how enthusiastic the performance is of someone who dances, skates, sings, rides a horse, or runs to catch a train. But that is only because in those cases the actor knows precisely what he is doing. When portraying a great emotion, the film actor rarely ever can do more than guess where it ultimately will be used—or which of the many attempts to squeeze it from him will finally be shown.

There is another man who may know where all these pieces fit and who is capable of determining what is required of the actor who stands on his stage and who, on occasion with the patience of Job, compels everyone to something which can resemble a work of art. But that is not the actor.

I, therefore, suggest that the motion picture actor cannot function as an artist, and will deal with him not as I might deal with the actor who *appears!* to dominate the stage of the theatre, but only as one of the complex materials of our work. Since he has been magnified in importance, you may detect a tendency on my part to incline in the other direction. But my purpose is neither to reduce nor to increase his stature, but simply to study him. In order to do so properly, further analysis is necessary of the personalities who are literally multiplied into three or four hundred images, each of whom can attract a great audience, and can return to the original fame and fortune such as is not gained by a statesman, a poet, a musician, a painter, a scientist, teacher and physician, or anyone else whose approach to his work cannot be reconciled with a failure to master his profession.

Orson Welles

*

F R A N C I S
K O V A L
I N T E R V I E W S
W E L L E S

THAT NIGHT the curtain rose twenty minutes late in the Paris Theatre where Orson Welles was the main attraction; Orson Welles, the producer and principal actor of *The Blessed and The Damned* written by himself in collaboration with Milton, Dante and Marlowe, as the program explains.

The angry audience, stamping their feet impatiently, fortunately never suspected that my own dinner-table interview with Welles had been the cause of that delay; the fact was that, engrossed in conversation, we both completely forgot to look at the time. Much as I regretted the result, I could not help feeling that —from the mere journalistic point of view—this was not exactly a failure, considering that Orson Welles had started our talk with the plain statement: "You highbrows writing on movies are nuts! In order to write about movies you must first make them. . . ."

He was still as unconventional and unafraid of shocking anybody as when I first met him three years ago on his arrival in England. On that occasion, towards the end of a reception given in his honor by Sir Alexander Korda, he started a heated discussion on *Hamlet* with Eileen Herlie (just then playing in Laurence Olivier's film) and myself. When the executives of London Films

From *Sight and Sound,* December 1950, pp. 314-16.

257

approached him, pointing out that the reception was practically finished and they were going home, Welles replied undisturbed, "I bid you farewell then, gentlemen, but I am just having a most interesting talk with these folks here, and I would like to continue if you don't mind." And then, while the lights went out one after another and the waiters were clearing the tables, Welles— with a stunning abundance of Shakespearian quotations—proceeded to psychoanalyze Ophelia and to explain to us his conception of *Hamlet* as Shakespeare's most anti-feminist play.

He must have behaved with the same dazzling self-assurance when in 1932—at the age of 17—he arrived in Dublin and obtained a part at the Gate Theatre, pretending to the manager-director, Hilton Edwards, to be one of the stars of the New York Theatre Guild. Very soon Hilton Edwards—like the rest of the world—discovered that the self-assurance was backed by original genuine talent, and he became one of Welles' closest friends. (As a matter of fact, he is co-producer of the show running in Paris at present, and plans to direct Welles' next film.) The prodigy attracted worldwide attention in 1936 with his production of *Macbeth* with an all Negro cast, and again in 1938 with his radioplay on the invasion from Mars. Its unsurpassed realism created a panic in the United States at the time and led to an abrupt end of the young author's brilliant broadcasting career.

Undismayed by countless failures, Orson Welles founded his own theatre, wrote, produced, acted and concentrated on the study of Shakespeare, poured out new ideas. In 1939 he turned to the cinema and in 1941 produced *Citizen Kane,* one of the most controversial films of the last decade. Admired by a discerning minority, hated and bitterly attacked by more or less inarticulate majorities in most countries, the picture did not bring the financial results expected, but it established Welles' name in the cinema. It cost him that unlimited freedom hardly ever given before to a film-maker by Hollywood executives; a freedom that is to him an essential condition of creative film-work. Lack of this condition is discernible in the pictures that followed: *The Magnificent Ambersons, Journey into Fear, The Lady from Shanghai, The Stranger.*

The derogatory statement about serious cinema journalists coming from a man of such achievements—a man who at 35 still gives the impression of an exuberant, brilliantly seductive child prodigy—did not sound offensive at all. It was pronounced with a twinkling smile and in a perfectly charming manner, so typical of Welles—but when I asked him to substantiate it, he erupted:

"Well, I cannot swallow all the sacrosanct principles and accepted truths underlying the writings of people who try to deal seriously with the problems of films. For one, you all seem to start from the article of faith that a silent picture is necessarily better than a sound one. . . ."

My puzzled expression and a timid attempt at interruption were of no avail. All signs of my disagreement and bewilderment were swept aside by a grandiloquent hand movement.

"What I mean to say," he continued, "is that you always overstress the value of images. You judge films in the first place by their visual impact instead of looking for content. This is a great disservice to the cinema. It is like judging a novel only by the quality of its prose. I was guilty of the same sin when I first started writing about the cinema. It was the experience of film-making that changed my outlook.

"Now I feel that only the literary mind can help the movies out of that cul-de-sac into which they have been driven by mere technicians and artificers. That is why I think that today the importance of the director in film-making is exaggerated, while the writer hardly ever gets the place of honor due to him. To me people like Marcel Pagnol or Jacques Prévert mean more than any others in the French cinema. In my opinion the writer should have the first and the last word in film-making, the only better alternative being the writer-director, but with the stress on the first word."

When I pressed for actual examples to illustrate this theory (which sounds somewhat startling from a man made famous by the visual impact of *Citizen Kane*), Orson Welles produced one without hesitation:

"Take a picture that has become a classic, and deservedly so: *La Femme du Boulanger*. What have you got there? Bad photography, inadequate cutting and a lot of happenings which are told instead of shown. But there is a story and an actor—both superb—which makes it a perfect movie. The story is not even particularly "cinema." I think I could make a play out of it in one evening, if I wanted to.

"This example illustrates perhaps better than anything else what I mean when I talk about the primary importance of the film story. I certainly don't refer merely to the anecdotal value, that you can summarize in a brief outline like: 'She slaves for 20 years to repay that pearl necklace, and then it proved to be a fake. . . .' It is really more a combination of human factors and basic ideas that makes a subject worth putting on the screen."

It turns out that Orson has been considerably impressed by the Italian neo-realists, but for reasons which fit into the line of his argument. He was struck by Vittorio de Sica's lyric power, particularly as expressed in *Sciuscia,* while he thinks *Bicycle Thieves* more commercial and slick, but less observed. To him de Sica's greatness lies in his being a *writer*-director in the Chaplin tradition. Together with Carol Reed he has been fighting tooth and nail to get one particular de Sica story which was just "an ideal subject for a great movie." But in the end de Sica decided to make the film himself. Among the younger generation he considers Renato Castellani one of the most promising directors, and is very enthusiastic about his *E Primavera.*

Although in the course of conversation Orson underlines several times that he is essentially a theatre man and "rather hazy on the subject of movies," the continuous flow of ideas cascading from his lips with fervor and conviction belies these affirmations.

"I definitely prefer to act on the stage than before the camera," he says. "I find film-acting extremely exhausting, both mentally and physically, and I honestly believe I am not a good movie-actor. Even so, I prefer acting to directing, and I prefer writing to anything. Cinema as a medium of expression fascinates me, of course, but ever so often—when directing—I ask myself whether we really know what we are doing and whether there is any reasonable proportion between the thousands of man-hours spent on the director's job and the final result. And then, I hate the worries connected with the financial and administrative side of film-making. . . ."

But between statements brought forward with utmost sincerity there are flashes of half humorous exaggeration obviously designed to produce a certain effect. They make me think of André Bazin's most fitting remark: *"Welles possède en effet, parmi beaucoup d'autres, le génie du bluff. Il le traite comme l'un des beaux-arts au même titre que la prestidigitation, le cinéma ou le théâtre."*

When discussing contemporary Italian films, for instance, he suddenly remarks with a mischievous glint in his eyes: "Good as some of them are, they are largely overestimated by snobs who avidly swallow the subtitles and don't understand a word of Italian. I can see it, now that I have mastered the language. . . . You would probably like them only half as much, if you understood the dialogue."

At my slow-witted reply that my more than superficial knowledge of Italian led me to disagree, Welles with superb versatility turned his flash of irony into a firework of sarcasm:

"Oh, you know, this is part of a theory I once elaborated with Hitchcock in a happy moment. We decided then that in order to have a sweeping success in all the highbrow cinemas of the Anglo-Saxon world we should make a picture about nothing, in no language at all and with bad photography—but copiously subtitled. We agreed that people would scream their heads off with delight."

I asked Welles whether his achievements of the last fifteen years or so had satisfied his ambitions. Of course they had not.

"I have lost years and years of my life," he exclaims, "fighting for the right to do things my own way, and mostly fighting in vain. I have wasted five years writing film-scripts which no producer would accept. Among the pictures I have made I can only accept full responsibility for one: *Citizen Kane*. In all the others I have been more or less muzzled, and the narrative line of my stories was ruined by commercially-minded people.

"I came to Europe because in Hollywood there was not the slightest chance for me (or for anybody, at that) to obtain freedom of action. With *Othello* I have now at least made a picture for which I can again accept full responsibility. It is true that I would have never embarked on that project, had I known that my financial backers would withdraw. This will be in any case the last of my 'adaptations,' as I am only interested now in putting my own stories on the screen. But left high and dry in the middle of shooting I have put every ounce of energy into this picture, and also every penny I had earned working on *The Third Man, Black Rose, Prince of Foxes* and *Black Magic*. Many people will certainly not understand why I accepted some of the parts in question. Well, the requirements of *Othello* are the explanation.

"I frankly don't think that I am particularly good as Othello but even so I firmly believe that this will be a remarkable picture. I have kept as closely as possible to the original, and the only change I introduced concerns the character of Iago, as played by the Irish actor Michael MacLiammoir; I have taken from him the diabolic quality and made him more human. The motive for his actions is supplied by the implication of impotence."

Orson is, of course, less happy about his previous Shakespeare film, *Macbeth,* which during its extended run in Paris has provoked a variety of comment, most of it not very flattering.

"On the first night there was a fight in the cinema between the supporters and adversaries of the picture," he told me. "Indifference would hurt me much more. After all, the film cannot be worthless if people like Jean Cocteau like it. On the other hand I don't take it as a compliment that the picture is having terriffic success in Germany, where people are probably attracted by the medieval savagery of the subject. I now see its many shortcomings, particularly in the remade version, but I still think that it is better Shakespeare than most stage productions of *Macbeth* I have seen. The worst of all is that nobody seems to judge the picture on its own grounds: as an experiment achieved in 23 days and on an extremely low budget."

Orson Welles looks tired, and he admits he is. It is not so much the actual work on the *Othello* production (that took almost a year) as the worries around it that have lead to his feeling of exhaustion.

"Returning to the theatre for a while is to me a relaxation," he says with an ambiguous smile.

But his capacity for work is enormous. He treats his nightly appearances on the stage in two diametrically opposed parts as a welcome change from film-work, but his days are still occupied with the editing and dubbing of *Othello*. And in between he finds the time to prepare his next production.

And new films? Not for a while yet. But he entrusts me with the secret (an open one) that in his free moments (where on earth does he find them?) he is scripting a picture about sexual obsession called *Lovelife*.

"Despite the subject, it will not be endangered by any censorship," he proclaims. "It will be so respectable that families will take their children to see it without the slightest hesitation. But if I succeed—the picture will shock every adult with human feelings and social conscience."

Satyajit Ray

*
A
LONG
TIME
ON
THE
LITTLE
ROAD

I REMEMBER the first day's shooting of *Pather Panchali* very well. It was in the festive season, in October, and the last of the big *pujas* was taking place that day. Our location was 75 miles away from Calcutta. As our taxi sped along the Grand Trunk Road we passed through several suburban towns and villages and heard the drums and even had fleeting glimpses of some images. Someone said it would bring us luck. I had my doubts, but I wished to believe it. All who set about making films need luck as much as they need the other things: talent, money, perseverance and so on. We needed a little more of it than most.

I knew this first day was really a sort of rehearsal for us, to break in, as it were. For most of us it was a start from scratch. There were eight on our unit of whom only one—Bansi, the art director—had previous professional experience. We had a new cameraman, Subrata, and an old, much-used Wall camera which happened to be the only one available for hire on that particular day. Its one discernible advantage seemed to be a device to insure

From *Sight and Sound,* Spring 1957, pp. 203-205.

smoothness of panning. We had no sound equipment, as the scene was to be a silent one.

It was an episode in the screenplay where the two children of the story, brother and sister, stray from their village and chance upon a field of *kaash* flowers. The two have had a quarrel, and here in this enchanted setting they are reconciled and their long journey is rewarded by their first sight of a railway train. I chose to begin with this scene because on paper it seemed both effective and simple. I considered this important, because the whole idea behind launching the production with only 8,000 rupees in the bank was to produce quickly and cheaply a reasonable length of rough cut which we hoped would establish our bonafides, the lack of which had so far stood in the way of our getting a financier.

At the end of the first day's shooting we had eight shots. The children behaved naturally, which was a bit of luck because I hadn't tested them. As for myself, I remember feeling a bit strung up in the beginning; but as work progressed my nerves relaxed and in the end I even felt a kind of elation. However, the scene was only half finished, and on the following Sunday we were back on the same location. But was it the same location? It was hard to believe it. What was on the previous occasion a sea of fluffy whiteness was now a mere expanse of uninspiring brownish grass. We knew *kaash* was a seasonal flower, but surely they were not that shortlived? A local peasant provided the explanation. The flowers, he said, were food to the cattle. The cows and buffaloes had come to graze the day before and had literally chewed up the scenery.

This was a big setback. We knew of no other *kaash* field that would provide the long shots that I needed. This meant staging the action in a different setting, and the very thought was heart-breaking. Who would have known then that we would be back on the identical location exactly two years later and indulge in the luxury of reshooting the entire scene with the same cast and the same unit but with money provided by the Government of West Bengal?

When I look back on the making of *Pather Panchali,* I cannot be sure whether it has meant more pain to me than pleasure. It is difficult to describe the peculiar torments of a production held up for lack of funds. The long periods of enforced idleness (there were two gaps totaling a year and a half) produce nothing but the deepest gloom. The very sight of the scenario is sickening, let alone thoughts of embellishing it with details or brushing up the dialogue.

But work—even a day's work—has rewards, not the least of which is the gradual comprehension of the complex and fascinating nature of film-making itself. The edicts of the theorists, learnt assiduously over the years, doubtless perform some useful function at the back of your mind. But grappling with the medium in a practical way for the first time, you realize *(a)* that you know rather less about it than you thought you did; *(b)* that the theorists don't provide all the answers, and *(c)* that your approach should derive not from Dovzhenko's *Earth*, however much you may love that dance in the moonlight, but from the earth, the soil, of your own country—assuming, of course, that your story has its roots in it.

Bibhutibhusan Bannerji's *Pather Panchali (The Little Road)* was serialized in a popular Bengali magazine in the early 1930's. The author had been brought up in a village and the book contained much that was autobiographical. The manuscript had been turned down by the publishers on the grounds that it lacked a story. The magazine, too, was initially reluctant to accept it, but later did so on condition that it would be discontinued if the readers of the magazine so wished. But the story of Apu and Durga was a hit from the first installment. The book, published a year or so later, was an outstanding critical and popular success and has remained on the best-seller list ever since.

I chose *Pather Panchali* for the qualities that made it a great book: its humanism, its lyricism, and its ring of truth. I knew I would have to do a lot of pruning and reshaping—I certainly could not go beyond the first half, which ended with the family's departure for Benares—but at the same time I felt that to cast the thing into a mold of cut-and-dried narrative would be wrong. The script had to retain some of the rambling quality of the novel because that in itself contained a clue to the feel of authenticity; life in a poor Bengali village does ramble.

Considerations of form, rhythm or movement didn't worry me much at this stage. I had my nucleus: the family, consisting of husband and wife, the two children, and the old aunt. The characters had been so conceived by the author that there was a constant and subtle interplay between them. I had my time span of one year. I had my contrasts—pictorial as well as emotional: the rich and the poor, the laughter and the tears, the beauty of the countryside and the grimness of poverty existing in it. Finally, I had the two natural halves of the story culminating in two poignant deaths. What more could a scenarist want?

What I lacked was first hand acquaintance with the *milieu* of the story. I could, of course, draw upon the book itself, which was a kind of encyclopedia of Bengali rural life, but I knew that this was not enough. In any case, one had only to drive six miles out of the city to get to the heart of the authentic village.

While far from being an adventure in the physical sense, these explorations into the village nevertheless opened up a new and fascinating world. To one born and bred in the city, it had a new flavor, a new texture; and its values were different. It made you want to observe and probe, to catch the revealing details, the telling gestures, the particular turns of speech. You wanted to fathom the mysteries of "atmosphere." Does it consist in the sight, or in the sounds? How to catch the subtle difference between dawn and dusk, or convey the gray humid stillness that precedes the first monsoon shower? Is sunlight in Spring the same as sunlight in Autumn? . . .

The more you probed the more was revealed, and familiarity bred not contempt but love, understanding, tolerance. Problems of film-making began to recede into the background and you found yourself belittling the importance of the camera. After all, you said, it is only a recording instrument. The important thing is Truth. Get at it and you've got your great humanist masterpiece.

But how wrong you were! The moment you are on the set the three-legged instrument takes charge. Problems come thick and fast. Where to place the camera? High or low? Near or far? On the dolly or on the ground? Is the thirty-five O.K. or would you rather move back and use the fifty? Get too close to the action and the emotion of the scene spills over; get too far back and the thing becomes cold and remote. To each problem that arises you must find a quick answer. If you delay, the sun shifts and makes nonsense of your light continuity.

Sound is a problem, too. Dialogue has been reduced to a minimum, but you want to cut down further. Are these three words really necessary, or can you find a telling gesture to take their place? The critics may well talk of a laudable attempt at a rediscovery of the fundamentals of silent cinema, but you know within your heart that while there may be some truth in that, equally true was your anxiety to avoid the uninspiring business of dubbing and save on the cost of sound film.

Cost, indeed, was a dominant determining factor at all times, influencing the very style of the film. Another important factor— and I wouldn't want to generalize on this—was the human one. In handling my actors I found it impossible to get to that stage of impersonal detachment where I could equate them with so much raw material to be molded and remolded at will. How can you make a woman of eighty stand in the hot midday sun and go through the same speech and the same actions over and over again while you stand by and watch with half-closed eyes and wait for that precise gesture and tone of voice that will mean perfection for you? This meant, inevitably, fewer rehearsals and fewer takes.

Sometimes you are lucky and everything goes right in the first take. Sometimes it does not and you feel you will never get what you are aiming at. The number of takes increases, the cost goes up, the qualms of conscience become stronger than the urge for perfection and you give up, hoping that the critics will forgive and the audience will overlook. You even wonder whether perhaps you were not being too finicky and the thing was not as bad or as wrong as you thought it was.

And so on and on it goes, this preposterous balancing act, and you keep hoping that out of all this will somehow emerge Art

At times when the strain is too much you want to give up. You feel it is going to kill you, or at least kill the artist in you. But you carry on, mainly because so much and so many are involved, and the day comes when the last shot is in the can and you are surprised to find yourself feeling not happy and relieved, but sad. And you are not alone in this. Everybody, from "Auntie," for whom it has been an exciting if strenuous comeback after thirty years of oblivion, down to the little urchin who brought the live spiders and the dead toad, shares this feeling.

To me it is the inexorable rhythm of its creative process that makes film-making so exciting in spite of the hardships and the frustrations. Consider this process: you have conceived a scene, any scene. Take the one where a young girl, frail of body but full of some elemental zest, gives herself up to the first monsoon shower. She dances in joy while the big drops pelt her and drench her. The scene excites you not only for its visual possibilities but for its deeper implications as well: that rain will be the cause of her death.

You break down the scene into shots, make notes and sketches. Then the time comes to bring the scene to life. You go out into the open, scan the vista, choose your setting. The rain clouds approach. You set up your camera, have a last quick rehearsal. Then the "take." But one is not enough. This is a key scene. You must have another while the shower lasts. The camera turns, and presently your scene is on celluloid.

Off to the lab. You wait, sweating—this is September—while the ghostly negative takes its own time to emerge. There is no hurrying this process. Then the print, the "rushes." This looks good, you say to yourself. But wait. This is only the content, in its bits and pieces, and not the form. How is it going to join up? You grab your editor and rush off to the cutting room. There is a grueling couple of hours, filled with aching suspense, while the patient process of cutting and joining goes on. At the end you watch the thing on the moviola. Even the rickety old machine cannot conceal the effectiveness of the scene. Does this need music, or is the incidental sound enough? But that is another stage in the creative process, and must wait until all the shots have been joined up into scenes and all the scenes into sequences and the film can be comprehended in its totality. Then, and only then, can you tell—if you can bring to bear on it that detachment and objectivity—if your dance in the rain has really come off.

But is this detachment, this objectivity, possible? You know you worked honestly and hard, and so did everybody else. But you also know that you had to make changes, compromises—not without the best of reasons—on the set and in the cutting room. Is it better for them or worse? Is your own satisfaction the final test or must you bow to the verdict of the majority? You cannot be sure. But you can be sure of one thing: you are a better man for having made it.

Akira Kurosawa

*

JAPAN'S

POET

LAUREATE

OF

FILM

OF THE 200-odd directors adrift on Japan's celluloid torrents, about nine confine themselves to one film a year and among them divide up more than half of the industry's annual Oscar-type awards. Of the nine, only one is known as *Tenno*—the Emperor —and is addressed by his underlings at the Toho Studios in formal language only one inflection removed from that reserved for Hirohito himself. So awesome, in fact, is the reverence accorded Akira Kurosawa that on one occasion, when he was seeing rushes in a screening room, studio guides forced female visitors on the lot to remove their jewelry lest the tinkle of bracelets and earrings distract the master.

The man commanding such imperial dignities is tall and lean, with thinning hair, reflective, yet a rapid talker when his thoughts have taken shape. Kurosawa, whose films (beginning with *Rashomon* in 1950) were the first to make Western audiences aware of Japanese movies, came to his profession almost by accident. "In 1937," he told *Show Business Illustrated* in the course of a rare interview, "I was a struggling young painter. I saw a newspaper advertisement. PCL, which later became Toho Stu-

From *Show Business Illustrated,* April 1962.

271

dios, wanted an assistant director. They asked applicants to write essays on the basic weaknesses of Japanese films and what should be done to overcome them. In my answer I suggested, humorously, that if weaknesses were basic, there could be no cure. I also said that films could always be made better. To my surprise, I was offered a job, which I took, planning to return to painting after one or two months. But I found films were my medium, and I stayed."

The medium was then dominated by Kajiro Yamamoto, a director with whom Kurosawa served as assistant while he studied the work of other moviemakers. In Japan a first-class director is expected, through his apprenticeship, to have mastered the technical angles of his business and, above all, to be able to devise his own scripts. Yamamoto laid it down as a rule that "to understand motion pictures fully, one must be able to write a script." Disciple Kurosawa now even has principals selected when starting a screenplay. "Unless I have a specific actor in mind," he says, "I can't write the script. For the supporting roles I look for individuals who both fit their parts and complement the lead characters."

Other top Japanese directors have followed much the same method—but their results, far more parochial than Kurosawa's, have seldom been seen in America or the West. How do they differ from the Emperor? The greatest of the "traditional" or so-called "purely Japanese" directors, Yasujiro Ozu, will sit up all night with writer Kogo Noda and a bottle of sake, meticulously pondering each emotional or visual shading. Ozu has won six Kinema Jumpo prizes, but remains unknown beyond his own country. This lack of appreciation abroad of Ozu's austere, economic, subtle and almost entirely plotless films confirms a belief of many Japanese that no foreigner can comprehend their civilization, isolated for such long centuries, much less penetrate their "purely Japanese" movies. Concentrating almost wholly on the inner core of Japanese family life, Ozu has refused to make concessions to alien tastes. "The ends of the world," he has said of his quietly intimate vignettes, "are no farther than the outside of the house."